REEF FISH Identification

GALÁPAGOS

PAUL HUMANN

EDITED BY
NED DELOACH

Exclusive European Distributor
Coral Marine International Ltd
2 Des Roches Square, Witan Way,
Witney, Oxfordshire, OX8 6BE, England.
Tel: 01628 810654 Fax: 01628 810669
Europe's Largest Supplier of Diving and Marine Life Books
Please contact us for your free catalogue

CREDITS

Editor: Ned DeLoach
Copy Editors: Mary DeLoach & Jackie Jones
Layout & Design: Paul Humann & Ned DeLoach
Art Director, Drawings & Typography: Michael O'Connell
Printing & Color Separations: Paramount Miller Graphics, Inc. Jacksonville, FL
First Printing: 1993
ISBN 1-878348-06-X
Library of Congress #93-086620
Cartography authorized by the Instituo Geografico Militar of Ecuador. Permit number 930493-IGM-d, Dated September 14, 1993.
Copyright, ©1993 by Paul Humann
All rights reserved. No part of this book may be reproduced without prior written consent.
Co-Publishers: New World Publications, Inc., 1861 Cornell Road, Jacksonville, FL 32207, USA
Phone (904) 737-6558, FAX (904) 731-1188; Libri Mundi, Juan León Mera 851, Castilla 3029, Quito, Ecuador, Phones (5932) 544185 -234791 - 529587, FAX (5932) 504209

Acknowledgments

This book was the result of considerable encouragement, help, and advice from many friends and acquaintances. It became a much larger undertaking and involved many more people than ever expected. I wish to express my sincere gratitude to everyone involved. Naturally, the names of a few who played especially significant roles come to mind.

Dr. John E. McCosker, Director of the Steinhart Aquarium, California Academy Of Sciences, undertook the Herculean task of principal ichthyological advisor. An authority on Galapagos fishes, he tutored me through the many pitfalls of visual identification. He gave freely of his time, bountiful knowledge, personal diving experiences and advice, as a result the text was enhanced immeasurably. Several additional ichthyologists, all recognized authorities, assisted with some identifications and information; they include: **Dr. Robert Lavenberg**, Los Angeles County Museum; **Dr. Kenyon Lindeman**, American Coastal Research & Education; **Dr. Richard Rosenblatt**, Scripps Institution of Oceanography; **Dr. John E. Randall**, Bishop Museum; **Dr. William Smith-Vaniz**, U.S. Fish & Wildlife Service, National Fishery Research Center. Every attempt was made to keep the text and identifications accurate. Where errors may exist, they are my sole responsibility.

Good friends, **Eduardo** and **Deloris Diez** of Quasar Nautica in Quito, Ecuador, persuaded me to undertake this project. They felt it was important for both Galapagos and their country to have the book published. Without their continued support and personal commitment the venture would have floundered. An equally important role was played by **Marcela Garcia Grosse - Luemern** of Libri Mundi, Quito, Ecuador. Her vision and personal knowledge of book markets and distribution are essential elements in the success of this book. She had the foresight to support the project from its inseption.

Over the years, many naturalist guides have patiently nurtured my knowledge of life in Galapagos. Those especially assisting with this book include: **Claire Dallies**, **Juan Carlos Naranjo**, **Patsy Topke Dousdebes** and **Francisco "Pancho" Dousdebes**. Patsy and Pancho also researched the Spanish common names for the fish. Close friends and naturalist photographers, **Tui de Roy** and **Mark Jones** provided valuable knowledge from their personal experiences in Galapagean waters. Special friend, fellow diver and Galapagos native, **Captain Rafael Gill** was an endless source of information, drawing from his years of experience in the waters of the archipelago. **Captain Guillermo Sevilla** has also been most helpful through the years.

Mary DeLoach and **Jackie Jones** gave valuable assistance in the editing process. **Michael O'Connell**'s fish drawings are superb. He was also most helpful with advice and assistance in design, layout, typesetting and production. Finally, I must mention dear friend, editor and business partner **Ned DeLoach**, without whose continued encouragement and support my books would never be published.

Photo Credits

Ned DeLoach 5 & 19; ***Howard Hall*** 176a & b, 187a & b; ***Tui de Roy*** 192 top; all other pictures were taken by the author, ***Paul Humann.***

Editor's Note

For most world travelers a visit to the Galapagos is a fantasy fulfilled. More common than not, the dream to one day explore the distant archipelago sprang from the pages of childhood travel books. What impressionable youngster could resist the images of a mystical moonscape on earth, inhabited by giant tortoises large enough to ride, prehistoric iguanas that share a sea filled with fishes, sea lions and whales, and spreading above it all, a blue equatorial sky alive with the sailing silhouettes and sounds of ocean-going birds on the wing? So the strange name Galapagos is placed high on a mental list of natural wonders to someday see. It may take 20, 30 or over 50 years, but at some point, time, finances, and personal commitments fall into place and the dreamer is off to live a dream.

When the Galapagos' most famous visitor, Charles Darwin, wandered her shores in 1835 he discovered a naturalist's fantasyland so exotic that it would forever alter the course of Western thought. As today's modern jets lift off from Guayaquil and bank west over the Ecuadorian coastline for the 600 mile flight to the archipelago, it is difficult for visitors not to reflect on how the islands' wondrous creatures have fared since the days of Darwin. Had the isolated ecosystems, that gave rise to such unique flora and fauna, suffered irreversible wounds from the abuses of a modern world, or is her celebrated wildlife still diverse, abundant and unafraid?

The news is good! After three centuries of exploitation, first by hungry buccaneers who harvested the tortoises to near extinction, followed by uncontrolled whaling and sealing, and finally, the great destructive pressures from domesticated species, mankind took a heroic step forward in 1959 when the government of Ecuador proclaimed the entire archipelago a national park. A year later the Charles Darwin Research Station began research and conservation programs to protect native species. Thanks to the Ecuadorian people's resolve to safeguard their natural treasure, and the efforts of worldwide conservation organizations, visitors will find the islands' captivating natural history robust as we near the end of the twentieth century.

Recently, a new world of wonder has been discovered hidden within the Galapagos' fertile sea of currents. The islands' dramatic parade of terrestrial species is reflected underwater by the diversity, quantity and vitality of its marine life. The term "wild diving" could well apply to underwater exploration here, not because of physical danger, although the diving is beyond the skill of the novice, but because the rich waters are alive with breathtaking creatures. Large charismatic animals — eagle rays, dolphin, turtles, sea lions and hammerheads are sighted so frequently and in such numbers that their majestic presence becomes the ordinary. But the real treasure under the waves is the bountiful variety of life, most noticeably the fishes.

Paul Humann's text *Reef Fish Identification—Galapagos* provides the underwater naturalist with a lavishly illustrated, comprehensive yet easy-to-use guide into this exciting submarine frontier. It is hoped that the author's pioneering efforts in the waters of Galapagos will stimulate continued marine life research, and honor the exemplary tradition of preservation set in motion by the people of Ecuador.

About The Author

It is difficult to imagine how Paul Humann could possibly spend sufficient time underwater to capture the thousands of images required for his award-winning series of marine life identification books. From the many factors contributing to his success, sheer tenacity and an enduring enthusiasm for discovery head the list.

Paul took his first underwater photographs in the early 1960's. His hobby became a way of life in 1970 when he left a successful law practice in Wichita, Kansas to become captain/owner of the *Cayman Diver*. His next eight years were spent documenting the biological diversity of the Caribbean's coral reefs. The dive charter business was sold in 1979 to gain the freedom to study and photograph the great reefs of the world. Since that time Paul has traveled and photographed extensively. His desire to learn and teach about sea life has produced numerous magazine articles, four large-format photographic books and the *Reef Set* — a comprehensive, three volume visual identification guide to the marine life of Florida, the Bahamas and Caribbean.

Of all the exotic underwater destinations explored, he most cherishes the Galapagos. Over the past fifteen years, he has made 40 extended trips and 1,400 photographic dives in the islands. During this period he pioneered many now popular dive sites, including Darwin and Wolf, and documenting seven previously unreported and two new fish species from the region.

Watching Paul work a reef system is the best way to understand his photographic success. Although generally among the first divers in the water he is always last back on the boat by a wide margin. Nothing more than an old-style horse collar is necessary for him to maintain neutral buoyancy at any depth. In difficult currents, heavily encrusted outcroppings are skillfully negotiated with minimum effort.

Years of underwater observations have trained him well in the subtleties of the reef. Every nook and cranny is meticulously searched with the keen eye of the experienced hunter. Gliding slowly along a submerged cliff Paul finds well-camouflaged frogfish, hidden seahorses, and the tiniest goby where others spot nothing at all. While many fish are easily located and cooperate for the camera, others are rare or wary. Patience is required. Often one or two entire dives are spent waiting motionlessly outside the refuge of a cryptic species in the hope of snapping a single exposure. At other times a lonely ocean drift far from shore is the only way to chance a brief glimpse of a great open-water fish.

Even after a lifetime of underwater adventure and marked photographic accomplishments Paul is far from content; so he continues to search and discover, linger and drift all for another image on a piece of thin plastic film no larger than a postage stamp, that will tell an untold story about the sea.

Contents

Twelve Identification Groups

Butterflyfish

Angelfish

Surgeonfish

Jack

Porgy

Chub

Mojarra

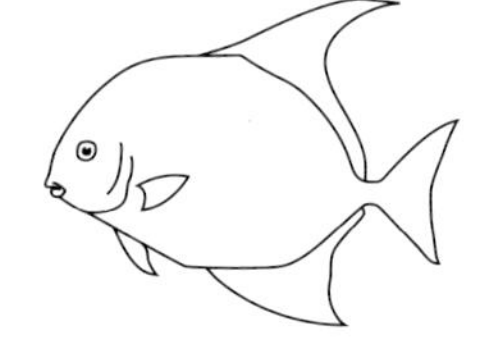

Spadefish

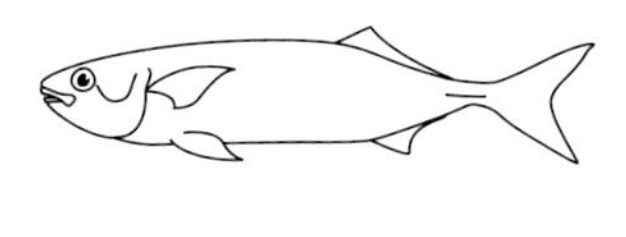

Mullet

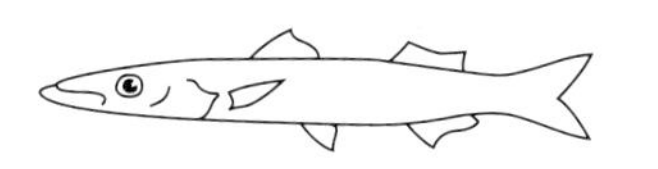

Barracuda

Mackeral

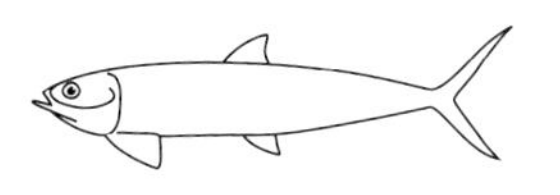

Machete

3. Sloping Head/Tapered Body 54-65

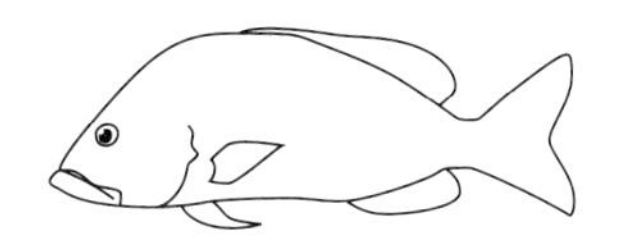

Snapper

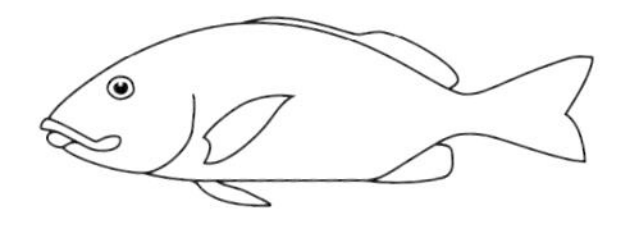

Grunt

Grunt

4. Small Ovals 66-75

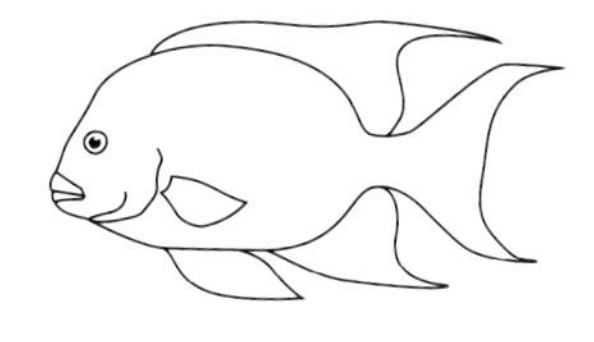

Damselfish

Chromis

5. Heavy Body/Large Lips 76-87

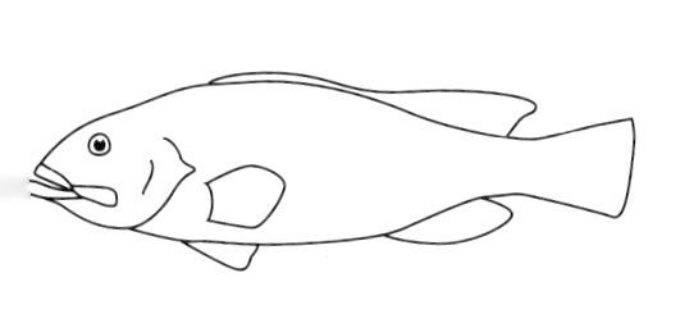

Seabass

Seabass

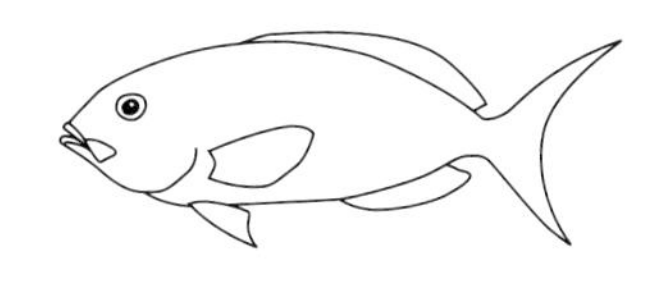

Creole Fish

6. Swim With Pectoral Fins/Obvious Scales 88-105

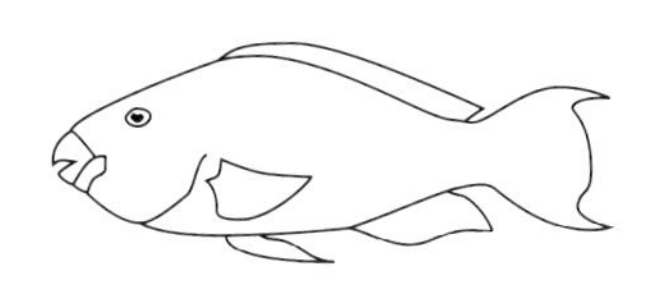

Parrotfish

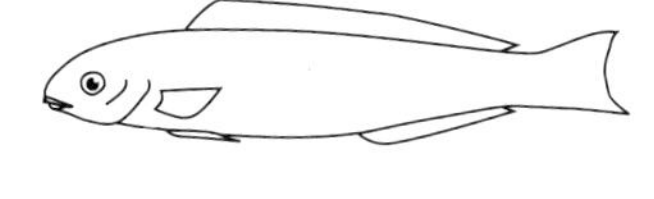

Wrasse

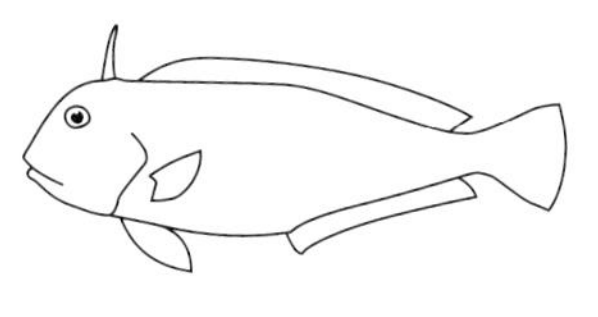

Wrasse/Razorfish

7. Reddish/Big Eyes 106-113

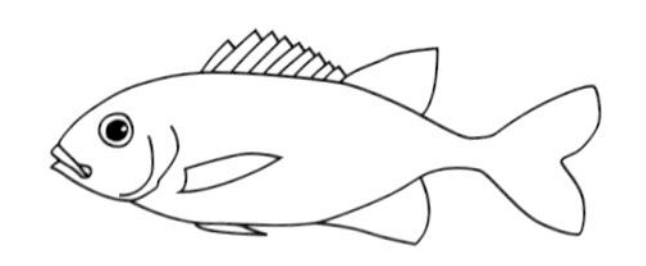
Squirrelfish

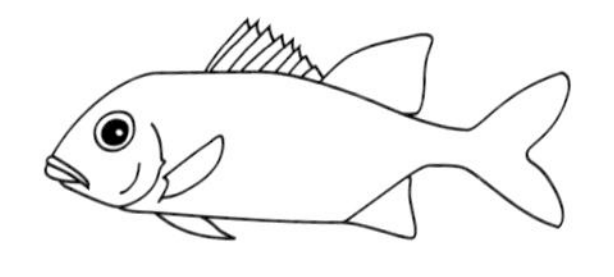
Squirrelfish/Soldierfish

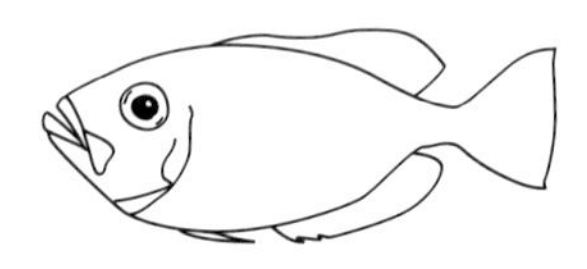
Bigeye

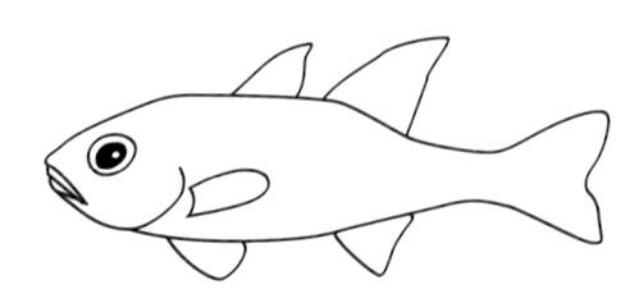
Cardinalfish

8. Small, Elongated Bottom-Dwellers 114-127

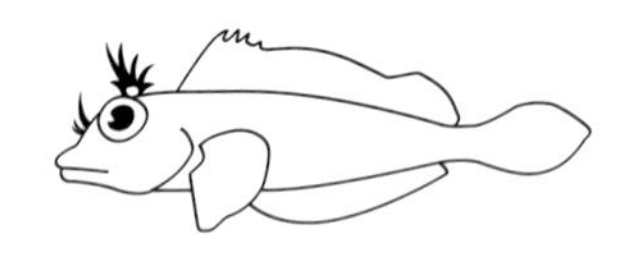
Blenny

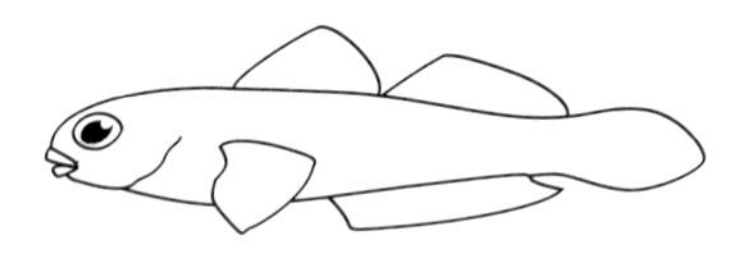
Goby

9. Odd-Shaped Bottom Dwellers 128-141

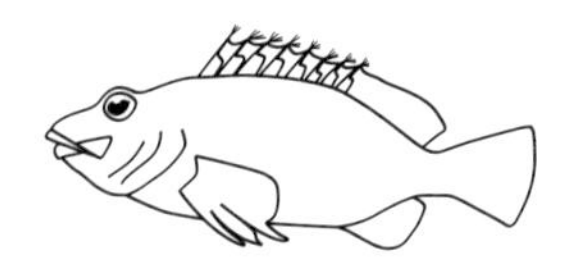
Hawkfish

Scorpionfish

Soapfish

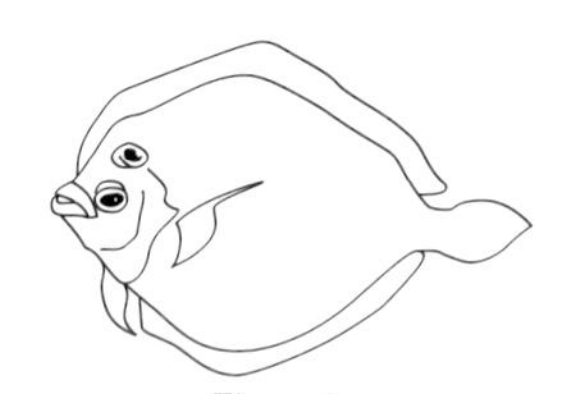
Flounder

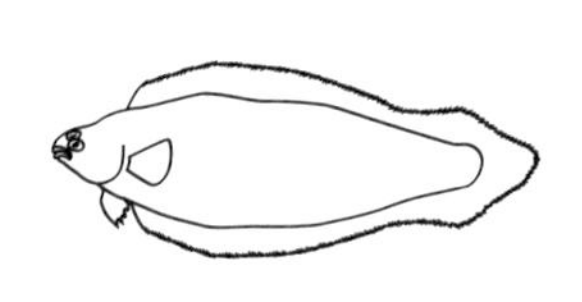
Tonguefish

Sea Robin

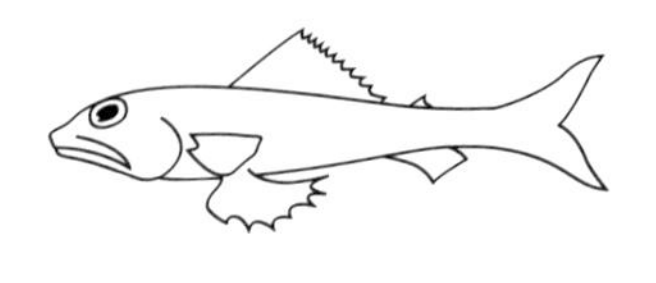
Lizardfish

Frogfish

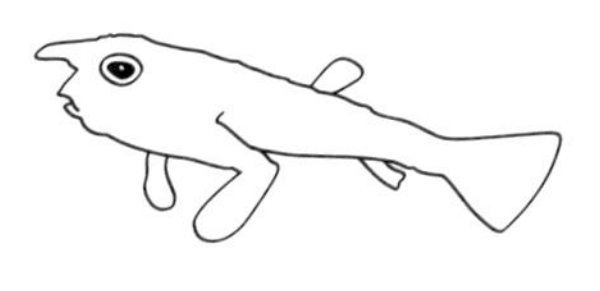
Batfish

10. Odd-Shaped Swimmers 142-165

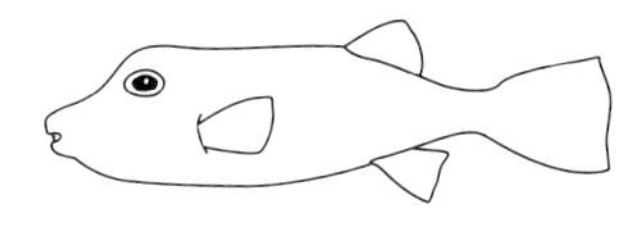

Smooth Puffer

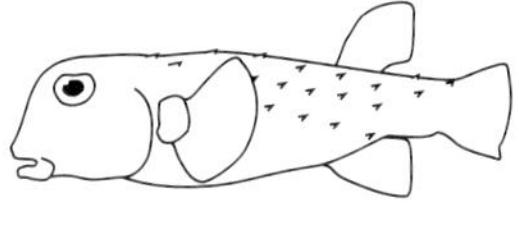

Spiny Puffer

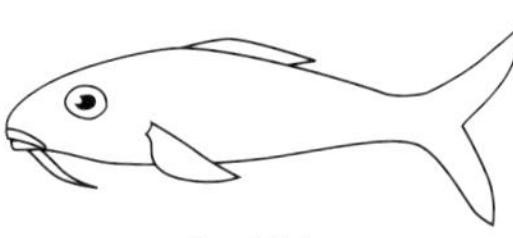

Goatfish

Triggerfish

Filefish

Drum

Beakfish

Boxfish

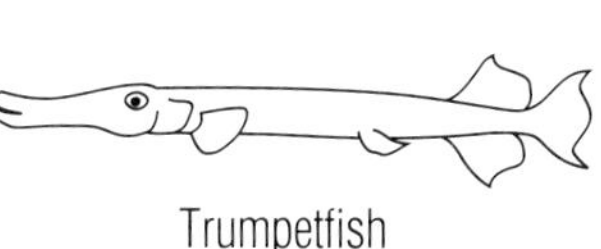

Trumpetfish

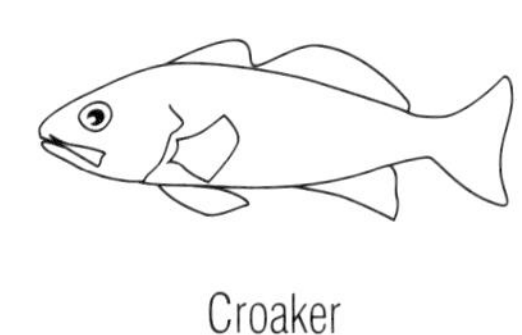

Croaker

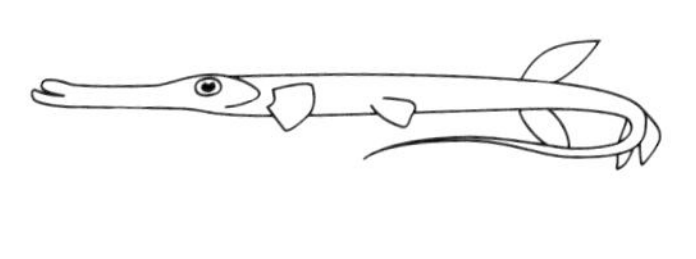

Cornetfish

Seahorse

11. Eels 166-177

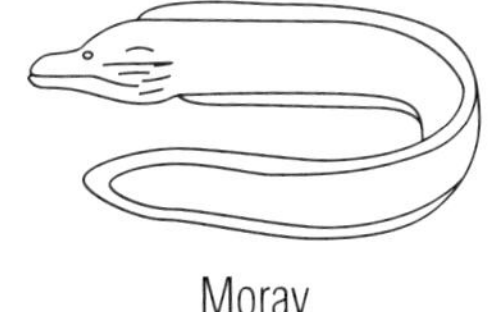

Moray

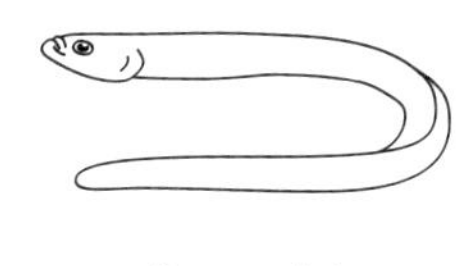

Conger Eel

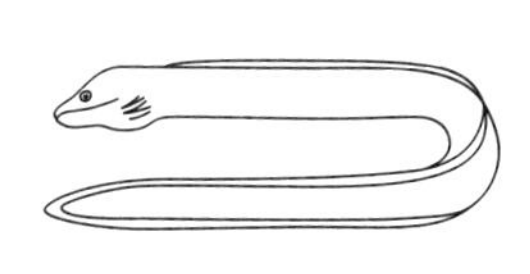

Snake Eel

12. Sharks & Rays 178-187

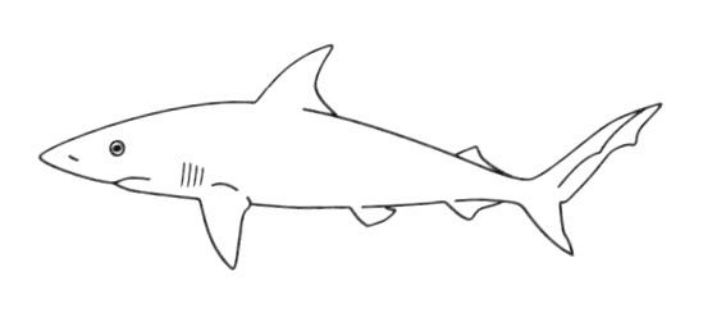

Pointed-Nose Shark

Hammerhead

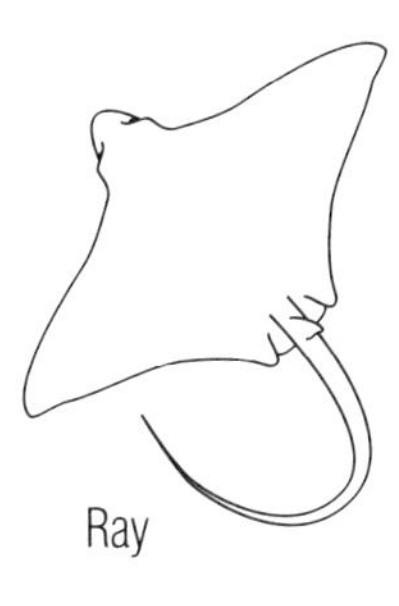

Ray

Galapagos Overview

Over five million years ago successive volcanic eruptions in the depths of the Pacific Ocean formed an underwater platform with projecting mountains. Ultimately the tallest peaks pushed their way above the surface, creating an island chain officially named Archipelago de Colon, but commonly known as the Galapagos. This violent geological process continues. Today, the islands remain one of the most active oceanic volcanic regions in the world with numerous eruptions this century. Thirteen major islands, six minor islands, and numerous islets and rock formations make up the archipelago. The islands lie uniquely isolated on the equator 600 miles west of the Ecuadorian coast of South America, 1000 miles south of Guatemala, 2000 miles north of Easter Island, and just over 3000 miles from the Marquesas Islands to the west.

The seven major oceanic currents that bathe the islands are responsible for an unusual assemblage of over 300 species of fish — a marine mosaic from tropical to cool water regions. The primary influence is the cool South Equatorial Current formed by the Peru Coastal (Humbolt) and Peru Oceanic Currents, pushed by southeastern trade winds from June to December. Surprisingly however, the nearby Peru-Chile province accounts for only seven percent of the fish species. This is due to the weak influence of these currents during that region's primary breeding season from January through May, and the fact that most resident species produce short-lived larval stages. Conversely, the Nino Flow or Panama Current that sweeps southwest from the tropical Panamic Province is responsible for over half of the fish species in the Galapagos. The flow is at its strongest during a lengthy breeding season when many species produce long-lived larval stages. An additional 14 percent, including the colorful Coral and Long-nosed Hawkfishes, Moorish Idols and several butterflyfishes have tropical Indo-pacific origins. Circumglobal species, primarily pelagic sharks and jacks, and western Atlantic fishes, account for roughly eight percent.

The remaining 17 percent, about 50 species, are endemic (seven of these are also reported from Malpelo and the Cocos Islands to the northeast). Some of the more commonly observed endemic species include: Galapagos Grunt, Yellowtail Damsel, Camotillo, Galapagos Cardinalfish, Galapagos Barnacle Blenny, Galapagos Triple-fin Blenny, Bravo Clinid, Galapagos Blue-banded Goby, Galapagos Puffer, Galapagos Drum, Galapagos Garden Eel, Galapagos Snake Eel, and the White-tailed Damselfish (subspecies).

Diving in Galapagos is richly rewarding. The sheer abundance of fish life is stunning. Great schools of inshore grunts and snappers are encountered on nearly every dive, while immense schools of open water jacks, barracuda, bonito, eagle rays and scalloped hammerheads are regularly sighted. Adding to the excitement is the constant expectation of spotting Manta Rays, Wahoo, Yellowfin Tuna and even Whale Sharks. Drop-offs and the boulder strewn sea floor are home to many strange and exotic species such as the Wrasse Ass Bass, Red-lipped Batfish, Sanguine Frogfish, Pacific Seahorse, Dragon Wrasse and Galapagos Clingfish. The ability to correctly identify the many species sighted adds an exciting dimension to underwater exploration in the archipelago.

Because of varying water temperatures, many fish species tend to inhabit one of three ocean zones. The central islands, including eastern Isabela, and the north side of the southern islands are home to the largest number of species. A few tropical species, including several butterflyfishes, Red-tailed Triggerfish, and Convict Tang, exclusively inhabit the warmer northern waters around Darwin, Wolf, Tower, Pinta and Roca Redonda.The Grape-eye, Scythe Butterflyfish and Horn Shark are among those that typically congregate in the cooler waters of western Isabela, Fernandina and on the south side of the southern islands.

Unfortunately, Galapagos diving is not for everyone. Waters can be cool and/or murky with strong currents or surge. Open water drifting is often required. Full wet suits with hood are preferred. Only those comfortable with such demanding conditions should plan a diving vacation here. Live-aboard dive boats provide the best way to visit the majestic underwater terrain. Most charters visit several islands during one-to-two week trips including regular land excursions to enjoy the dramatic landscapes and view the unique terrestrial flora and fauna.

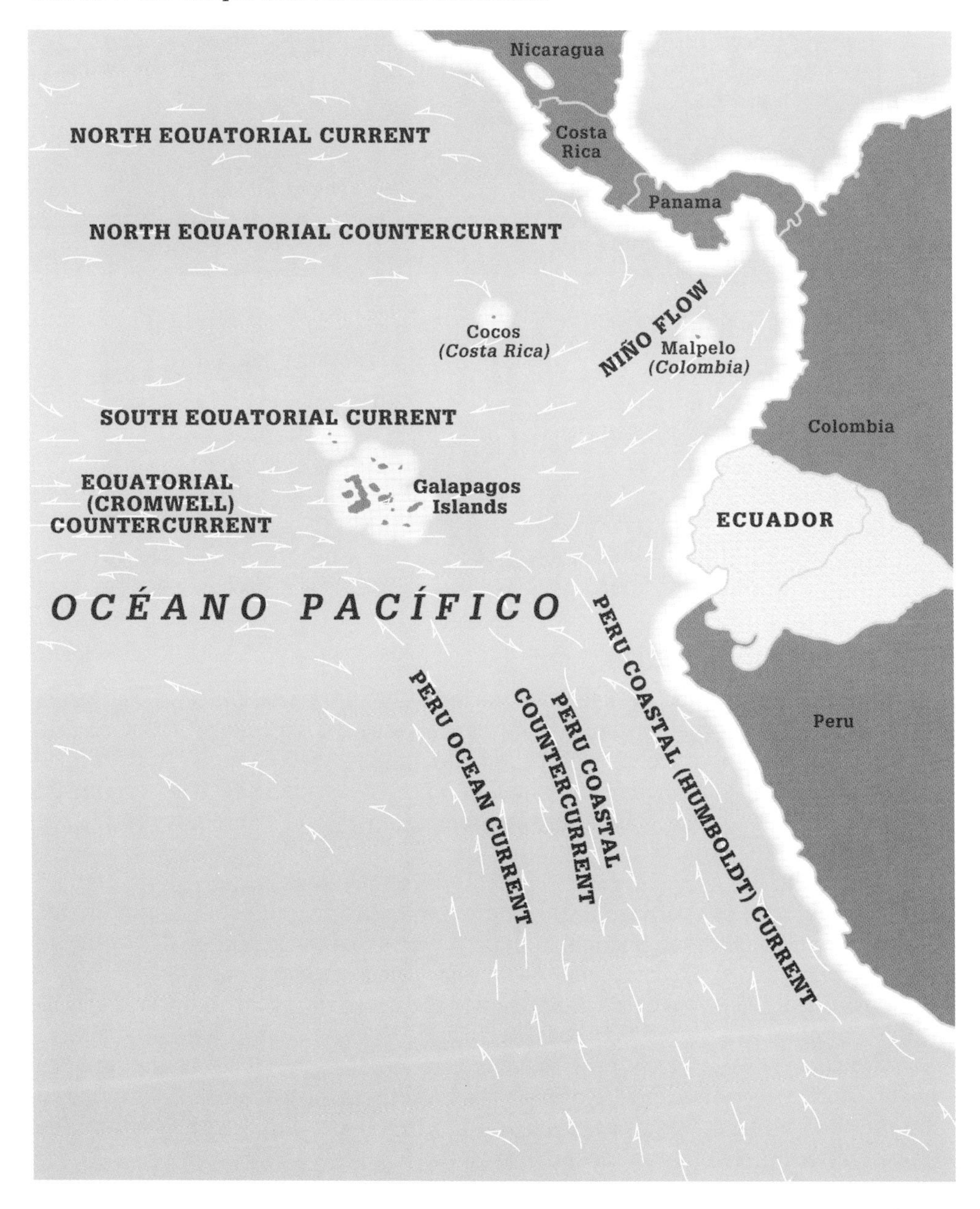

How To Use This Book

Identification Groups

Trying to identify a specific fish from the nearly four hundred sighted in the waters of the Galapagos Archipelago can be a perplexing task. To help simplify the process, families are arranged in twelve color-coded and numbered ID Groups. Each group is distinguished by similar physical or behavioral characteristics that can be recognized underwater. Although there are a few anomalies, most species integrate easily into this system.

The ID Groups and their families are displayed on the content pages. Each group's similar characteristics are listed at the beginning of the chapters. It is important for beginning fish watchers to become familiar with the make-up of each ID Group, so they can go quickly to the correct chapter to start the identification process.

The next step is to learn to recognize the major families that comprise each ID Group. Families are scientific groupings that are based upon similar physical characteristics. An overview of the family's behavioral and physical characteristics (that are observable by divers) is presented at the beginning of each ID Group. The total number of family members described in this book, along with diagrams of representative family body shapes, is also given.

Names

Information about each fish begins with the English common name (that used by the general public). Using common names exclusively for identification is impractical because several fish are known by more than one name. For example, Dragon Wrasse [pg. 105], is also know as the Reindeer Wrasse, Rockmover Wrasse, Clown Razorfish, and Pearlscale Razorfish. The common names used in this text are based on previously published names. If more than one name has been published, the one most commonly used in Galapagos or the name which best incorporated an anatomical feature that would help the layman remember and recognize the species was selected. Additional previously published names are listed in a "NOTE" at the end of the text describing the species. Several species included have never had a common name published. In these instances, a name was selected that describes a distinctive feature that can be used for visual identification. Following the English name is the Spanish common name typically used by locals in Galapagos. In this book common species names are capitalized to help set them apart, although this practice is not considered grammatically correct.

Below the common names is the two-part scientific name, which always appears in italics. The first word (always capitalized) is the genus. The genus name is given to a group of animals with very similar physiological characteristics (for example, approximately half of the region's species in the jack family in Galapagos belong to the genus *Caranx*). The second word (never capitalized) is the species. A species includes only animals that are sexually compatible and produce fertile offspring (continuing our example of jacks, the Black Jack is *Caranx lugubris*, while the Blue Spotted Jack is *Caranx melampygus*, and so on). Genus and species names, rooted in Latin and Greek, are used by scientists throughout the world.

The common and scientific family names are listed next. Because of its importance in identification, the common family name is also printed at the top of the left page.

Phases

Many species are shown in more than one photograph. This is necessary to show the differences in color, markings and shape that occur in these species.

Occasionally, the maturation phases in certain fish are so dramatic that they may be confused as a different species altogether. These phases can include JUVENILE, INTERMEDIATE and ADULT. Most parrotfish and wrasse have an additional phase called SUPERMALE (an example, the Bicolor Parrotfish, pg. 93). When the maturation phase is not given, the photograph is that of an adult. No attempt has been made to include juveniles that resemble the adults, or that live in habitats not frequented by divers.

Many fishes are able to alter both color and markings, either for camouflage or with mood changes. If these changes confuse identification, they may also be pictured (examples: Harlequin Wrasse, pg. 103, Sanguine Frogfish, pg. 131). In a few species the appearance of the MALE and FEMALE also differs (an example is the Pacific Boxfish, pg. 151).

Size

The size range of a species that divers are most likely to observe, followed by the generally accepted maximum size.

Depth

The reported depth range in scientific literature, although species are occasionally found outside these limits. When significant, the depths at which a species is most commonly found is given in "HABITAT & BEHAVIOR." Depths below the recommended safe diving limit of 130 feet are given only as a matter of scientific interest. Species that live exclusively below 130 feet are not included.

Distinctive Features

Colors, markings and anatomical differences that distinguish the fish from similar appearing species. In most cases, these features are readily apparent to divers, but occasionally they are quite subtle. When practical, the locations of these distinctive features are indicated by numbered arrows on the drawing next to the photograph. The numbers are keyed to the explanation in bold type on the left page.

Description

A general description of colors, markings and anatomical features. The information given in "DISTINCTIVE FEATURES" is not repeated in this section unless it is qualified or expanded.

Colors – The colors of many species vary considerably from individual to individual. In these situations the DESCRIPTION might read: "Bright red to reddish brown, olive-brown or gray." This means that the fish could be any of the colors and shades between. Many fish also have an ability to pale, darken, and change color. Because of this, color alone is rarely used for identification.

Markings – The terminology used to describe fish markings is indicated on the following drawings.

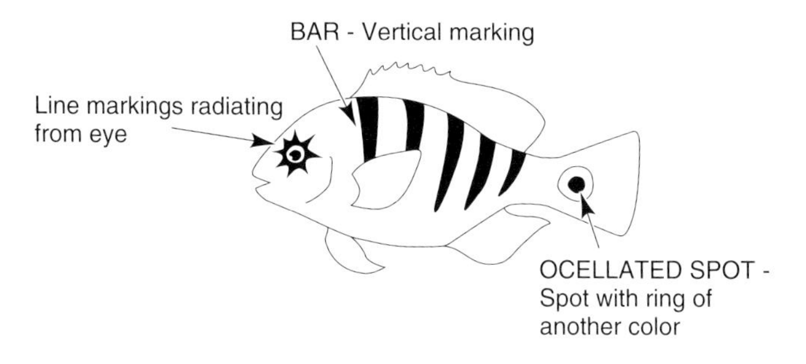

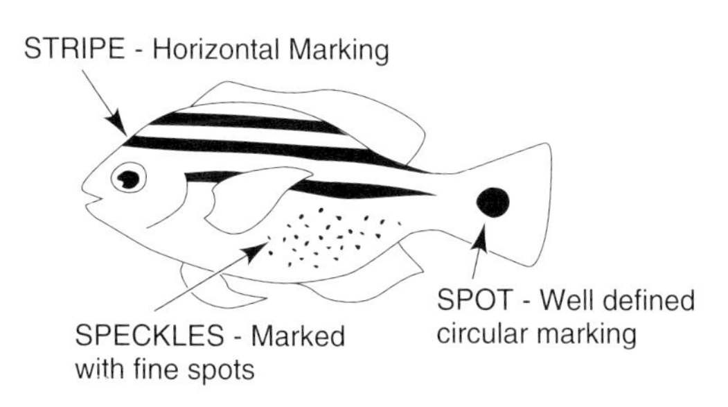

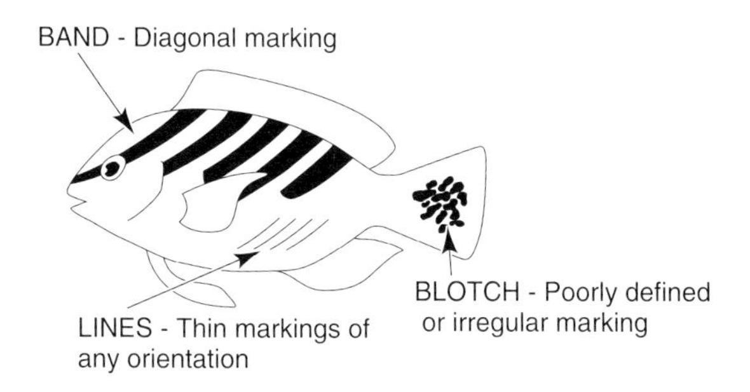

Anatomy – Anatomical features used for identification purposes are indicated on the following drawings.

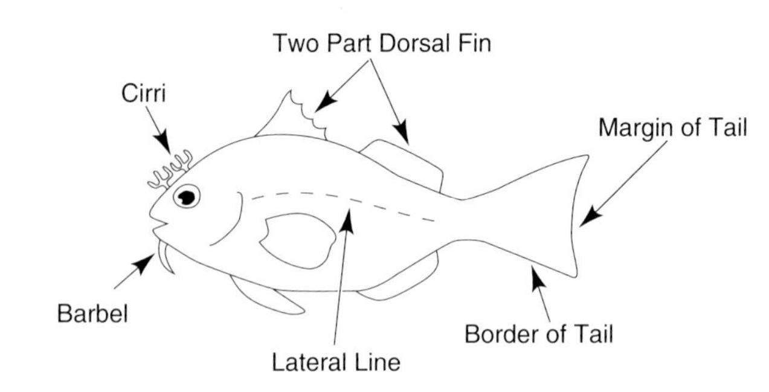

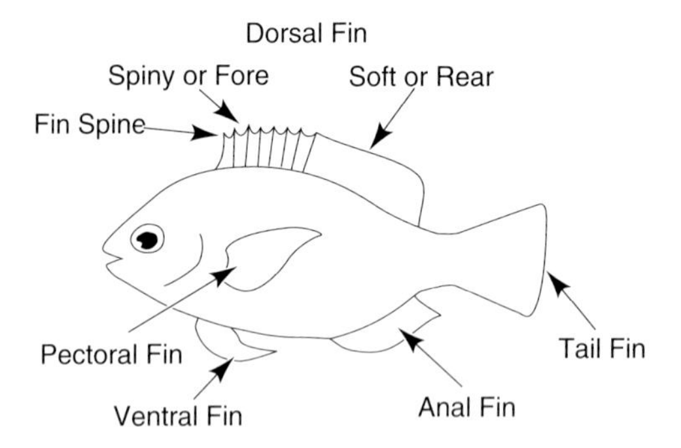

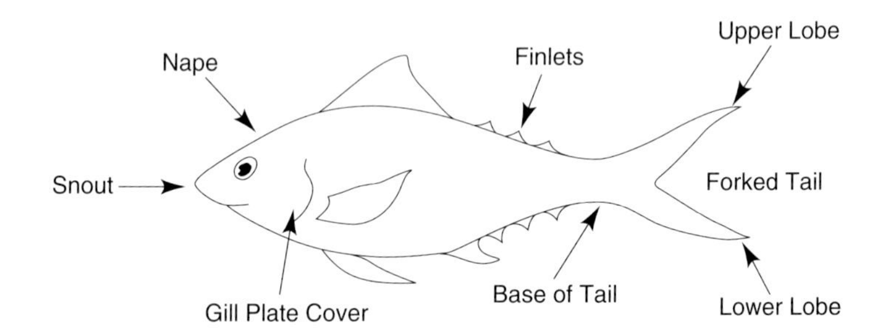

Abundance & Distribution

Abundance refers to a diver's likelihood of observing a species in its normal habitat and depth range on any given dive. This is not always indicative of the actual population. Definitions are as follows:

Abundant – At least several sightings can be expected on nearly every dive.

Common – Sightings are frequent, but not necessarily expected on every dive.

Occasional – Sightings are not unusual, but are not expected on a regular basis.

Uncommon – Sightings are unusual.

Rare – Sightings are exceptional.

Not reported – Indicates the fish is not known from these waters and is probably absent in the area.

Distribution describes where the fish may be found in Galapagos. This is followed by "ENDEMIC," if the species is found only in Galapagos; or if not endemic, its geographical distribution outside the archipelago is listed last.

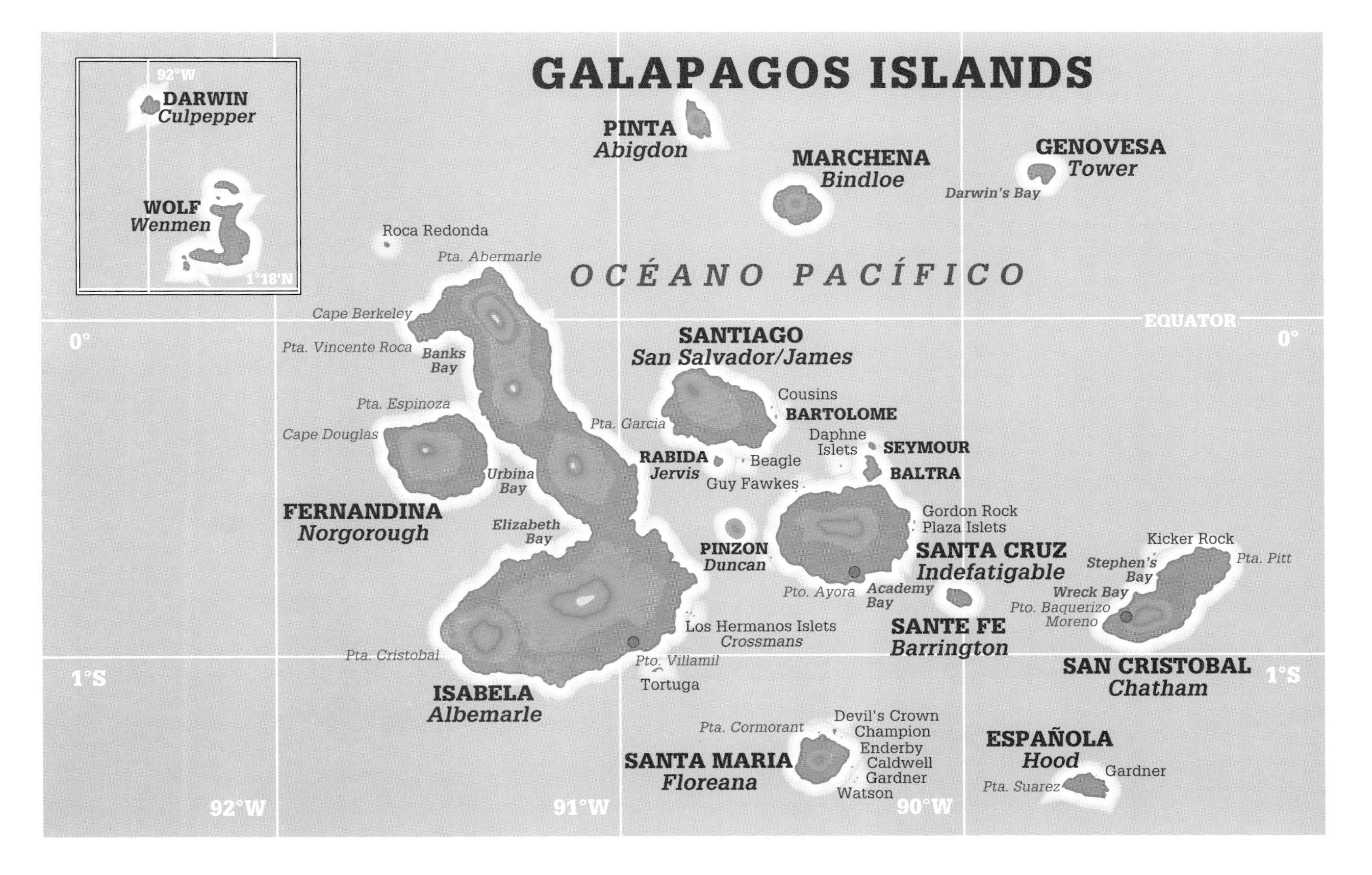

GALAPAGOS ISLANDS
92°W
DARWIN
Culpepper
WOLF
Wenmen
1°18'N
PINTA
Abigdon
MARCHENA
Bindloe
GENOVESA
Tower
Darwin's Bay
Roca Redonda
Pta. Abermarle
OCÉANO PACÍFICO
Cape Berkeley
EQUATOR
0°
0°
Pta. Vincente Roca
Banks Bay
SANTIAGO
San Salvador/James
Cousins
BARTOLOME
Pta. Espinoza
Cape Douglas
Pta. Garcia
Daphne Islets
SEYMOUR
RABIDA
Jervis
Beagle
BALTRA
Urbina Bay
Guy Fawkes
FERNANDINA
Norgorough
Elizabeth Bay
Gordon Rock
Plaza Islets
PINZON
Duncan
SANTA CRUZ
Indefatigable
Kicker Rock
Pta. Pitt
Stephen's Bay
Pto. Ayora
Academy Bay
Wreck Bay
Pto. Baquerizo Moreno
Los Hermanos Islets
Crossmans
SANTE FE
Barrington
Pta. Cristobal
Pto. Villamil
1°S
1°S
SAN CRISTOBAL
Chatham
Tortuga
ISABELA
Albemarle
Pta. Cormorant
Devil's Crown
Champion
Enderby
Caldwell
Gardner
Watson
SANTA MARIA
Floreana
ESPAÑOLA
Hood
Gardner
Pta. Suarez
92°W
91°W
90°W

Habitat & Behavior

Habitat is the type of underwater terrain where a particular species is likely to be found. Habitats frequented by divers, such as walls, boulder strewn slopes, and adjacent areas of sand and rubble have been emphasized.

Behavior is the fish's normal activities that may be observed by a diver and help in identification. Some of the behaviors discussed in this book include schooling and cleaning which are explained below.

Schooling – Many fish congregate in groups commonly called schools. The two primary reasons for this behavior are predator protection and cooperative hunting. It is theorized that when schooling fish pack together and move in unison, predators have a difficult time picking out and attacking a single target and, in the confusion of numbers, all members of the school may survive the attack. If, however, a fish gets separated from the school, the predator can concentrate on the lone fish and the attack is often successful. Some predators also school. They facilitate hunting by cooperating with each other in separating and confusing potential victims. The advantage of schooling also extends to algae-grazing fish such as Yellowtail Surgeonfish who, by sheer force of numbers, may overcome the territorial defenses of damselfish.

There are several types of congregations. Polarized schools are those in which all fish swim together in the same direction, at the same speed, keeping the same relative distance between one another. Non-polarized schools, or simply "schools," are those where the fish stay together, but do not display the rigid uniformity of movement seen in polarized schools. Fish may also come together for reasons other than protection or hunting. These types of gatherings often include a mixing of species and should, more properly, be called aggregations, rather than schools. For example, they may drift together in the shade of a coral head, or be attracted to the same area because of food. There is considerable gradation between the three types of congregations, making clear-cut categorizations difficult at times.

Polarized School

Aggregation

Reaction to Divers

This information relates to the fish's normal reaction to divers, and what a diver can do to try to get a closer look.

Similar Species

Occasionally there are similar appearing species that are not pictured. Usually they are fish that are rarely observed by divers. Characteristics and information are given that distinguish them from the pictured species.

Note

Includes any additional information that may be of interest or help in the identification process. Also, included are additional common names.

IDENTIFICATION GROUP 1

Disks & Ovals/Colorful

Butterflyfish—Angelfish—Surgeonfish

This ID Group consists of fish that are thin-bodied and have round or oval profiles. All have small mouths and are generally quite colorful.

FAMILY: Butterflyfish—Chaetondontidae

8 Species Included

Butterflyfish
(Typical Shape)

Longsnout
Butterflyfish

Reminiscent of their butterfly namesake, these small, colorful fish flit about the reefs in search of food. They travel alone or often in pairs, and occasionally in schools, using keen eyesight to spot tiny worms, exposed polyps and other marine invertebrates.

These round, thin-bodied fish are easy to recognize. Their small size (usually less than 6 inches) and slightly concave foreheads make them easy to distinguish from the larger, similar-shaped Angelfish which have rounded foreheads.

Butterflyfish are most commonly silver to white, with yellow tints and dark markings. Their eyes are concealed by dark bars on the head. This, and the false eyespots found on many juvenile and adult species, are characteristics thought to confuse predators. At night they become inactive, and may change color and markings.

The colors and markings of juveniles are somewhat different from those of adults, though their body shapes are nearly identical. Identifying adults is not difficult; however, learning to differentiate their similar-appearing juveniles is more of a challenge.

FAMILY: Angelfish—Pomacanthidae
1 Species Included

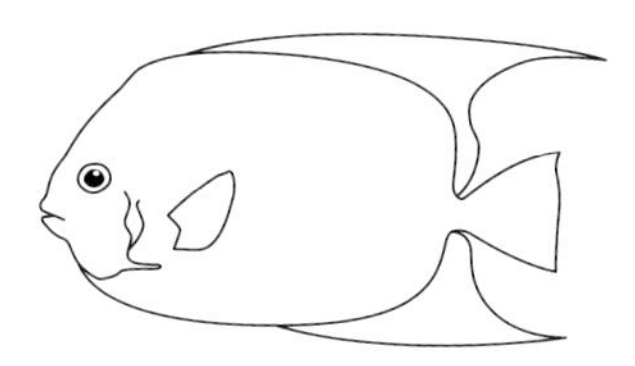

King Angelfish

Beautiful, disc-shaped angelfish are similar in habits and shape to butterflyfish; in fact, they were included in the same family for many years. Angelfish swim more gracefully and generally grow to more than one foot in length (although in tropical waters species called pygmy angelfish may grow to only 3 inches). Adult angelfish have long dorsal and anal fins, and rounded foreheads. A spine extending from the rear cheek over the lower gill cover conclusively distinguishes them from butterflyfish. Generally they travel alone or in pairs, although they may occasionally school. They forage on shallow reefs during daylight hours. Many feed on sponges. Only one member of this family is represented in Galapagos, the King Angelfish.

FAMILY: Surgeonfish—Acanthuridae
4 Species Included

Yellowtail

Goldrimmed

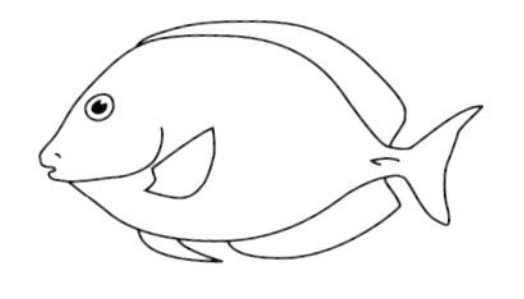

Convict Tang

A spine as sharp as a surgeon's scalpel, located on each side of the body at the tail's base, is the origin of this family's common name. They use these spines as defensive weapons by slashing them from side to side. When not in use, they fold forward against the body. Surgeonfish are thin-bodied and oval, with relatively long dorsal and anal fins, and a crescent tail. Their scales are not as conspicuous as those of butterfly and angelfish. All are frequently seen reef inhabitants that often mix in loose aggregations as they move about the reefs, feeding on algae.

DISTINCTIVE FEATURES: 1. White bar behind pectoral fin. 2. Yellow tail. Only angelfish in Galapagos.

DESCRIPTION: Dark blue body. Yellow to orange markings on dorsal and anal fins. Round area, "crown" of light blue spots on forehead. Ventral fin of females yellow, males white [right]. Juvenile body yellow to orange with bright blue bands [below right].

ABUNDANCE & DISTRIBUTION: Abundant entire archipelago. Northern Peru to Baja including offshore islands.

HABITAT & BEHAVIOR: Inhabit rocky boulder strewn areas. Often solitary, also in large, non-polarized schools [below]. Occasionally clean large fish, including hammerheads.

REACTION TO DIVERS: Tend to ignore divers, but move away when approached. Best way to get a closer look is to wait quietly in a concealed position near their course of travel.

Large School

DISTINCTIVE FEATURES: 1. Black eye ring. 2. Black bar from mid-dorsal fin to base of tail.

DESCRIPTION: Silver head; silver-yellow body. Black ring around snout. Black bar from in front of dorsal fin to above eye.

ABUNDANCE & DISTRIBUTION: Abundant entire archipelago. North to Baja, including offshore islands.

HABITAT & BEHAVIOR: Flit about rocky, boulder strewn areas. Often in large schools.

REACTION TO DIVERS: Tend to ignore divers, but move away when approached. Best way to get a closer look is to wait quietly in a concealed position near their course of travel or make a slow approach.

KING ANGELFISH
Pez Bandera
Holacanthus passer

FAMILY:
Angelfish –
Pomacanthidae

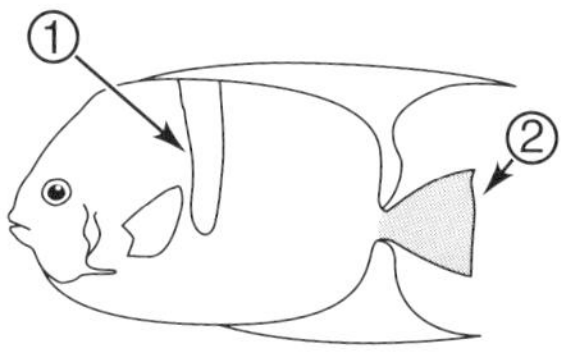

SIZE: 1/2 - 1 ft.,
max. 1 1/4 ft.
DEPTH: 15 - 100 ft.

**Juvenile,
Note Yellow-orange
Body And Blue Bands**

BARBERFISH
Mariposa Barbero
Johnrandallia nigrirostris

FAMILY:
Butterflyfish –
Chaetodontidae

SIZE: 3 - 4 in., max. 6 in.
DEPTH: 10 - 70 ft.

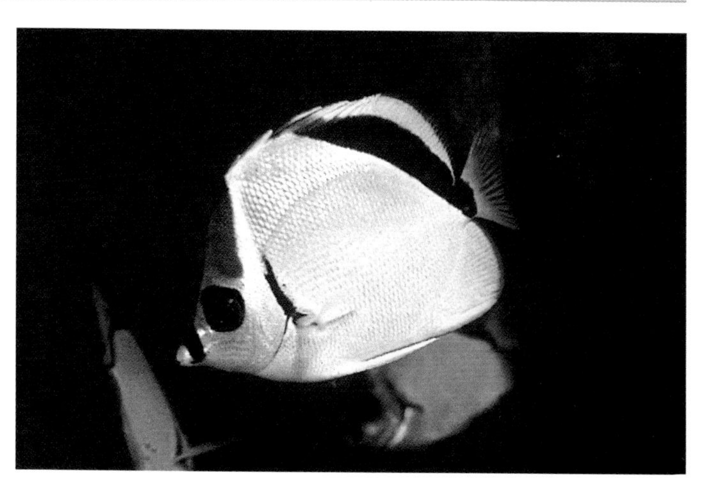

DISTINCTIVE FEATURES: 1. Three black bands: through eye, from foredorsal fin to pectoral fin base, and rear.

DESCRIPTION: Silver-gray. Black border on rear dorsal and anal fins. Three black bands on tail.

ABUNDANCE & DISTRIBUTION: Common entire archipelago. Peru to Southern California.

HABITAT & BEHAVIOR: Flit about rocky, boulder strewn areas. Often in pairs.

REACTION TO DIVERS: Tend to ignore divers, but move away when approached. Best way to get a closer look is to wait quietly in a concealed position near their course of travel.

DISTINCTIVE FEATURES: 1. Black scythe-shaped bar/stripe from gill cover to upper back continuing to below base of tail.

DESCRIPTION: Yellowish silver. Black soft dorsal fin and anal fin edged with white. Yellow foredorsal fin spines.

ABUNDANCE & DISTRIBUTION: Occasional entire archipelago. North to Southern California.

HABITAT & BEHAVIOR: Flit about rocky, boulder strewn areas; often solitary. Prefer cooler, deep water.

REACTION TO DIVERS: Tend to ignore divers, but move away when approached. Best way to get a closer look is to wait quietly in a concealed position near their course of travel.

DISTINCTIVE FEATURES: 1. Diagonal black bands across body. 2. All fins yellow.

DESCRIPTION: Silver with black band encircling body; black bar through eye; black band encircles mouth.

ABUNDANCE & DISTRIBUTION: Rare, known only from Darwin and Wolf. Tropical Indo-Pacific.

HABITAT & BEHAVIOR: Flit about rocky, boulder strewn areas; often solitary.

REACTION TO DIVERS: Tend to ignore divers, but move away when approached. Best way to get a close look is to wait quietly in a concealed position near their course of travel.

THREEBANDED BUTTERFLYFISH
Mariposa de Tres Bandas
Chaetodon humeralis

FAMILY:
Butterflyfish – Chaetodontidae

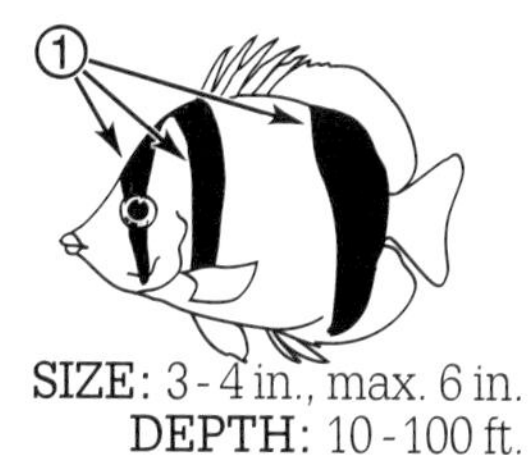

SIZE: 3 - 4 in., max. 6 in.
DEPTH: 10 - 100 ft.

SCYTHE BUTTERFLYFISH
Mariposa de Scythe
Chaetodon falcifer

FAMILY:
Butterflyfish – Chaetodontidae

SIZE: 3 - 4 in., max. 6 in.
DEPTH: 50 - 130 ft.

MEYER'S BUTTERFLY
Mariposa de Meyer
Chaetodon meyeri

FAMILY:
Butterflyfish – Chaetodontidae

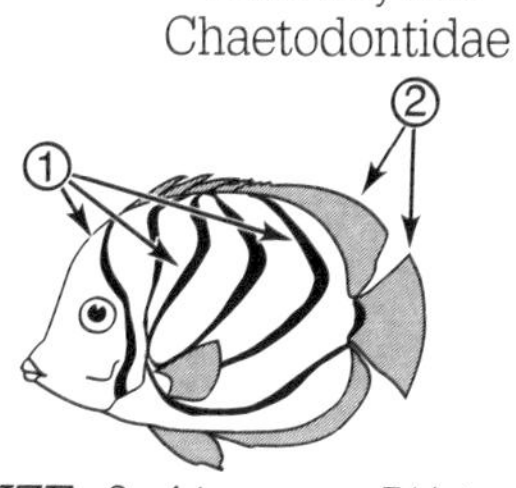

SIZE: 3 - 4 in., max. 5 1/2 in.
DEPTH: 15 - 75 ft.

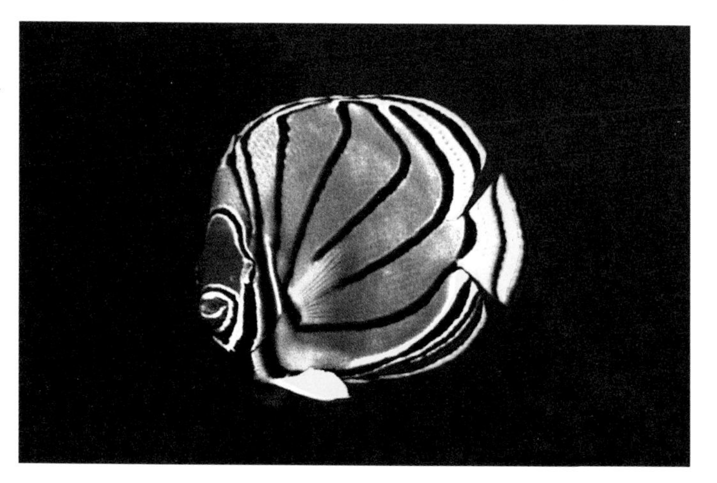

DISTINCTIVE FEATURES: 1. Long thread-like extension of upper rear dorsal fin. 2. Black spot on upper rear of dorsal fin.

DESCRIPTION: Silver forebody; yellow rear body, including fins. Black bar through eye; diagonal black banding runs from forehead upward toward dorsal fin and on body toward anal fin.

ABUNDANCE & DISTRIBUTION: Rare, known only from Darwin and Wolf. Red Sea and tropical Indo-Pacific, including Hawaii.

HABITAT & BEHAVIOR: Flit about rocky, boulder strewn areas; often solitary.

REACTION TO DIVERS: Tend to ignore divers, but move away when approached. Best way to get a closer look is to wait quietly in a concealed position near their course of travel.

DISTINCTIVE FEATURES: 1. Wide black bar (mask) across eye with white bar behind.

DESCRIPTION: Yellow body with dusky diagonal bands and black diagonal band from white bar behind eye to dorsal fin; black blotch at base of tail.

ABUNDANCE & DISTRIBUTION: Rare, known only from Darwin and Wolf. Tropical Indo-Pacific, including Hawaii.

HABITAT & BEHAVIOR: Flit about rocky, boulder strewn areas; often solitary.

REACTION TO DIVERS: Tend to ignore divers, but move away when approached. Best way to get a closer look is to wait quietly in a concealed position near their course of travel.

DISTINCTIVE FEATURES: 1. Dark bar across eye. 2. Broad, dusky yellow-brown bar behind pectoral fin.

DESCRIPTION: Whitish forebody; yellow-brown rear with horizontal rows of small dusky brown spots. Dorsal, anal and tail fins yellow.

ABUNDANCE & DISTRIBUTION: Rare, known only from Darwin and Wolf. Tropical Indo-Pacific, including Hawaii.

HABITAT & BEHAVIOR: Flit about rocky, boulder strewn areas. Often solitary, occasionally in pairs.

REACTION TO DIVERS: Tend to ignore divers, but move away when approached. Best way to get a closer look is to wait quietly in a concealed position near their course of travel.

THREADFIN BUTTERFLY
Mariposa de Aleta Ribeteada
Chaetodon auriga
FAMILY:
Butterflyfish – Chaetodontidae

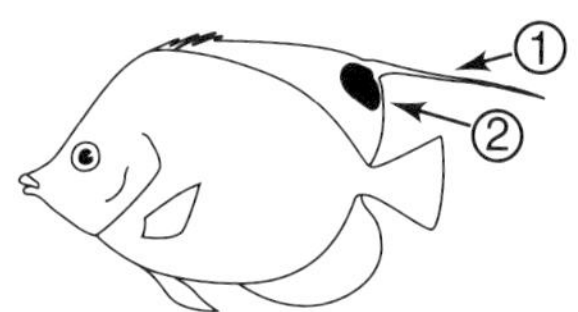

SIZE: 3-4 in., max. 6 in.
DEPTH: 15-90 ft.

RACOON BUTTERFLY
Mariposa Mapache
Chaetodon lunula
FAMILY:
Butterflyfish – Chaetodontidae

SIZE: 3-4½ in., max. 6¼ in.
DEPTH: 15-100 ft.

DUSKYBARRED BUTTERFLY
Mariposa de Barra Penumbre
Chaetodon kleinii
FAMILY:
Butterflyfish – Chaetodontidae

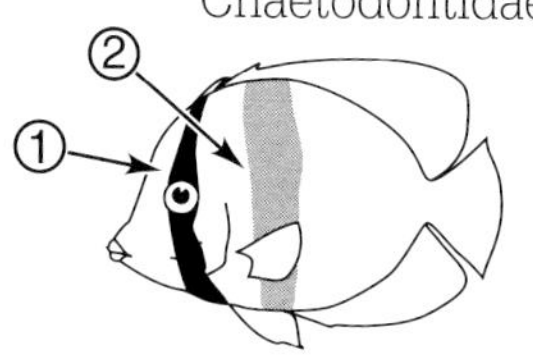

SIZE: 3-4 in., max. 4½ in.
DEPTH: 35-190 ft.

DISTINCTIVE FEATURES: 1. Elongated snout. 2. Black spot on anal fin below base of tail.

DESCRIPTION: Yellow body; black upper half of head, silver below; translucent tail.

ABUNDANCE & DISTRIBUTION: Rare, known only from Darwin and Wolf. North to Baja including offshore islands; also tropical Indo-Pacific.

HABITAT & BEHAVIOR: Flit about rocky, boulder strewn areas; often solitary.

REACTION TO DIVERS: Tend to ignore divers, but move away when approached. Best way to get a close look is to wait quietly in a concealed position near their course of travel.

DISTINCTIVE FEATURES: 1. Yellow tail. 2. White band behind eye bordered in black.

DESCRIPTION: Gray to brown. Row of three retractile spines on base of tail. Many have a few black spots near base of tail.

ABUNDANCE & DISTRIBUTION: Abundant entire archipelago. Cocos and Revillagigedos Islands.

HABITAT & BEHAVIOR: Swim about reefs in large schools.

REACTION TO DIVERS: Tend to ignore divers, but move away when approached. Best way to get a closer look is to wait quietly in a concealed position near their course of travel.

NOTE: Do not confuse with a similar appearing Yellowtail Surgeonfish, *P. punctatus*, (not in Galapagos) distinguished by numerous black spots on body. Upper Gulf of California to El Salvador and offshore islands.

DISTINCTIVE FEATURES: 1. Yellow-gold stripes along base of dorsal and anal fins.

DESCRIPTION: Dark blue; white tail. Blotch below eye. Single, yellow, retractile spine at base of tail.

ABUNDANCE & DISTRIBUTION: Abundant Darwin, Wolf, Roca Redonda, Genovesa; uncommon or rare remainder of archipelago. North to Baja and offshore islands; also tropical Pacific.

HABITAT & BEHAVIOR: Swim rapidly about reefs.

REACTION TO DIVERS: Shy; tend to avoid divers, swim away when approached. Best way to get a closer look is to wait quietly in a concealed position near their course of travel.

LONGNOSE BUTTERFLYFISH
Mariposa Nariz Larga
Foreipiger flavissimus

FAMILY:
Butterflyfish – Chaetodontidae

SIZE: 3 - 4 in., max. 6 in.
DEPTH: 30 - 130 ft.

YELLOWTAILED SURGEONFISH
Chancho
Prionurus laticlavius

FAMILY:
Surgeonfish – Acanthuridae

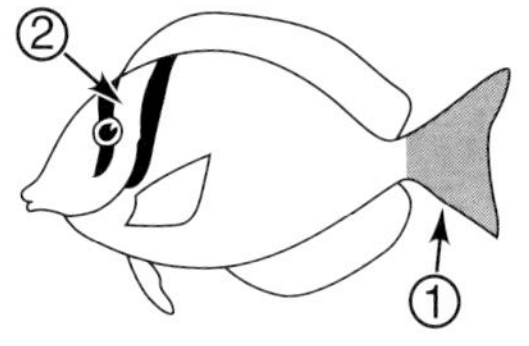

SIZE: ½ - 1 ft., max. 1½ ft.
DEPTH: 10 - 100 ft.

GOLDRIMMED SURGEONFISH
Pez Cirujano de Filo Amarillo
Acanthurus nigricans

FAMILY:
Surgeonfish – Acanthuridae

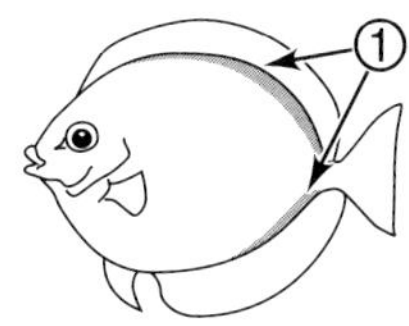

SIZE: 5 - 7 in., max. 8 in.
DEPTH: 10 - 80 ft.

DISTINCTIVE FEATURES: 1. Yellow pectoral fin. 2. Yellow mask runs horizontally over eyes.

DESCRIPTION: Light blue to dark purple. Narrow, light blue to yellow stripe along base of dorsal and anal fins; thin, light stripes on dorsal, anal and tail fins; often whitish blotch on base of tail. Retractile spine at base of tail.

ABUNDANCE & DISTRIBUTION: Occasional entire archipelago. North to Baja, including offshore islands; also tropical West Africa and Indo-Pacific.

HABITAT & BEHAVIOR: Swim in open water above reefs and off walls. Most common 10 to 25 feet of water.

REACTION TO DIVERS: Shy, but curious. Tend to approach when diver appears disinterested.

DISTINCTIVE FEATURES: 1. Six black bands.

DESCRIPTION: Yellowish cream to white or silvery. Single retractile spine at base of tail.

ABUNDANCE & DISTRIBUTION: Uncommon Darwin, Wolf, Tower; rare to absent balance of archipelago. North to Baja, including offshore islands; also tropical Pacific.

HABITAT & BEHAVIOR: Swim singly and in small schools about shallow reefs.

REACTION TO DIVERS: Tend to ignore divers, but move away when approached. Best way to get a closer look is to wait quietly in a concealed position near their course of travel.

DISTINCTIVE FEATURES: 1. Long dorsal fin end with thread-like tip. 2. Long snout. 3. Three bold black bands over eye to ventral fins, rear body and on tail.

DESCRIPTION: White with yellowish areas. Orange saddle outlined in black on snout. Short horns or spines over eyes; no spines at base of tail.

ABUNDANCE & DISTRIBUTION: Common to occasional entire archipelago. North to Baja, including offshore islands; also tropical Indo-Pacific.

HABITAT & BEHAVIOR: Inhabit rocky boulder strewn areas and along walls. Swim singly, in pairs or in small aggregations, occasionally in large schools.

REACTION TO DIVERS: Tend to ignore divers, but move away when approached. Best way to get a closer look is to wait quietly in a concealed position near their course of travel.

NOTE: Closely related to surgeonfish. Only family member.

PURPLE SURGEONFISH
Pez Cirujano Púrpura
Acanthurus xanthopterus

FAMILY:
Surgeonfish –
Acanthuridae

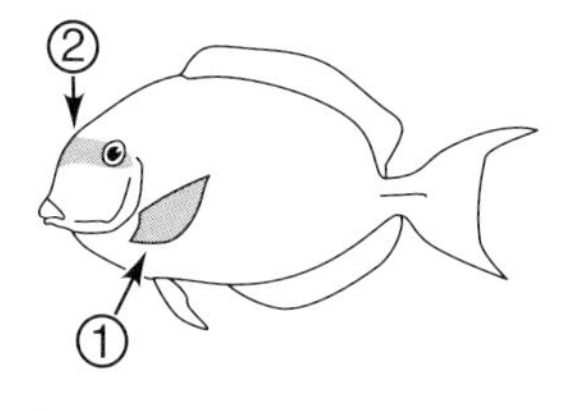

SIZE: 8 - 12 in., max. 20 in.
DEPTH: 10 - 80 ft.

CONVICT TANG
Lancero Convicto
Acanthurus triostegus

FAMILY:
Surgeonfish –
Acanthuridae

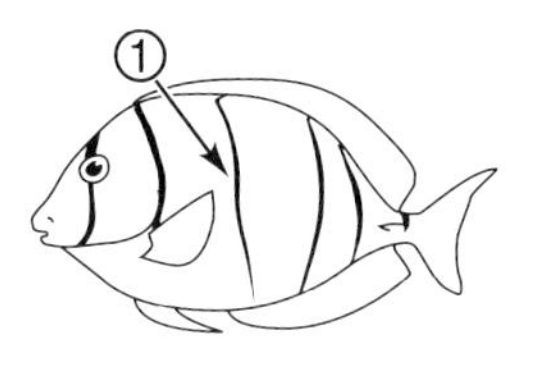

SIZE: 4 - 6 in., max. 9 in.
DEPTH: 10 - 50 ft.

MOORISH IDOL
Idolo moro
Zanclus cornutus

FAMILY:
Moorish Idol – Zanclidae

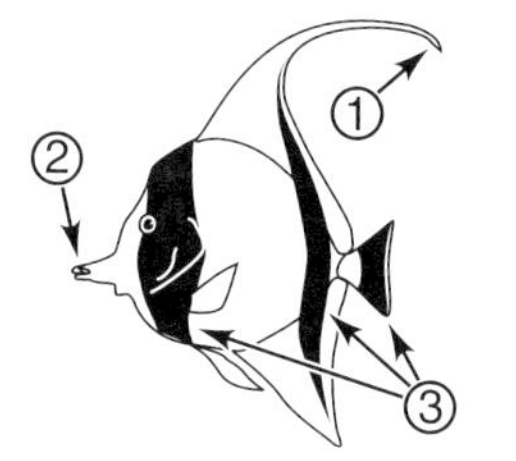

SIZE: 4 - 6 in., max. 9 in.
DEPTH: 10 - 150 ft.

IDENTIFICATION GROUP 2

Silvery

Jack—Chub—Porgy—Others

This ID Group consists of fish that are silver to gray in color, and are generally unpatterned; however, several species have bluish, yellowish or greenish tints and occasional markings. All have forked tails.

FAMILY: Jack—Carangidae

14 Species Included

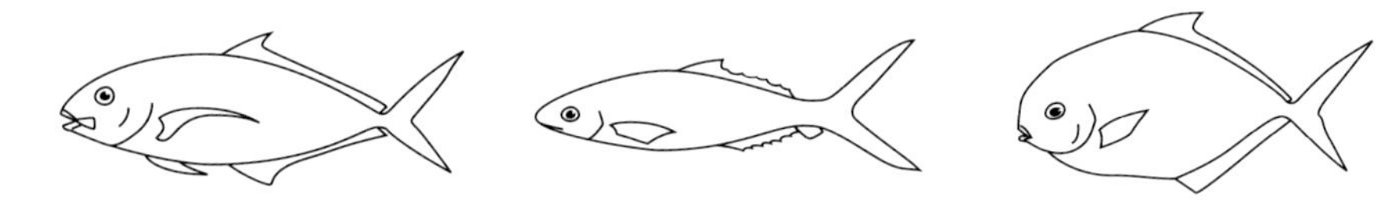

Jack (typical shape) Rainbow Runner Steel Pompano

Jacks are strong swimming predators of the open sea. They spawn at sea. The juveniles have bar markings, and hover under floating objects; with maturity they begin to school. Though schools occasionally pass over reefs in search of small fish and crustaceans, only a few species are seen about reefs on a regular basis.

Most jacks have silvery sides, darkish backs and large eyes. They are thin, and have small tail bases that reduce drag. All have deeply forked tails that facilitate speed, and two-part dorsal fins (high in the front, low in the rear) that extend to the tail.

As a family, jacks are easy to recognize, but it takes a sharp eye to distinguish between similar-appearing species such as the Almaco, Bigeye Jack, Black Jack. Body shape, color tints, and inconspicuous markings are the keys to correct identification.

FAMILY: Mackerels, Tunas & Bonitos — Scombridae

6 Species Included

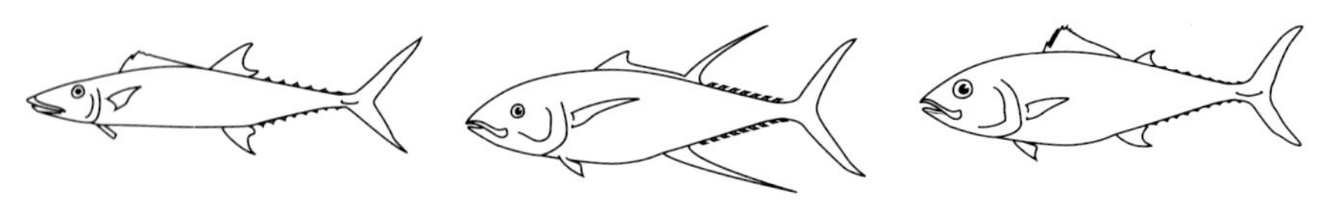

Sierra Mackerel Yellowfin Tuna Indo-Pacific Bonito

Mackerels, tunas and bonitos are silvery, strong, fast swimming predators of the open sea. They have two dorsal fins that fold into grooves. Between the dorsal and anal fins and the tail is a series of small fins, called finlets. The base of tail is slender with two or more keels on each side. Scales are small and not obvious. Keys to identification are body shape, size of fins and occasional subtle darkish markings that can fade or intensify.

FAMILY: Chubs — Kyphosidae

4 Species Included

Cortez Rainbow Dusky

Chubs are moderately deep-bodied, oval shaped fish with forked tails. They are generally silver and have noticeable scales. The head and terminal mouth are small. The Cortez and Striped Chubs are difficult to distinguish from one another; careful attention to detail is required to make identification. The remaining species are quite distinctive and easy to identify.

FAMILY: Others

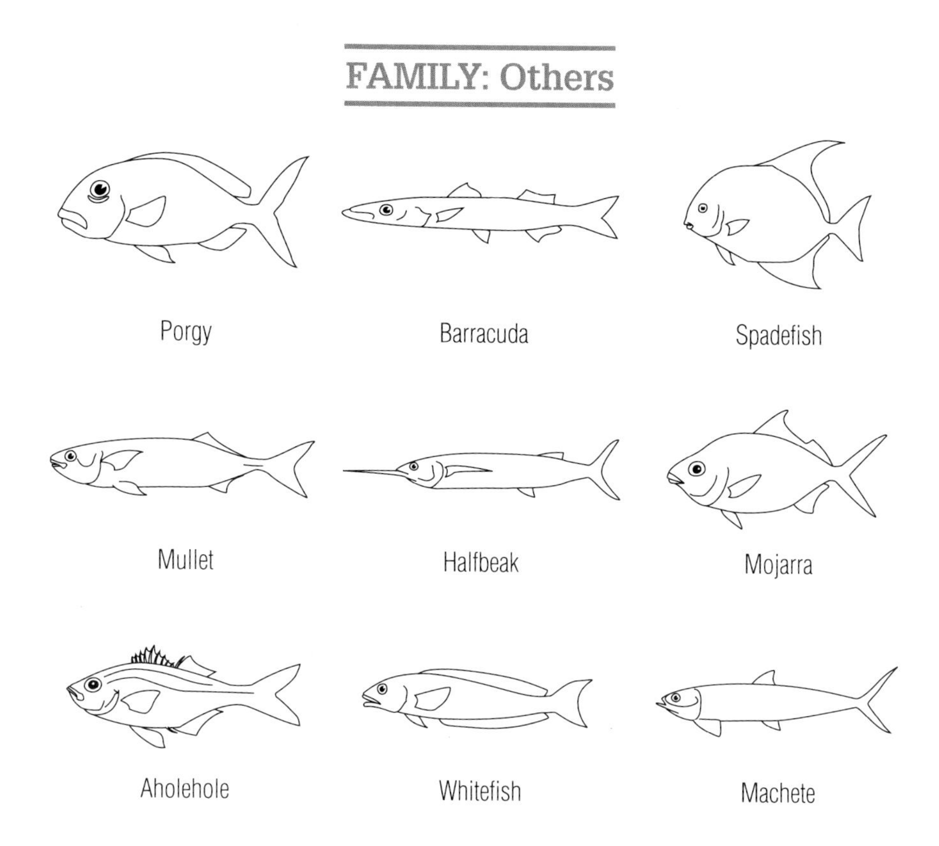

DISTINCTIVE FEATURES: 1. Black spot rear upper edge of gill cover. 2. White tipped dorsal fin.

DESCRIPTION: Silver to silvery gray. Large eye. Forehead (nape) steep.

ABUNDANCE & DISTRIBUTION: Common to occasional entire archipelago. North to Baja, including offshore islands; also tropical Indo-Pacific.

HABITAT & BEHAVIOR: Swim rapidly in large, somewhat polarized schools in open water over deep reefs, steep slopes and along walls. Travel in pairs when mating, male turns almost black [pictured].

REACTION TO DIVERS: Apparently attracted by bubbles; often make rapid approach, circle several times and depart.

SIMILAR SPECIES: Pacific Crevalle Jack, *C. canius*, has dark blotch at pectoral fin base; deeper body.

DISTINCTIVE FEATURES: Black to brown, can be silvery. No distinctive markings.

DESCRIPTION: Forehead (nape) steep. Dorsal and anal fins long.

ABUNDANCE & DISTRIBUTION: Common to occasional entire archipelago. Circumtropical.

HABITAT & BEHAVIOR: Swim in open water over deep reefs, steep slopes and along walls. Travel solitary or several individuals in loose aggregations; never form large schools.

REACTION TO DIVERS: Tend to ignore divers, but move away when approached. Somewhat curious, occasionally approach when diver appears disinterested.

DISTINCTIVE FEATURES: Iridescent blue tinting and highlights.

DESCRIPTION: Silvery; neon blue, gold and black spots and speckles; blue dorsal, anal and tail fins.

ABUNDANCE & DISTRIBUTION: Occasional entire archipelago. North to Baja, including offshore islands; also tropical Indo-Pacific.

HABITAT & BEHAVIOR: Swim rapidly in small, somewhat polarized groups or schools in open water over deep reefs, along walls and drop-offs. Often in areas with current.

REACTION TO DIVERS: Apparently attracted by bubbles; often make rapid, single pass and depart.

BIGEYE JACK
Jurel Ojón
Caranx sexfasciatus
FAMILY:
Jack – Carangidae

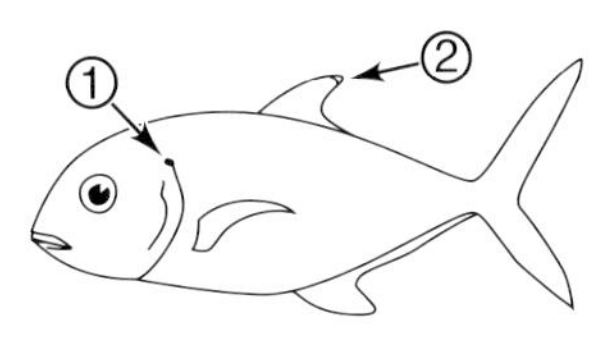

SIZE: 1¼-2 ft., max. 2½ ft.
DEPTH: 10-180 ft.

BLACK JACK
Jurel Negro
Caranx lugubris
FAMILY:
Jack – Carangidae

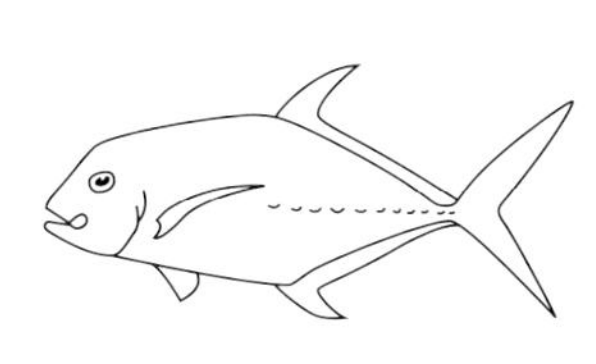

SIZE: 1¼-2 ft., max. 3 ft.
DEPTH: 10-650 ft.

BLUE SPOTTED JACK
Jurel Azul
Caranx melampygus
FAMILY:
Jack – Carangidae

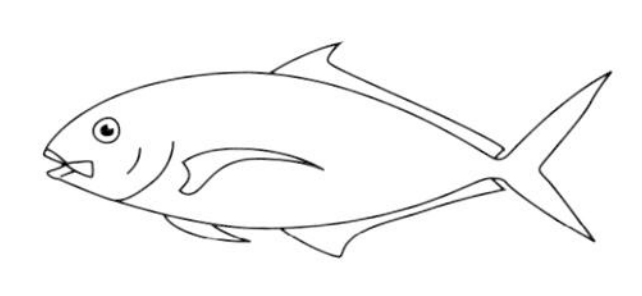

SIZE: 1¼-2 ft., max. 3 ft.
DEPTH: 10-180 ft.

DISTINCTIVE FEATURES: 1. Black to dusky band runs from foredorsal fin across eye to upper lip.

DESCRIPTION: Silvery to gray.

ABUNDANCE & DISTRIBUTION: Occasional entire archipelago. Peru north to Southern California, including offshore islands; circumtropical.

HABITAT & BEHAVIOR: Swim rapidly in large, somewhat polarized schools in open water over deep reefs, along walls and steep slopes.

REACTION TO DIVERS: Apparently attracted by bubbles; often make rapid approach, circle several times and depart.

NOTE: Also commonly known as "Pacific Amber Jack."

DISTINCTIVE FEATURES: 1. Black spot on upper rear gill cover with white body streak behind.

DESCRIPTION: Silvery. Body more slender than other members of genus. Often show thin, dusky, rib-like bars.

ABUNDANCE & DISTRIBUTION: Occasional entire archipelago. Peru north to Southern California, including offshore islands; also tropical Indo-Pacific.

HABITAT & BEHAVIOR: Swim rapidly in small, somewhat polarized groups or schools in open water over deep reefs, along walls and drop-offs.

REACTION TO DIVERS: Apparently attracted by bubbles; often make rapid, single pass and depart.

DISTINCTIVE FEATURES: 1. Two blue stripes from head to tail with pale to brilliant yellow or gold stripe between. 2. Yellow tail.

DESCRIPTION: Silvery to gray; back dark, belly light. Rear dorsal and anal fins, serrate pattern, with a single finlet before tail.

ABUNDANCE & DISTRIBUTION: Occasional entire archipelago. North to Baja, including offshore islands; circumtropical.

HABITAT & BEHAVIOR: Swim rapidly in small, somewhat polarized groups to large aggregations in open water over deep reefs, along walls and drop-offs. Prefer areas with current.

REACTION TO DIVERS: Apparently attracted by bubbles; often make rapid, single pass and depart.

ALMACO JACK
Palometa
Seriola rivoliana
FAMILY:
Jack – Carangidae

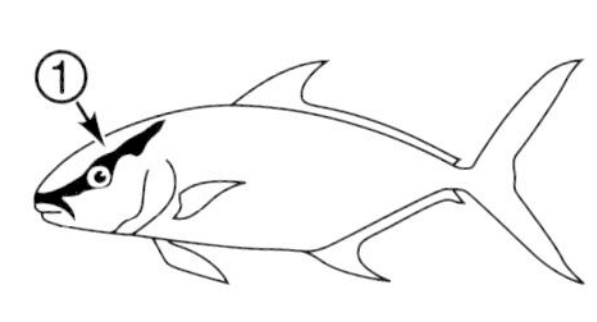

SIZE: 1½ - 2½ ft., max. 5 ft.
DEPTH: 10 - 180 ft.

GREEN JACK
Jurel Verde
Caranx caballus
FAMILY:
Jack – Carangidae

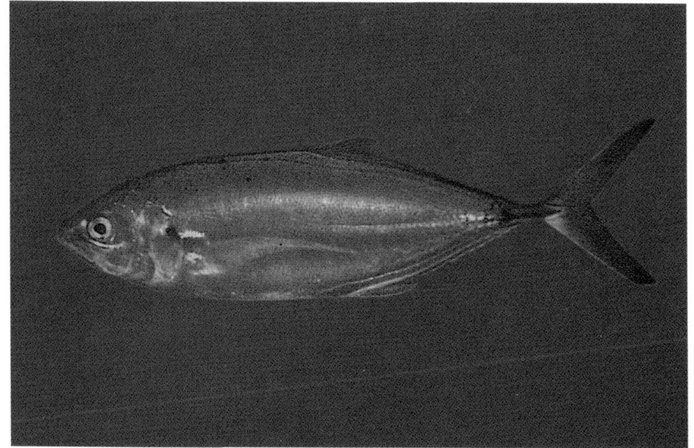

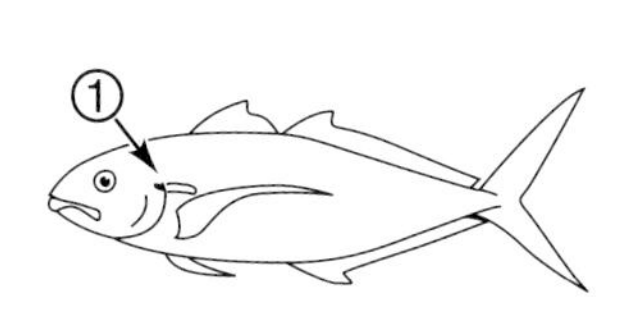

SIZE: 6 - 12 in., max. 1¼ ft.
DEPTH: 10 - 180 ft.

RAINBOW RUNNER
Macarela Arco Iris
Elagatis bipinnulata
FAMILY:
Jack – Carangidae

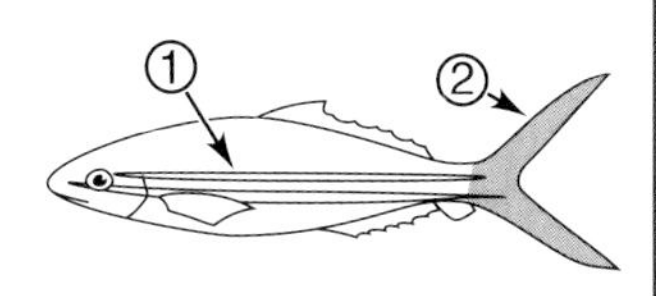

SIZE: 1 - 2½ ft., max. 4 ft.
DEPTH: 10 - 100 ft.

DISTINCTIVE FEATURES: Silvery, oval body. No distinctive markings.

DESCRIPTION: Often darkish; dorsal, anal and tail fins dark. Pectoral fins long, spinous dorsal fin low. Young have six to eight narrow pale bars. Tongue, roof and floor of mouth white (origin of common name), sides and throat black.

ABUNDANCE & DISTRIBUTION: Occasional Darwin, Wolf, Roca Redonda; uncommon to absent balance of archipelago. North to California; tropical circumglobal.

HABITAT & BEHAVIOR: Pelagic, form schools in open water. Frequent islands, sweeping by steep slopes and walls.

REACTION TO DIVERS: Tend to ignore divers, but move away when approached. Somewhat curious; apparently attracted by bubbles, may make close pass.

DISTINCTIVE FEATURES: 1. White bar behind head extends to pectoral fin.

DESCRIPTION: Silvery to gray. Deep body; thin, deeply forked tail. Dusky rib pattern often shows on body.

ABUNDANCE & DISTRIBUTION: Abundant entire archipelago. Peru north to Baja.

HABITAT & BEHAVIOR: Swim rapidly in large, polarized schools near surface of open water close to shore. Prefer areas with current.

REACTION TO DIVERS: Tend to ignore divers, but move away if rapidly approached. Can occasionally enter school with a very slow, non-threatening approach.

DISTINCTIVE FEATURES: 1. Steep, blunt forehead. Deep bodied.

DESCRIPTION: Silvery, often with bluish or greenish tints; scales not obvious. Compressed body, deeply forked tail. Diamond-shaped juveniles trail long thread-like filaments from dorsal and anal fins; as fish mature, filaments usually become progressively shorter, disappearing in large adults.

ABUNDANCE & DISTRIBUTION: Uncommon Darwin, Wolf, Roca Redonda; rare balance of archipelago. Circumtropical.

HABITAT & BEHAVIOR: Inhabit clear open water, occasionally cruise along steep slopes and walls. Adults are solitary.

REACTION TO DIVERS: Apparently attracted by bubbles; often make rapid, single pass and depart.

NOTE: Also, especially juveniles, commonly called "Threadfin" or "Threadfish."

COTTONMOUTH JACK
Jurel Boca Algodón
Uraspis secunda
FAMILY:
Jack – Carangidae

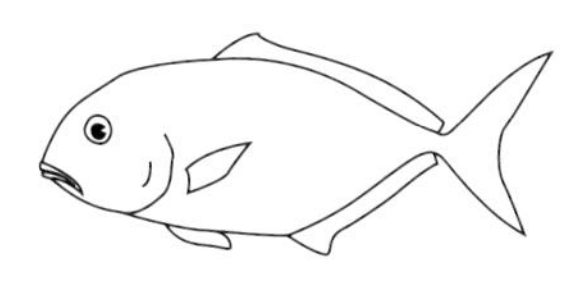

SIZE: 8-14 in.,
max. 18½ in.
DEPTH: 3-120 ft.

STEEL POMPANO
Pámpano Acerado
Trachinotus stilbe
FAMILY:
Jack – Carangidae

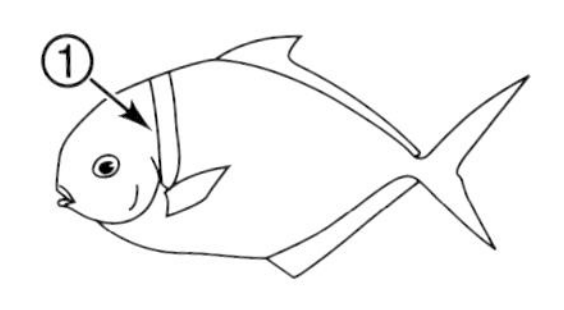

SIZE: 5-8 in., max. 10 in.
DEPTH: 0-20 ft.

AFRICAN POMPANO
Pámpano Africano
Alectis ciliaris
FAMILY:
Jack – Carangidae

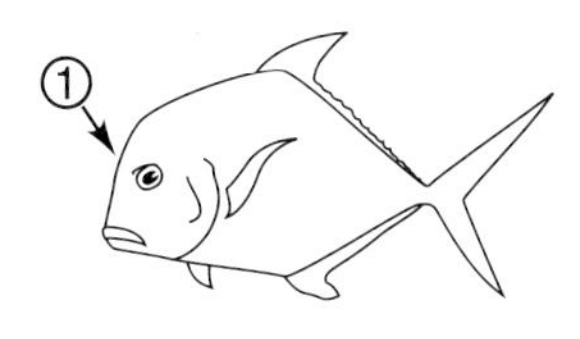

SIZE: 6-12 in., max. 16 in.
DEPTH: 3-325 ft.

DISTINCTIVE FEATURES: 1. Large eye (diameter greater than snout length).

DESCRIPTION: Bright, reflective silver. Rib pattern on body; scutes on rear lateral line; forked tail.

ABUNDANCE & DISTRIBUTION: Occasional entire archipelago. North to Baja; also circumtropical and sub-tropical.

HABITAT & BEHAVIOR: Form small to large, rapidly swimming schools. Often sweep over reefs, shallow bays and along walls.

REACTION TO DIVERS: Tend to ignore divers, but keep their distance, moving away if approached. Apparently attracted by bubbles; occasionally make one or two rapid passes.

DISTINCTIVE FEATURES: 1. Dark spot at base of pectoral fin. 2. Two dorsal fins.

DESCRIPTION: Long, cigar-shaped body. Bluish silver with yellowish forked tail.

ABUNDANCE & DISTRIBUTION: Occasional entire archipelago. North to Monterey Bay, California, including offshore islands.

HABITAT & BEHAVIOR: Rapidly swimming schools inhabit open water. Often sweep over reefs, shallow bays and along walls.

REACTION TO DIVERS: Tend to ignore divers. Apparently attracted by bubbles; occasionally make one or two rapid passes. Move away if approached.

DISTINCTIVE FEATURES: 1. Five to seven bold dark bars encircle body.

DESCRIPTION: Silvery white to gray. Long, torpedo-shaped body and forked tail.

ABUNDANCE & DISTRIBUTION: Uncommon entire archipelago. Peru north to southern Canada; worldwide in tropical to warm temperate water.

HABITAT & BEHAVIOR: Accompany large fish, including sharks, rays, whales and, occasionally, ships.

REACTION TO DIVERS: Ignore divers.

BIGEYE SCAD
Jurelito Ojo Grande
Selar crumenophthalmus
FAMILY
Jack/Scad – Carangidae

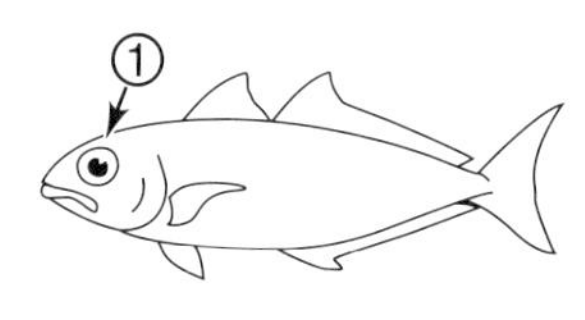

SIZE: 6-10 in., max. 18 in.
DEPTH: 0-500 ft.

YELLOWTAIL SCAD
Jurelito de Cola Amarilla
Decapterus sanctae-helenae
FAMILY
Jack/Scad – Carangidae

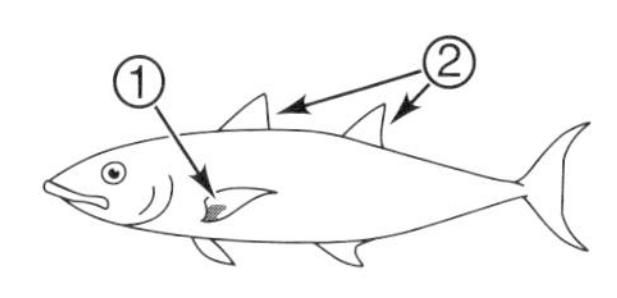

SIZE: 8-12 in., max. 18 in.
DEPTH: 0-80 ft.

PILOT FISH
Pez Piloto
Naucrates ductor
FAMILY:
Jack – Carangidae

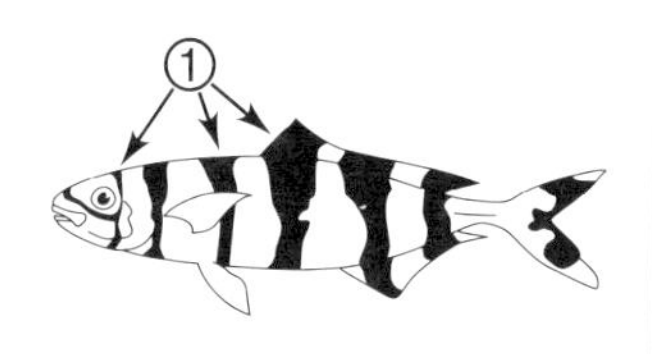

SIZE: 6-15 in., max. 2 ft.
DEPTH: 3-100 ft.

DISTINCTIVE FEATURES: 1. Long, yellow rear dorsal and anal fins. 2. Yellow finlets.

DESCRIPTION: Silvery, often with iridescent bluish or yellowish tints. Widely forked tail; pectoral fin extends to base of anal fin.

ABUNDANCE & DISTRIBUTION: Abundant (but rarely observed by divers) entire archipelago. Peru north to Baja; circumtropical. Commercially harvested.

HABITAT & BEHAVIOR: Inhabit clear, open oceanic water. Run in large schools. Occasionally along deep walls of offshore rocks and small islands.

REACTION TO DIVERS: Apparently attracted by bubbles; may make one or two rapid passes and depart.

SIMILAR SPECIES: Albacore or Longfin Tuna, *Thunnus alalunga*, distinguished by relatively short, rear dorsal and anal fins and long pectoral fin extending beyond base of anal fin. Both species also commonly called "Albacora."

DISTINCTIVE FEATURES: 1. Large, dark spots on belly under pectoral fin. (Similar Indo-Pacific Bonito, [next] lack these spots.) **2. Dark stripes above midline on back.**

DESCRIPTION: Dark, silver-blue back; silvery to white sides and belly. May have a few faint stripes on belly behind spots.

ABUNDANCE & DISTRIBUTION: Occasional entire archipelago. North to Southern California.

HABITAT & BEHAVIOR: Prefer open water, but occasionally sweep in close to island drop-offs. Swim in large, rapidly moving, polarized schools. Occasionally small groups swim along walls feeding on Creolefish.

REACTION TO DIVERS: Tend to ignore divers, but move away if rapidly approached.

NOTE: Also commonly known as "Mexican Little Tunny" and "Negra."

DISTINCTIVE FEATURES: 1. Black, horizontal stripes on back above lateral line. (Similar Black Skipjack [previous] distinguished by large black spots on belly.)

DESCRIPTION: Dark, silver-blue back; silvery to white sides and belly. Wide forked tail.

ABUNDANCE & DISTRIBUTION: Occasional entire archipelago. Peru north to Baja; also tropical Indo-Pacific from Red Sea to Hawaii.

HABITAT & BEHAVIOR: Prefer open water, but occasionally sweep in close to island drop-offs. Swim in large, rapidly moving, polarized schools.

REACTION TO DIVERS: Tend to ignore divers, but move away if rapidly approached.

NOTE: Also commonly known as "Mexican Bonito" and "Striped Bonito." Do not confuse with a similar appearing Eastern Pacific Bonito, *S. chiliensis*, (not in Galapagos, although [incorrectly] reported) distinguished by slanting stripes on back above lateral line. Peru and Chile; Alaska to Baja; also tropical and temperate South Pacific.

YELLOWFIN TUNA
Atún de Aleta Amarilla
Thunnus albacares

FAMILY:
Mackerel & Tuna – Scombridae

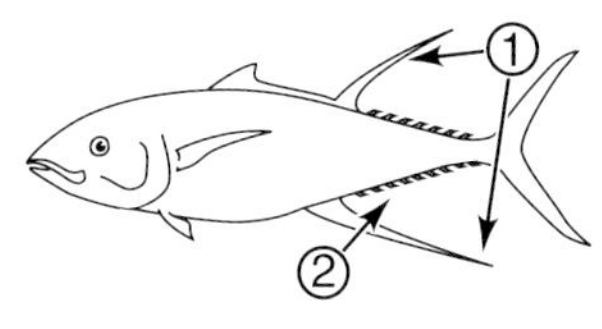

SIZE: 3-5 ft., max. 6½ ft.
DEPTH: 3-100 ft.

BLACK SKIPJACK
Barrilete Negro
Euthynnus lineatus

FAMILY:
Mackerel & Tuna – Scombridae

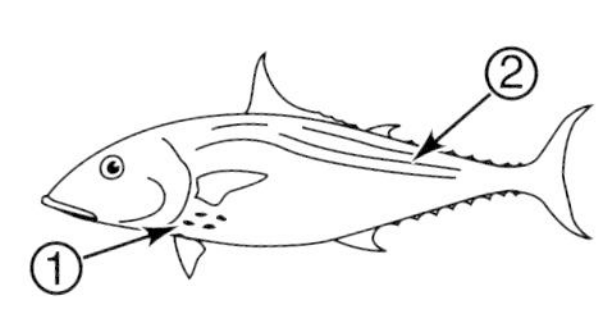

SIZE: 1-2 ft., max. 3¼ ft.
DEPTH: 0-130 ft.

INDO-PACIFIC BONITO
Bonito
Sarda orientalis

FAMILY:
Mackerel & Tuna – Scombridae

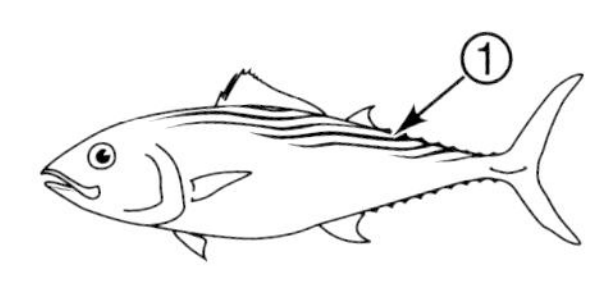

SIZE: 1-2 ft., max. 2½ ft.
DEPTH: 3-100 ft.

DISTINCTIVE FEATURES: 1. Gold spots on sides.

DESCRIPTION: Dark, silver-blue back; silvery to white sides and belly. Long, widely forked tail lobes.

ABUNDANCE & DISTRIBUTION: Common to occasional eastern and southern Isabela, southern Fernandina; occasional to uncommon balance of archipelago. Peru north to Southern California.

HABITAT & BEHAVIOR: Swim near shore in shallow water, feeding on schools of small fish. Often solitary, occasionally in large schools.

REACTION TO DIVERS: Apparently attracted by bubbles; often make rapid, single pass and depart.

DISTINCTIVE FEATURES: 1. Sharply pointed snout. Long, cigar-shaped body.

DESCRIPTION: Bright silver to dark gray. May display numerous dark bars, especially when stressed. Nine dorsal finlets and widely forked tail.

ABUNDANCE & DISTRIBUTION: Common to occasional Darwin, Wolf, Roca Redonda, Pinta, Marchena and Genovesa; occasional to uncommon balance of archipelago. North to Baja, including offshore islands; circumtropical.

HABITAT & BEHAVIOR: Open water surface feeders; occasionally along walls and over reefs. Solitary or in pairs.

REACTION TO DIVERS: Curious; apparently attracted by bubbles. During an open water safety stop, may circle, making several close passes, and depart.

DISTINCTIVE FEATURES: Long, thin, silvery body. **1. Long jaws with protruding teeth.**

DESCRIPTION: Often have darkish bars on back.

ABUNDANCE & DISTRIBUTION: Common to occasional entire archipelago. South to Peru.

HABITAT & BEHAVIOR: Swim in large, polarized schools. Often hold position over reef, facing current.

REACTION TO DIVERS: Tend to ignore divers, but move away if rapidly approached. Occasionally may be able to enter school with a very slow, non-threatening approach.

SIERRA MACKEREL
Sierra
Scomberomorus sierra

FAMILY:
Mackerel & Tuna – Scombridae

SIZE: 1-2 ft., max. 3 ft.
DEPTH: 0-40 ft.

WAHOO
Guaho
Acanthocybium solandri

FAMILY:
Mackerel & Tuna – Scombridae

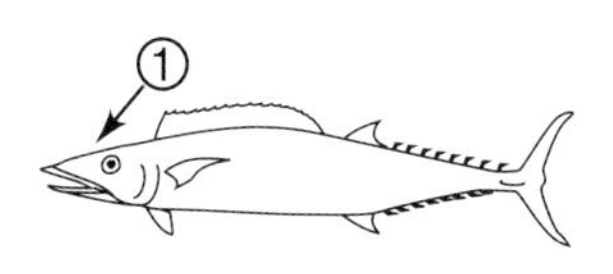

SIZE: 4-5 ft., max. 7 ft.
DEPTH: 0-40 ft.

BARRACUDA
Barracuda
Sphyraena idiastes

FAMILY:
Barracuda – Sphyraenidae

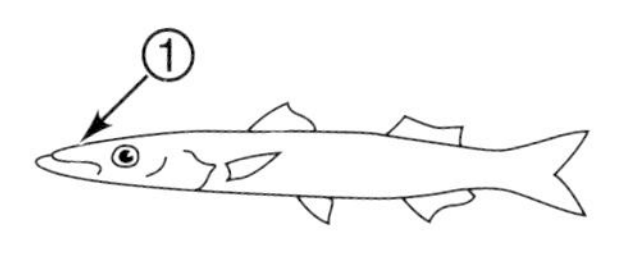

SIZE: 1-2 ft., max. 3 ft.
DEPTH: 10-80 ft.

DISTINCTIVE FEATURES: Football-shaped, silvery gray body. **1. Two white stripes below eye with thin dark border between.**

DESCRIPTION: Thin, dark stripes run length of body; tail dusky. Can display silvery white spot pattern over entire body. An imaginary line extended upward along rear edge of the anal fin would pass in front of upper tail fin lobe. (See illustration and compare Striped Chub [next].)

ABUNDANCE & DISTRIBUTION: Common to occasional entire archipelago. North to Baja.

HABITAT & BEHAVIOR: Swim in large, somewhat polarized schools; occasionally in small groups or solitary. Commonly over shallow protected areas near shore. Often mix with Striped Chubs.

REACTION TO DIVERS: Tend to ignore divers, but move away if rapidly approached. Apparently attracted by bubbles; may make one or two close passes and depart. May be able to enter school with a very slow, non-threatening approach.

DISTINCTIVE FEATURES: Football-shaped, silvery gray body. **1. Yellowish bronze stripe runs from mouth to rear gill cover.**

DESCRIPTION: Dusky to yellow-bronze pinstripes run length of body; tail dusky. Can display silvery white spot pattern over entire body. An imaginary line extended upward along rear edge of the anal fin would pass into upper tail fin lobe. (See illustration and compare Cortez Chub [previous].)

ABUNDANCE & DISTRIBUTION: Occasional entire archipelago. Peru north to Southern California.

HABITAT & BEHAVIOR: Swim in somewhat polarized schools; occasionally in small groups or solitary. Commonly over shallow protected areas near shore. Often mix with Cortez Chubs.

REACTION TO DIVERS: Tend to ignore divers, but move away if rapidly approached. Apparently attracted by bubbles; may make one or two close passes and depart. May be able to enter school with a very slow, non-threatening approach.

DISTINCTIVE FEATURES: 1. Broad blue body stripe, bordered by narrower yellow-gold stripes.

DESCRIPTION: Bluish silver overall; yellowish dorsal, anal and tail fins. Tail deeply forked. Body more elongated than other members of family.

ABUNDANCE & DISTRIBUTION: Occasional entire archipelago. North to Southern California.

HABITAT & BEHAVIOR: Rapidly swim in small, somewhat polarized groups or schools in open water over deep reefs, along walls and drop-offs. Often in areas with current.

REACTION TO DIVERS: Apparently attracted by bubbles; often make rapid, single pass and depart.

CORTEZ CHUB
Chopa de Cortez
Kyphosus elegans
FAMILY:
Chub – Kyphosidae

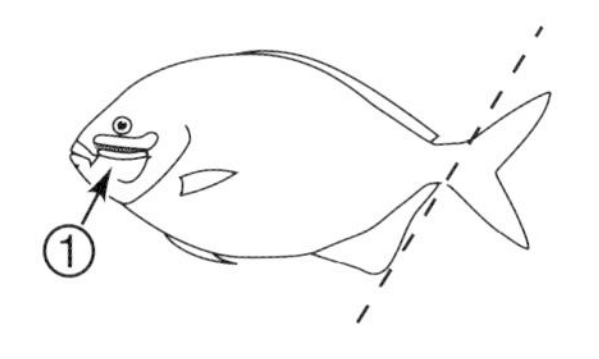

SIZE: 6-12 in., max. 1¼ ft.
DEPTH: 3-40 ft.

STRIPED CHUB
Chopa Rayada
Kyphosus analogus
FAMILY:
Chub – Kyphosidae

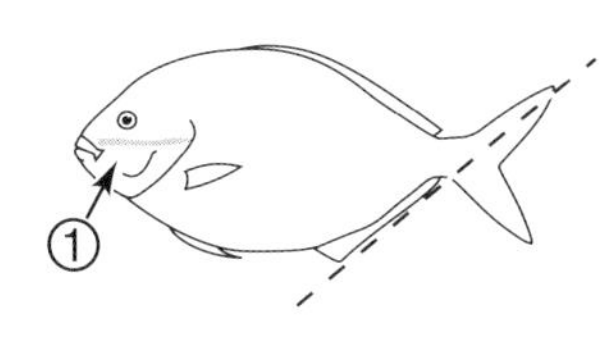

SIZE: 6-12 in., max. 1½ ft.
DEPTH: 3-40 ft.

RAINBOW CHUB
Chopa Arco Iris
Sectator ocyurus
FAMILY:
Chub – Kyphosidae

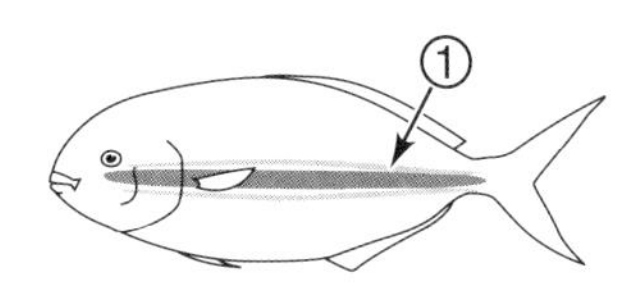

SIZE: 6-10 in., max. 1 ft.
DEPTH: 3-40 ft.

DISTINCTIVE FEATURES: 1. White "tear-drop" spot in front of eye. 2. Large lips.

DESCRIPTION: Somewhat silvery gray to brown body. Body heavy compared to other members of family.

ABUNDANCE & DISTRIBUTION: Common to occasional entire archipelago. ENDEMIC.

HABITAT & BEHAVIOR: Swim in small aggregations over shallow reefs. Occasionally mix with schools of other species.

REACTION TO DIVERS: Tend to ignore divers, but move away when approached. May be able to enter school with a very slow, non-threatening approach.

DISTINCTIVE FEATURES: 1. Black margin on gill cover. Back silver, belly whitish silver.

DESCRIPTION: Steep forehead (nape) and snout, smooth convex dorsal outline and highly arched midline. Large lips. Scales relatively large and obvious. Small dark spot base of pectoral fin. Snout may be silver or dramatically darkened [pictured].

ABUNDANCE & DISTRIBUTION: Uncommon entire archipelago. ENDEMIC (has been reported from coastal Ecuador and Peru, but recent scientific evidence suggests these identifications were in error).

HABITAT & BEHAVIOR: Generally over sandy substrates.

REACTION TO DIVERS: Tend to ignore divers, but move away when approached. Occasionally curious and swim in for close look.

NOTE: The similar Pacific Porgy, *C. brachysomus*, has been reported in Galapagos several times, but recent scientific evidence suggests these identifications were in error. Southern California to Peru.

DISTINCTIVE FEATURES: 1. Seven golden stripes 2. Black spot above pectoral fin.

DESCRIPTION: Oval body. Back bluish silver, belly silver to whitish silver.

ABUNDANCE & DISTRIBUTION: Uncommon central islands. ENDEMIC.

HABITAT & BEHAVIOR: Generally over sandy, protected bottoms, especially in bays and lagoons.

REACTION TO DIVERS: Tend to ignore divers, but move away when approached. Occasionally curious and swim in for close look.

NOTE: Also commonly known as "Galapagos Seabrim" and "Blue Striped Porgy."

DUSKY CHUB
Chopa Penumbre
Girella freminvillei
FAMILY:
Chub – Kyphosidae

SIZE: 6-12 in., max. 1½ ft.
DEPTH: 3-40 ft.

GALAPAGOS PORGY
Pluma de Galápagos
Calamus taurinus
FAMILY:
Porgy – Sparidae

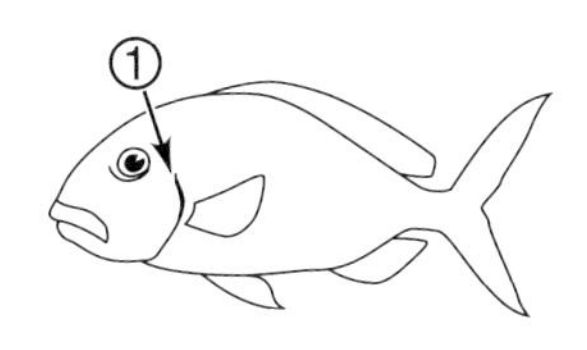

SIZE: 6-10 in., max. 1 ft.
DEPTH: 10-130 ft.

BLACKSPOT PORGY
Camiseta Rayada
Archosargus pourtalesii
FAMILY:
Porgy – Sparidae

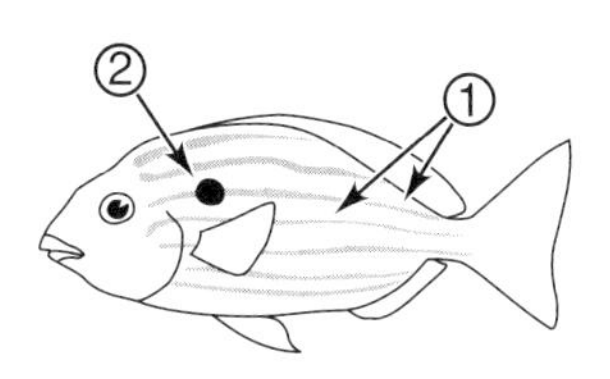

SIZE: 6-10 in., max. 15 in.
DEPTH: 10-100 ft.

DISTINCTIVE FEATURES: Silvery. No distinctive markings.

DESCRIPTION: Dorsal fin dusky. Protrusile mouth and deeply forked tail.

ABUNDANCE & DISTRIBUTION: Occasional entire archipelago (most common mojarra in Galapagos). Peru north to California.

HABITAT & BEHAVIOR: Inhabit shallow, inshore areas along sand beaches.

REACTION TO DIVERS: Tend to ignore divers, but move away when approached. Remaining still or making slow, non-threatening movements may allow close approach.

SIMILAR SPECIES: Pacific Flagfin Mojarra, *E. californiensis*, distinguished by black-tipped and banded spinous dorsal fin. Spotfin Mojarra, *E. gracilis*, distinguished by black tip on spinous dorsal fin. Peruvian Mojarra, *Diapterus peruvianus*, distinguished by darkish margin of dorsal fin and yellow ventral and anal fins. Yellowfin Mojarra, *Gerres cinereus*, distinguished by yellow ventral fins and seven darkish bars on sides.

DISTINCTIVE FEATURES: 1. Deeply forked tail with black stripes.

DESCRIPTION: Silver with large eye.

ABUNDANCE & DISTRIBUTION: Occasional Darwin and Wolf; rare balance of archipelago. North to Baja; also Hawaii.

HABITAT & BEHAVIOR: Inhabit shallow, rocky areas in dense, generally polarized schools. Often in small grottos and backwater areas near, but protected from strong current and surge.

REACTION TO DIVERS: Shy; move away when approached.

DISTINCTIVE FEATURES: 1. Long, deeply forked, darkish tail. 2. Slightly projecting lower jaw.

DESCRIPTION: Silvery with noticeable scales. Single dorsal fin. Upper jaw extends beyond rear of eye.

ABUNDANCE & DISTRIBUTION: Uncommon entire archipelago. Peru north to southern California.

HABITAT & BEHAVIOR: Inhabit surface waters near shore over reefs and sandy bottoms; also in brackish lagoons and estuaries. Often school.

REACTION TO DIVERS: Apparently attracted by bubbles; often make rapid, single pass and depart.

NOTE: Also commonly called "Ladyfish" and "Diabla."

SILVER MOJARRA
Mojarra Plateada
Eucinostomus argenteus
FAMILY:
Mojarra – Gerreidae

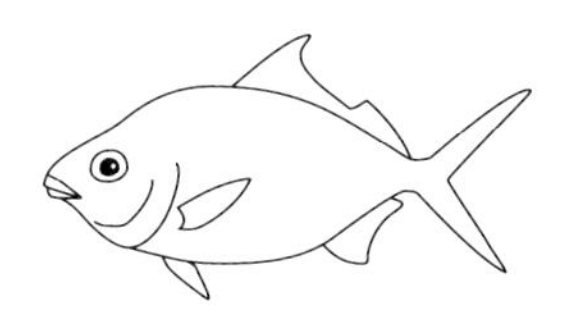

SIZE: 4-6 in., max. 8 in.
DEPTH: 1-40 ft.

STRIPE TAIL AHOLEHOLE
Aholehole Rabo Rayado
Kuhlia taeniura
FAMILY:
Aholehole – Kuhliidae

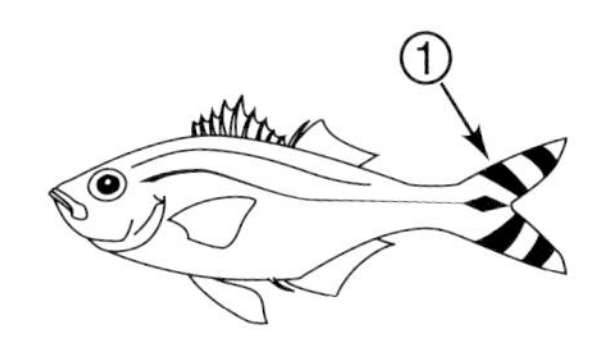

SIZE: 6-10 in., max. 12 in.
DEPTH: 10-60 ft.

MACHETE
Chiro
Elops affinis
FAMILY:
Machete – Elopidae

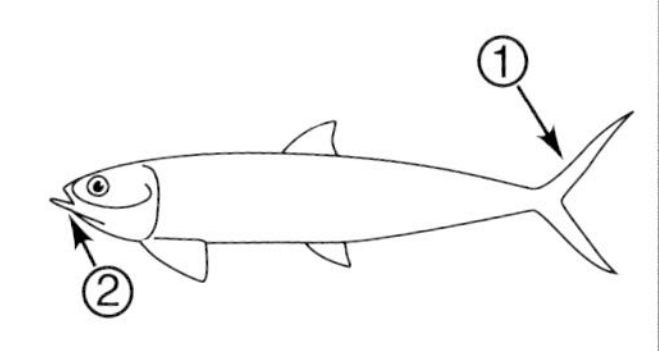

SIZE: 1-2½ ft., max. 3 ft.
DEPTH: 0-25 ft.

DISTINCTIVE FEATURES: 1. Forked yellow tail.

DESCRIPTION: Silvery elongated body. Pectoral, rear dorsal and anal fins yellowish.

ABUNDANCE & DISTRIBUTION: Common entire archipelago. SUBSPECIES ENDEMIC.

HABITAT & BEHAVIOR: Feed on plankton near surface in large schools.

REACTION TO DIVERS: Tend to ignore divers, but move away when approached.

SIMILAR SPECIES: Galapagos Mullet, Lisa de Galapagos, *M. galapagensis*, grayish silver to brownish silver back, whitish belly, black tail. Inhabit shallow water over sandy bottoms and in protected bays. ENDEMIC.

DISTINCTIVE FEATURES: Large, silvery disk-shaped.

DESCRIPTION: Six faint to distinct dark bars.

ABUNDANCE & DISTRIBUTION: Rare entire archipelago. Northern Peru north to South California.

HABITAT & BEHAVIOR: Swim in large schools in open water.

REACTION TO DIVERS: Tend to ignore divers. Occasionally curious; apparently attracted by bubbles, school may approach and encircle diver.

DISTINCTIVE FEATURES: 1. Red to orange tip on long, needle-like lower jaw.

DESCRIPTION: Bright bluish silver. Body elongated (generally more slender than other species of halfbeaks) with deeply forked tail. Scales form ribbed pattern on body.

ABUNDANCE & DISTRIBUTION: Occasional entire archipelago. Peru north to California; also tropical circumglobal.

HABITAT & BEHAVIOR: Swim in schools just below the surface.

REACTION TO DIVERS: Tend to ignore divers, but move away if approached.

SIMILAR SPECIES: Ribbon Halfbeak, *Euleptorhamphus longirostris*, distinguished by very long pectoral fins and large dorsal and anal fins near tail.

YELLOWTAIL MULLET
Lisa Rabo Amarillo
Mugil rammelsbergi
FAMILY:
Mullet – Mugilidae

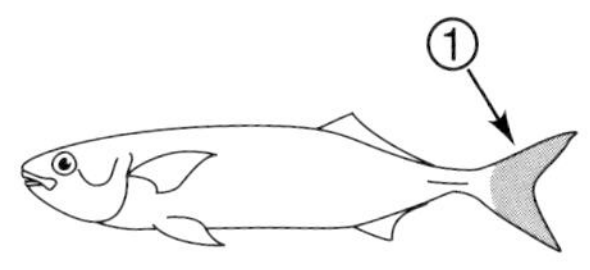

SIZE: 1-1½ ft., max. 2 ft.
DEPTH: 0-15 ft.

PACIFIC SPADEFISH
Chambo
Chaetodipterus zonatus
FAMILY:
Spadefish – Ephippidae

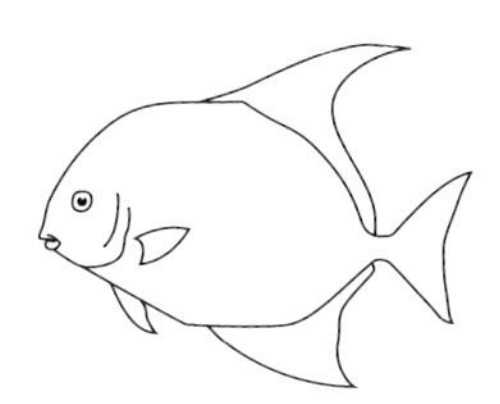

SIZE: 1-1½ ft., max. 2 ft.
DEPTH: 10-75 ft.

HALFBEAK
Picuda
Hyporhamphus unifasciatus
FAMILY:
Halfbeak – Hemirhampoidae

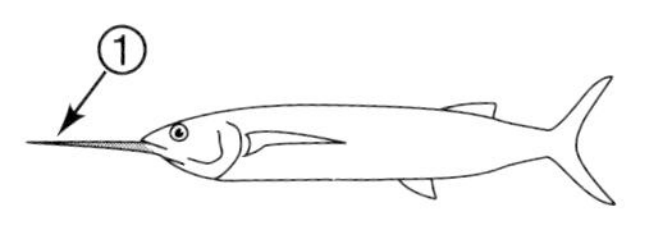

SIZE: 6-9 in., max. 12 in.
DEPTH: 0-15 ft.

IDENTIFICATION GROUP 3

Sloping Head/Tapered Body
Snapper—Grunt

This ID Group consists of fish that have what can best be described as a basic, "fish-like" shape, relatively large mouths and notched tails.

FAMILY: Snapper—Lutjanidae
6 Species Included

Snapper
(typical shape)

Mullet Snapper

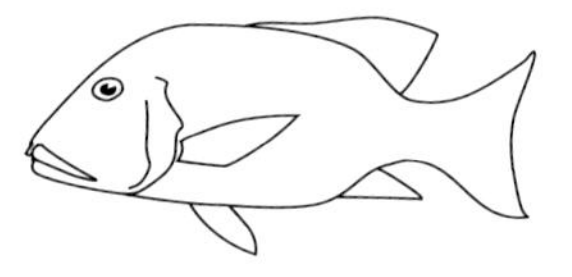

Barred Pargo

The behavior of snapping their jaws when hooked gives snappers their common family name. They are medium sized (usually 1 to 2 ½ feet), oblong shaped fish with triangular heads. All have a single, continuous dorsal fin that is often higher in the front, and shallow, notched tail. They have slightly upturned snouts, large mouths, and prominent canine teeth near the front of the jaw. Similar appearing grunts lack these canine teeth.

Snappers are nocturnal predators that feed on crustaceans and small fish. When seen on the reef in daytime, some species such as the Dog Snapper and Barred Pargo are solitary and wary, and swim near the bottom. Other family members including the Yellowtail, Bluestripe, Jordan's and Mullet Snappers school or swim in loose aggregations.

Most of the snappers have distinctive markings and colors making them easy to identify. Only the Dog and Yellowtail Snappers are occasionally confused, but attention to subtle detail makes identification possible.

FAMILY: Grunt—Pomadasyidae

7 Species Included

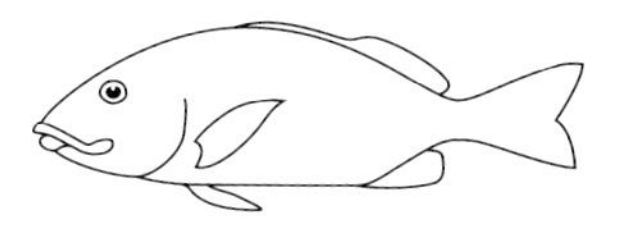

Grunt
(typical shape)

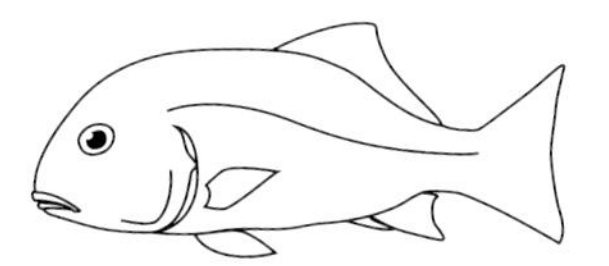

Peruvian Grunt

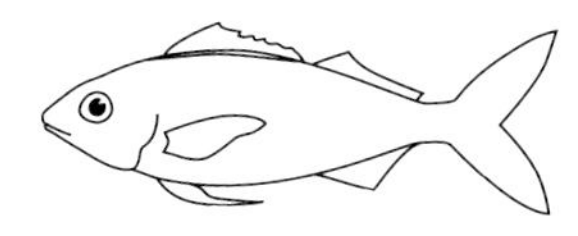

Salema
(typical shape)

The common family name is derived from the unusual "grunt" sound produced when teeth grinding deep within their throat is amplified by the air bladder. Grunts are closely related to snapper, but are generally smaller (normally between 12 and 18 inches), with more deeply notched tails. They also lack the snappers' sharp canine teeth. Most are colorful, and congregate during the day in small groups to large schools that drift in the reefs' shadows. At night, the nocturnal feeders scavenge the sand flats and grass beds near reefs for crustaceans.

Differences in color, body stripes and tail markings are keys to identifying grunts. Adults all have distinctive features and are fairly easy to distinguish. The Golden-eye, Graybar and Galapagos Grunts are more difficult. Distinguishing juvenile grunts underwater is almost impossible. Most are silver-white with similar dark body stripes, and many have a dot or blotch on the tail base.

Black Striped and White Salemas are also family members. They have slender, more elongated bodies, and form large, compact, polarized schools.

DISTINCTIVE FEATURES: 1. Golden eye. 2. Dark shadow-like border behind rear of gill cover.

DESCRIPTION: Silvery gray with darkish scale markings. Scales less obvious and more lightly marked than those of the Galapagos and Yellowtail Grunts [bottom and pg. 59].

ABUNDANCE & DISTRIBUTION: Abundant to common all islands. Peru north to Baja.

HABITAT & BEHAVIOR: School above rocky, boulder strewn reefs, and slopes and hard substrate with good water movement. Most common between 10-40 feet. May mix with Galapagos and Yellowtail Grunts.

REACTION TO DIVERS: Allow close approach with slow, non-threatening movements.

NOTE: Also commonly known as "Gray Grunt."

DISTINCTIVE FEATURES: 1. Several dark bars on back, which can pale or darken rapidly. 2. Eyes silvery (never golden like similar appearing Golden-eyed Grunt [previous]).

DESCRIPTION: Silvery gray with darkish scale markings; dusky spots on snout and gill cover; occasionally yellowish back. Scales less obvious and more lightly marked than those of Galapagos and Yellowtail Grunts [next].

ABUNDANCE & DISTRIBUTION: Occasional all islands. Peru north to Baja.

HABITAT & BEHAVIOR: Form large schools to small groups, occasionally solitary. Most common over sandy areas; occasionally above rocky, boulder strewn reefs and slopes with good water movement. Often feed by digging in sand. Most common between 10-40 feet.

REACTION TO DIVERS: Allow close approach with slow, non-threatening movements.

DISTINCTIVE FEATURES: Large, obvious scales with dark markings. (Similar Golden-eyed Grunt [top] has smaller, less obvious scales.) **1. Golden-eye.**

DESCRIPTION: Back silvery, yellowish brown fading to cream or white belly. (Similar Yellowtail Grunt [next] distinguished by yellow tail and fins and lack of golden eye.)

ABUNDANCE & DISTRIBUTION: Common to occasional all islands. ENDEMIC.

HABITAT & BEHAVIOR: School above rocky, boulder strewn reefs, and slopes and hard substrate with good water movement. Most common between 10-40 feet. May mix with Yellowtail Grunts [next] and Golden-eyed Grunts [top].

REACTION TO DIVERS: Allow close approach with slow, non-threatening movements.

GOLDEN-EYED GRUNT
Roncador Ojo Dorado
Haemulon scudderi
FAMILY:
Grunt – Haemulidae

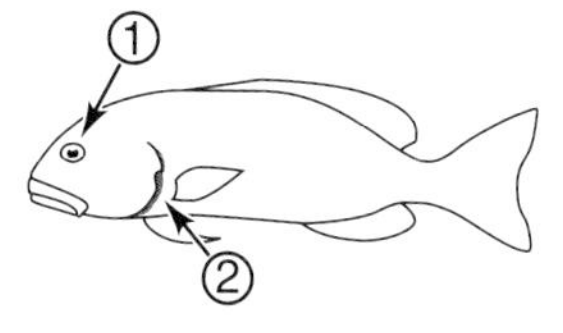

SIZE: 6-10 in., max. 1 ft.
DEPTH: 10-100 ft.

GRAYBAR GRUNT
Roncador Barra Gris
Haemulon sexfasciatum
FAMILY:
Grunt – Haemulidae

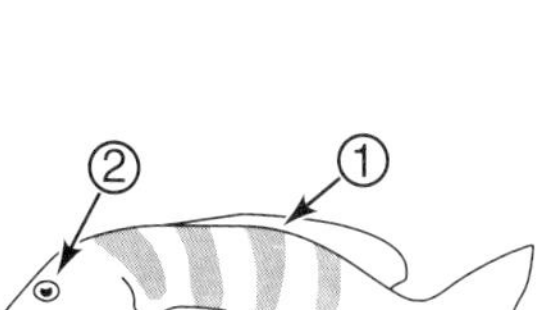

SIZE: 6-10 in., max. 1 ft.
DEPTH: 10-100 ft.

GALAPAGOS GRUNT
Roncador de Galápagos
Orthopristis forbesi
FAMILY:
Grunt – Haemulidae

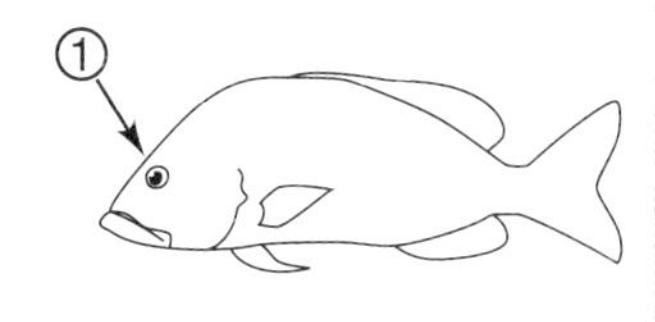

SIZE: 6-10 in., max. 1 ft.
DEPTH: 10-100 ft.

DISTINCTIVE FEATURES: 1. Yellow tail and fins. Large, obvious scales with dark markings.

DESCRIPTION: Back silvery, yellowish brown fading to silver, cream or white belly. (Similar Galapagos Grunt [previous] distinguished by golden eye and lack of golden tail.)

ABUNDANCE & DISTRIBUTION: Abundant to common all islands. Peru north to Baja.

HABITAT & BEHAVIOR: School above rocky, boulder strewn reefs, and slopes and hard substrate with good water movement. Most common between 10-40 feet. May mix with Galapagos Grunts [previous] and Golden-eyed Grunts [pg. 57].

REACTION TO DIVERS: Allow close approach with slow, non-threatening movements.

DISTINCTIVE FEATURES: 1. Obvious, light midline. 2. Steeper forehead than other grunts.

DESCRIPTION: Darkish silvery gray, fins generally darker shade. Scales not as obvious as those of Galapagos and Yellowtail Grunts [previous].

ABUNDANCE & DISTRIBUTION: Uncommon all islands. South to Chile.

HABITAT & BEHAVIOR: School in open water above rocky, boulder strewn reefs, and slopes and hard substrate with good water movement. Most common between 10-40 feet.

REACTION TO DIVERS: Allow close approach with slow, non-threatening movements.

DISTINCTIVE FEATURES: 1. Seven dark stripes on back and sides.

DESCRIPTION: Elongated, relatively thin body compared to other grunts. Back dark silver-gray, often with yellowish green, yellowish blue or blue-green tints, fading to lighter silver sides and silvery white belly.

ABUNDANCE & DISTRIBUTION: Occasional all islands. ENDEMIC.

HABITAT & BEHAVIOR: Form large, dense, polarized schools [see pg. 18] along walls and over rocky slopes, often in somewhat protected areas. Most common between 10-35 feet.

REACTION TO DIVERS: Allow close approach with slow, non-threatening movements.

NOTE: Also commonly known as "Brown-striped Snapper."

YELLOWTAIL GRUNT
Zapatilla
Anisotremus interruptus
FAMILY:
Grunt – Haemulidae

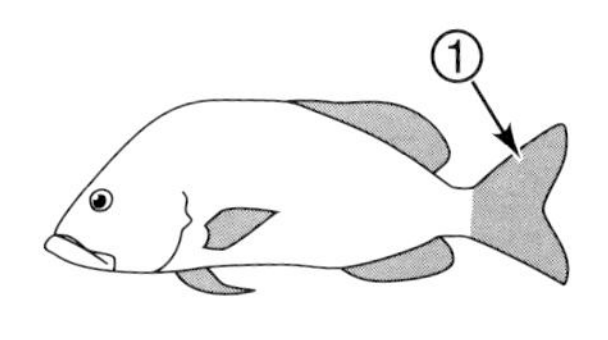

SIZE: 6 -10 in., max. 1 ft.
DEPTH: 10 -100 ft.

PERUVIAN GRUNT
Roncador Peruano
Anisotremus scapularis
FAMILY:
Grunt – Haemulidae

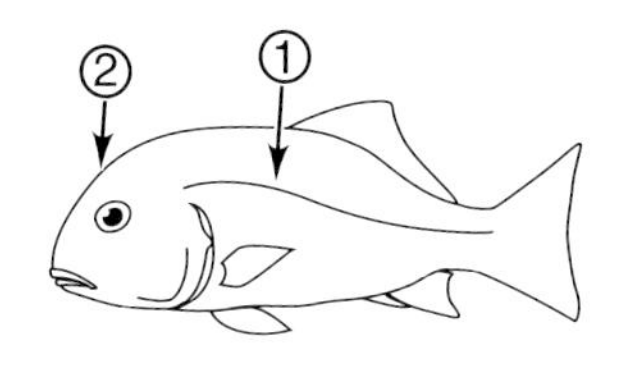

SIZE: 6 -10 in., max. 1 ft.
DEPTH: 10 -100 ft.

BLACK STRIPED SALEMA
Ojón
Xenocys jessiae
FAMILY:
Grunt – Haemulidae

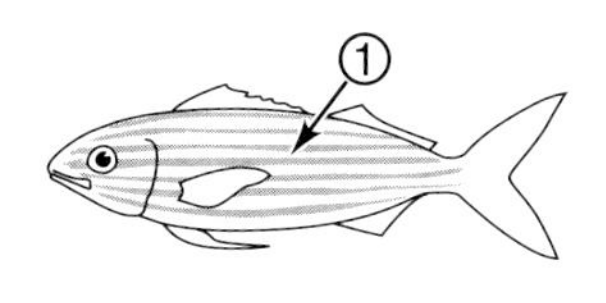

SIZE: 4 - 6 in.
DEPTH: 10 - 60 ft.

DISTINCTIVE FEATURES: No markings. **1. Large eyes.**

DESCRIPTION: Elongated, relatively thin body compared to other grunts. Back bright silver-gray fading to silvery white belly.

ABUNDANCE & DISTRIBUTION: Uncommon all islands. ENDEMIC.

HABITAT & BEHAVIOR: Form large, dense, polarized schools along walls and over rocky slopes, often in somewhat protected areas. Most common between 10-35 feet.

REACTION TO DIVERS: Allow close approach with slow, non-threatening movements.

VISUAL ID: 1. Dark stripe below dorsal fin and another on midbody run from head to tail; between runs a third, thinner stripe of varying length.

DESCRIPTION: Silver to white, often with bluish or greenish tints. Distinguishing visually between species of juvenile grunts is very difficult. Distinctions are based on the length of the middle stripe, and the size and shape of a spot on the base of the tail, if one is present. Often a specimen is required for positive species identification.

ABUNDANCE & DISTRIBUTION: Occasional entire archipelago. Circumtropical.

HABITAT & BEHAVIOR: Form somewhat polarized schools, commonly in sheltered, protected areas. Schools often contain more than one species, making identification even more difficult.

REACTION TO DIVERS: Tend to ignore divers, but move away if closely approached.

NOTE: Based on the relatively narrow body and long middle stripe, the pictured juveniles are probably in the genus *Xenichthys* or *Xenocys*.

DISTINCTIVE FEATURES: 1. Five blue to blue-green stripes with thin black borders. 2. Yellow tail.

DESCRIPTION: Golden yellow to yellow body and fins; white belly.

ABUNDANCE & DISTRIBUTION: Common to occasional all islands. North to Baja.

HABITAT & BEHAVIOR: Inhabit rocky reefs. Drift in small groups to medium schools, often in shade of cliffs and outcroppings. Most common between 30-50 feet.

REACTION TO DIVERS: Shy; move away when approached. Occasionally allow close approach with very slow, non-threatening movements.

WHITE SALEMA
Ojón Blanco
Xenichthys agassizi
FAMILY:
Grunt – Haemulidae

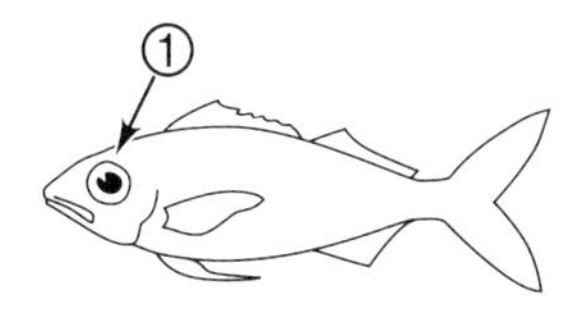

SIZE: 4 - 6 in.
DEPTH: 10 - 60 ft.

JUVENILE GRUNTS
Roncador Jovenes

FAMILY:
Grunt – Haemulidae

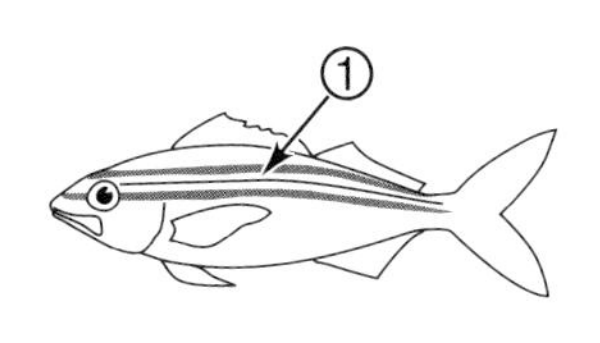

SIZE: ¾ - 1¼ in.

BLUE STRIPED SNAPPER
Rayado
Lutjanus viridis
FAMILY:
Snapper – Lutjanidae

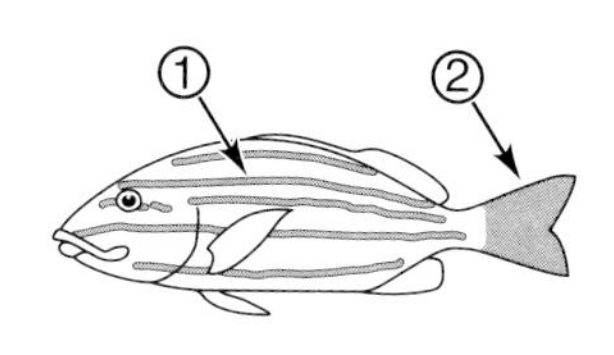

SIZE: 6 - 10 in., max. 1 ft.
DEPTH: 10 - 100 ft.

DISTINCTIVE FEATURES: 1. Prominent eye with dark center and reddish ring.

DESCRIPTION: Reddish silver.

ABUNDANCE & DISTRIBUTION: Occasional Darwin and Wolf; rare balance of archipelago. North to Panama.

HABITAT & BEHAVIOR: Form schools in areas of strong current, congregating in protected lees of large boulders and recesses in cliffs. Most common between 10-40 feet.

REACTION TO DIVERS: Shy; move away when approached.

DISTINCTIVE FEATURES: 1. Nine dusky, often obscure, bars on back.

DESCRIPTION: Silver to reddish silver. Two protruding canine teeth often visible. Fins silver, reddish silver or yellowish silver.

ABUNDANCE & DISTRIBUTION: Occasional all islands. North to Baja.

HABITAT & BEHAVIOR: Inhabit rocky reefs. Often lurk in caves and shaded recesses during day, occasionally mix in with aggregations of Yellow Snappers [next]. Feed in open from dusk to dawn. Most common between 15-40 feet.

REACTION TO DIVERS: Shy; move away when approached. Occasionally allow close approach with very slow, non-threatening movements.

DISTINCTIVE FEATURES: 1. Yellow rear body and tail.

DESCRIPTION: Silver forebody changing to yellow toward rear; all fins yellow to pale yellow. (Distinguished from similar appearing Dog Snapper [previous] by lack of dusky bars.)

ABUNDANCE & DISTRIBUTION: Occasional all islands. Peru north to Baja.

HABITAT & BEHAVIOR: Inhabit rocky reefs. Often drift in large aggregations. Occasionally organize into somewhat polarized schools, especially in areas of current. Most common between 15-40 feet.

REACTION TO DIVERS: Shy; move away when approached. Occasionally allow close approach with very slow, non-threatening movements.

NOTE: Also commonly known as "Yellowtail Snapper."

JORDAN'S SNAPPER
Pargo de Jordan
Lutjanus jordani
FAMILY:
Snapper – Lutjanidae

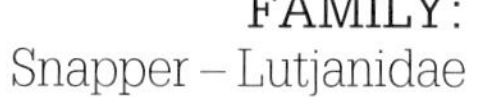

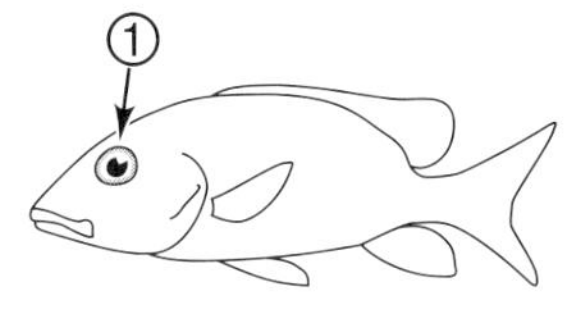

SIZE: 6-10 in., max. 1 ft.
DEPTH: 10-75 ft.

DOG SNAPPER
Pargo Prieto
Lutjanus novemfasciatus
FAMILY:
Snapper – Lutjanidae

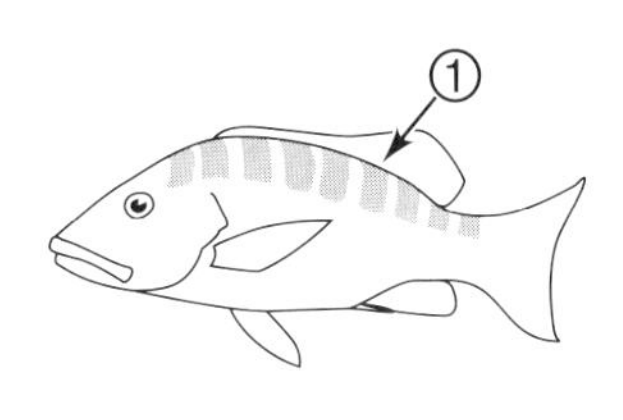

SIZE: 1¼-2¼ ft., max. 3½ ft.
DEPTH: 10-100 ft.

YELLOW SNAPPER
Pargo Amarillo
Lutjanus argentiventris
FAMILY:
Snapper – Lutjanidae

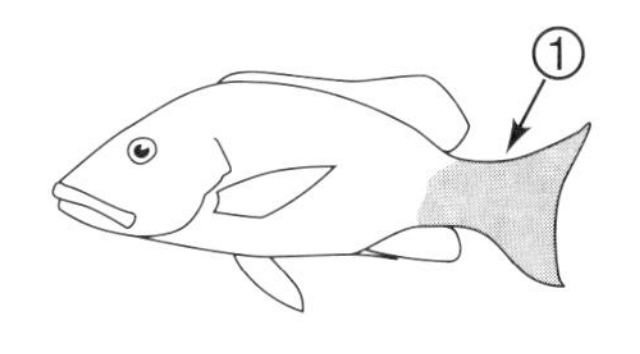

SIZE: 1-1½ ft., max. 2 ft.
DEPTH: 10-90 ft.

DISTINCTIVE FEATURES: 1. Prominent eye with black center and bright yellow-gold ring. 2. Numerous thin stripes formed by rows of large, conspicuous scales.

DESCRIPTION: Elongated body compared to other snappers. Body silver, with dark to faint bars on back; fins often dusky to black.

ABUNDANCE & DISTRIBUTION: Occasional to uncommon all islands. North to Baja.

HABITAT & BEHAVIOR: Form into somewhat polarized schools in areas of current over rocky reefs and slopes. Occasionally mix with schools of Yellow Snapper [previous]. Most common between 15-40 feet.

REACTION TO DIVERS: Shy; move away when approached. Occasionally make one or two relatively close passes, apparently attracted by bubbles.

DISTINCTIVE FEATURES: 1. Four pair of dark bars on body and two wide bars on base of tail. 2. Tubular nostrils extend beyond upper lip.

DESCRIPTION: Deeper bodied than other snappers. Back dark greenish brown to brown, fading to lighter shades of copper, reddish brown or maroon sides and belly.

ABUNDANCE & DISTRIBUTION: Occasional all islands. North to Baja.

HABITAT & BEHAVIOR: Solitary. Inhabit rocky reefs and slopes. May mix with Yellow Snappers [pg. 63]. Most common between 10-40 feet.

REACTION TO DIVERS: Shy; move away when approached.

DISTINCTIVE FEATURES: 1. Conspicuous, darkish lateral line. 2. Strongly projecting lower jaw.

DESCRIPTION: Light brown to olive snout, nape and above lateral line, silvery below. Large eye.

ABUNDANCE & DISTRIBUTION: Occasional western Isabela and Fernandina; not reported balance of archipelago. South to Chile.

HABITAT & BEHAVIOR: Inhabit deep rocky bottoms and boulder strewn slopes. Prefer cool water.

REACTION TO DIVERS: Unafraid; curiously watch divers' activities. Can be closely approached with slow, non-threatening movements.

MULLET SNAPPER
Pargo Lisa
Lutjanus aratus
FAMILY:
Snapper – Lutjanidae

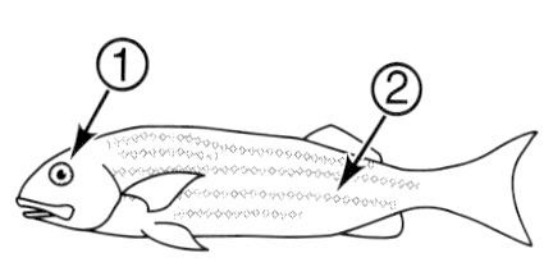

SIZE: 1½-2½ ft., max. 3 ft.
DEPTH: 10-75 ft.

BARRED PARGO
Pargo de Barras
Hoplopagrus guentheri
FAMILY:
Snapper – Lutjanidae

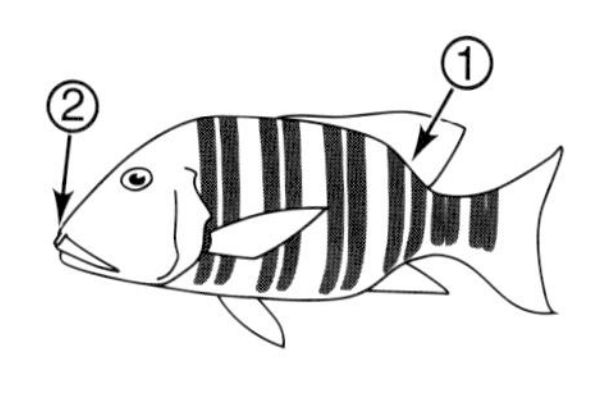

SIZE: 1-2 ft., max. 2½ ft.
DEPTH: 20-100 ft.

GRAPE EYE
Ojo de Uva
Hemilutjanus macrophthalmos
FAMILY:
Scientifically undescribed

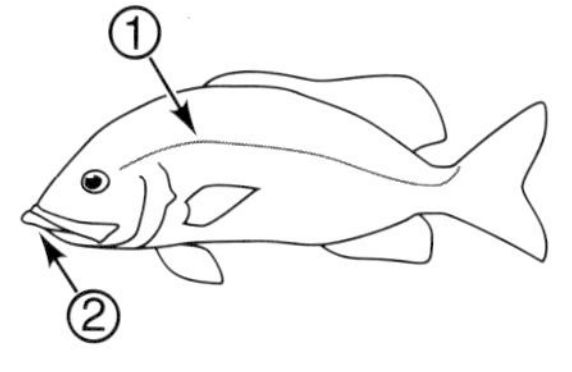

SIZE: 7-12 in., max. 15 in.
DEPTH: 80-180 ft.

IDENTIFICATION GROUP 4

Small Ovals

Damselfish–Damselfish/Chromis

This ID Group consists of small fish (generally 3 to 6 inches) that have a "perch-like" or oval profile.

FAMILY: Damselfish—Pomacentridae

7 Species Included

Damselfish
(typical shape)

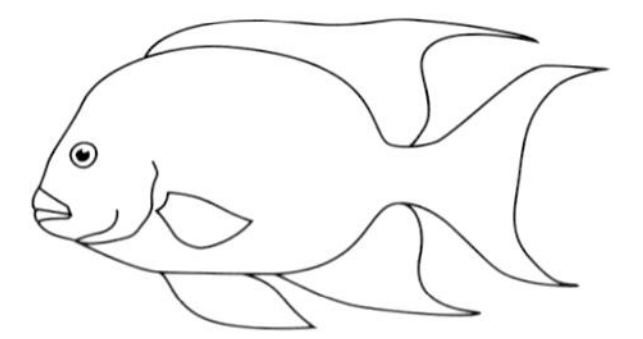

Giant Damselfish

Bumphead Damselfish

These energetic little fish are an evident part of the reef community. The most distinctive (but difficult to observe) family characteristic is a single nostril on each side of the snout, rather than the usual two. Although most of the adults are drab, the juveniles are quite colorful.

Several species spend their days busily tending and patrolling a private algae patch that is pugnaciously defended from intruders. When their domain is threatened, the fish dart back and forth with fins erect, ready to attack. Even divers are not immune to the aggressive assaults of these feisty fish. If the divers linger, they may receive a sharp nip on any exposed skin. Egg clusters are also defended in this manner by some males.

All have either distinctive colors, markings and/or shapes, making underwater identification easy.

FAMILY: Damselfish/Chromis—Pomacentridae

2 Species Included

Silver Stripe Chromis

Brown Chromis

Members of the genus *Chromis* are part of the damselfish family, but are discussed separately because the group carries its own common name, and its members are somewhat different in appearance. Both are somewhat elongated and have deeply forked tails.

During the day the Brown Chromis often swim in small to large aggregations well above the reefs, feeding on plankton. The Silver Stripe Chromis live in small groups near the bottom.

DISTINCTIVE FEATURES: 1. Long, trailing tips on dorsal, anal and tail fins, often with thin, pale blue to white borders.

DESCRIPTION: Large, somewhat elongated, disk-shaped. Bluish gray to gray; can change rapidly from pale shades to dark. Breeding males' forebodies often silvery gray [below left]. Juveniles more bluish with brilliant iridescent blue spots [below right].

ABUNDANCE & DISTRIBUTION: Common to occasional entire archipelago. North to Baja.

HABITAT & BEHAVIOR: Inhabit boulder strewn reefs and slopes with good water movement and algae growth. Territorial, will attempt to chase away intruders; especially aggressive when guarding nest during breeding season. Most common between 10-25 feet.

REACTION TO DIVERS: Often aggressively charge when approached, but retreat when confronted.

NOTE: Also commonly known as "Gray Mickey."

Breeding Male, Note Silvery Gray Head

DISTINCTIVE FEATURES: 1. Brilliant blue eyes. 2. Pronounced hump on forehead (nape).

DESCRIPTION: Large, somewhat elongated, disk-shaped. Usually dark brown, occasionally orangish brown or grayish; can pale or darken areas of body (such as head only) or entire body. Juveniles blue back and orange to yellow belly.

ABUNDANCE & DISTRIBUTION: Common to occasional entire archipelago. North to Baja.

HABITAT & BEHAVIOR: Inhabit boulder strewn reefs and slopes with good water movement and algae growth. Most common between 10-25 feet.

REACTION TO DIVERS: Often aggressively charge upon approach, but retreat when confronted.

NOTE: Also commonly known as "Sheepshead Mickey."

GIANT DAMSELFISH
Damisela Gigante
Microspathodon dorsalis
FAMILY:
Damselfish –
Pomacentridae

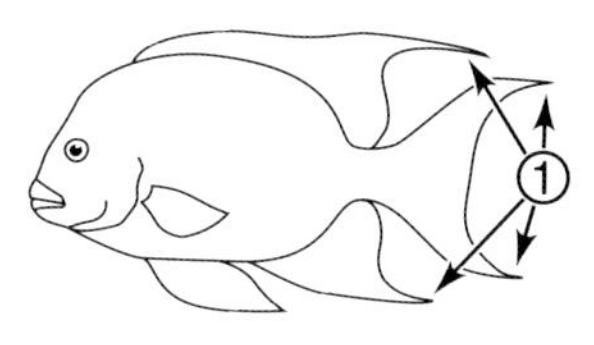

SIZE: 6 - 10 in.,
max. 1 ft.
DEPTH: 5 - 75 ft.

Juvenile,
Note Iridescent
Blue Spots

BUMPHEAD DAMSELFISH
Damisela Cabeza Chichón
Microspathodon bairdii
FAMILY:
Damselfish –
Pomacentridae

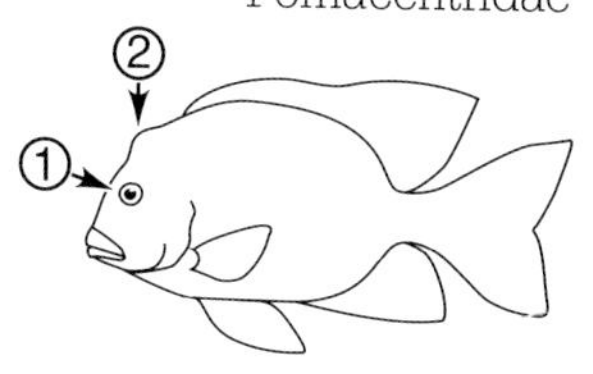

SIZE: 6 - 9 in.,
max. 1 ft.
DEPTH: 5 - 75 ft.

Damselfish

DISTINCTIVE FEATURES: 1. White band on base of tail (occasionally band is indistinct in mature adults [below left]). **2. Yellow edge on pectoral fins.**

DESCRIPTION: Elongated disk-shaped body. Grayish brown to dark charcoal; orangish crescent above eyes.

ABUNDANCE & DISTRIBUTION: Abundant to common all islands. SUBSPECIES ENDEMIC; species southern Baja to Mazatlan and Isla Revillagigedo.

HABITAT & BEHAVIOR: Inhabit rocky, boulder strewn areas with good water movement and algae growth. Somewhat territorial, chase away small intruders. Tend to be deeper than Yellow-tail Damselfish [next].

REACTION TO DIVERS: Tend to ignore divers. May charge and nip when approached, but retreat to protection of hole or crack when confronted.

DISTINCTIVE FEATURES: 1. Blue ocellated spot on middorsal fin. 2. Orange wash on back and dorsal fin.

DESCRIPTION: Navy blue with bright iridescent blue markings; translucent tail. Intermediate tail becomes opaque with distinct white band at base [below right].

Adult
Without White Band
at Base of Tail

WHITE-TAIL DAMSELFISH
Damisela Cola Blanca
Stegastes leucorus beebei

FAMILY:
Damselfish –
Pomacentridae

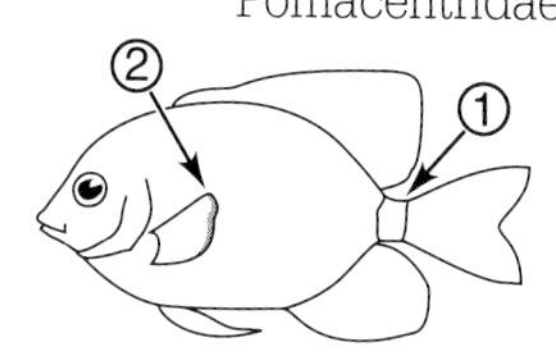

SIZE: 2½-5 in.,
max. 6 in.
DEPTH: 6-70 ft.

Juvenile

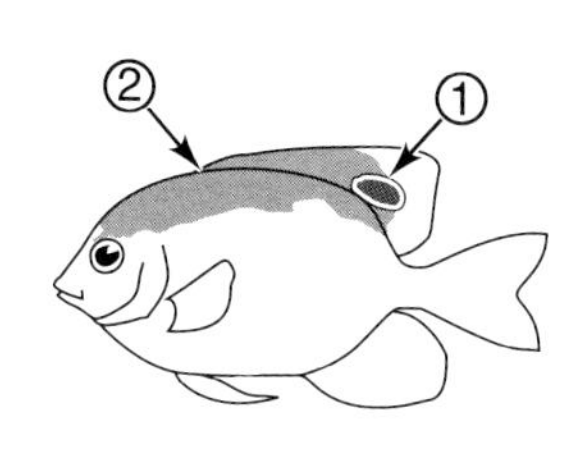

SIZE: 1-2 in.

Intermediate

Damselfish

DISTINCTIVE FEATURES: 1. Yellow tail. 2. Yellow lips.

DESCRIPTION: Elongated disk-shaped body. Grayish brown to dark charcoal; often lighter color on nape. Eyes blue.

ABUNDANCE & DISTRIBUTION: Abundant all islands. Malpelo, Cocos.

HABITAT & BEHAVIOR: Inhabit rocky, boulder strewn areas with good water movement and algae growth. Territorial, will actively attempt to chase away intruders. Tend to be more common in shallow water.

REACTION TO DIVERS: Pugnacious, will charge and nip.

SIMILAR SPECIES: Rusty Damselfish, *Nexilosus latifrons*, dark brown back, fading to lighter sides and whitish belly with orangish brown tinted head and midbody bar; rare western Isabela and Fernandina.

DISTINCTIVE FEATURES: 1. Five to six dark bars on body and base of tail.

DESCRIPTION: Elongated, disk-shaped. Usually yellow back and silver to white head and belly; often with bluish and blue-green tints. Breeding males change color to blue.

ABUNDANCE & DISTRIBUTION: Abundant to common entire archipelago, except uncommon western Isabela and Fernandina. Northern Peru north to Baja.

HABITAT & BEHAVIOR: Commonly form loose aggregations above boulder strewn reefs and slopes with good water movement. Most common between 10-25 feet. Breeding males aggressively guard their territories.

REACTION TO DIVERS: Tend to ignore divers. Breeding males aggressively charge and nip.

SIMILAR SPECIES: Night Sergeant, *Nexilarius concolor*, five or six light brown or yellowish brown bars on dark brown body; reclusive, rarely in open except at night.

Bright Color Phase

YELLOW-TAIL DAMSELFISH
Damisela Cola Amarilla
Stegastes arcifrons

FAMILY:
Damselfish – Pomacentridae

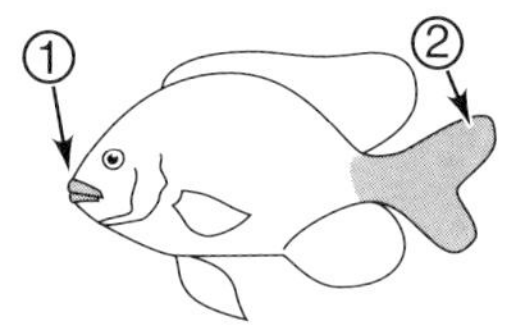

SIZE: 2½-5 in., max. 6 in.
DEPTH: 3-40 ft.

PANAMIC SERGEANT MAJOR
Sargento Mayor
Abudefduf troschelii

FAMILY:
Damselfish – Pomacentridae

SIZE: 3-5 in., max. 9 in.
DEPTH: 5-100 ft.

Breeding Male

DISTINCTIVE FEATURES: 1. Silver to white stripe below dorsal fin to tail.

DESCRIPTION: Elongated, disk-shaped body. Grayish brown to dark charcoal; often some iridescent blue markings. Juvenile has brilliant iridescent blue markings on head and body that fade with maturity.

ABUNDANCE & DISTRIBUTION: Common to occasional West Isabela, Fernandina; uncommon Roca Reodonda, Floreana, Espanola; rare balance of archipelago. North to Baja.

HABITAT & BEHAVIOR: Inhabit deep, rocky, boulder strewn areas with cool water upwellings.

REACTION TO DIVERS: Tend to ignore divers, but retreat to protection of hole or crack when closely approached.

NOTE: Also commonly known as "Deep-water Chromis."

Juvenile, Note Iridescent Blue Markings on Head and Body

DISTINCTIVE FEATURES: 1. White spot below rear of dorsal fin. 2. Scissortail has dark borders.

DESCRIPTION: Greenish brown to brown and gray; belly lighter shade to white.

ABUNDANCE & DISTRIBUTION: Common to occasional all islands. Northern Peru north to Baja.

HABITAT & BEHAVIOR: Commonly form large schools that feed on plankton in open water above rocky, boulder strewn reefs and slopes. Occasionally individuals or small groups hover above bottom near protective retreats. Most common between 20-60 feet.

REACTION TO DIVERS: Tend to ignore divers, but retreat upon close approach.

NOTE: Also commonly known as "Scissortail Damselfish" and "Whitespot Chromis."

SILVERSTRIPE CHROMIS
Chromis Dorso Plateado
Chromis alta
FAMILY:
Damselfish – Pomacentridae

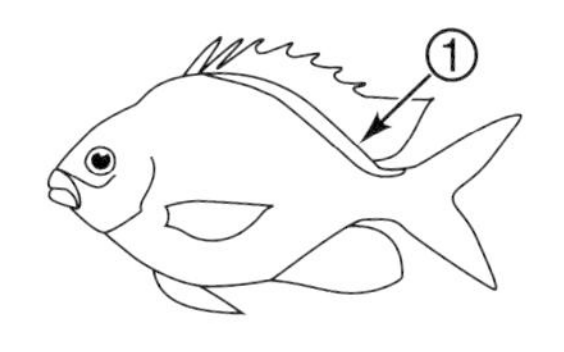

SIZE: 2½-4 in., max. 5 in.
DEPTH: 60-250 ft.

Intermediate, Note Blue Markings Partially Faded

BROWN CHROMIS
Castañeta
Chromis atrilobata
FAMILY:
Damselfish – Pomacentridae

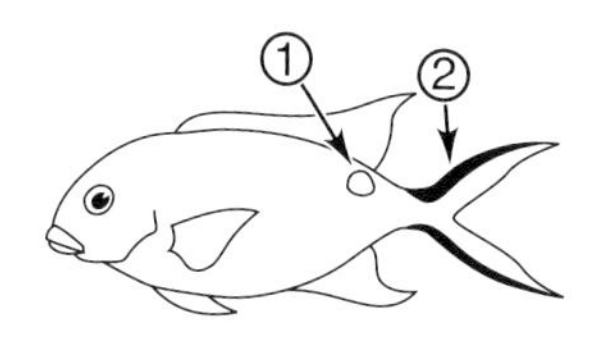

SIZE: 2½-4 in.,max. 5 in.
DEPTH: 10-250 ft.

IDENTIFICATION GROUP 5

Heavy Body/Large Lips

Seabass

This ID Group consists of fish with strong, well-built, "bass-like" bodies. They have large mouths and lips, and jutting lower jaws. The long, continuous dorsal fin is noticeably divided into two parts. The fore portion is constructed of sharp spines that can be held erect or lowered; the rear is soft and quite flexible.

FAMILY: Seabass—Serranidae

10 Species Included

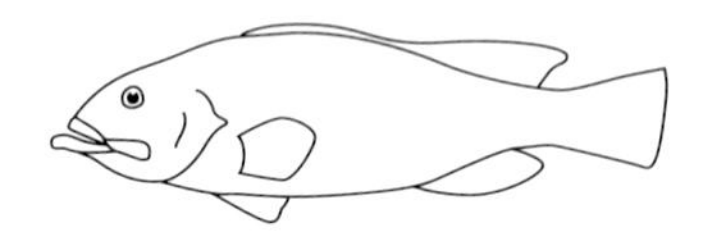

Seabass
(typical shape)

Leather Bass

Threadfin Bass

Mutton Hamlet

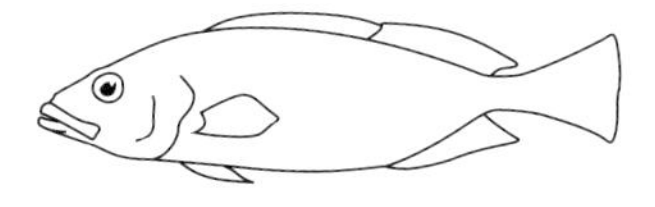

Barred Sarrano

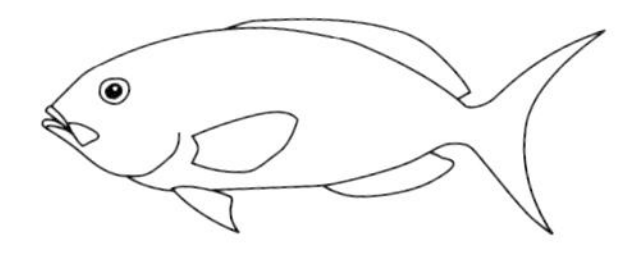

Creole Fish

Seabass have strong, stout bodies and large mouths. They vary in size from the Leather Bass and Bacalao that grow to three feet to the much smaller seven inch Barred Sarrano. They are solitary carnivores that live near the bottom. Most of their days are spent lurking in the shadows of reefs, ledges and wrecks where larger species blend with the background.

Although awkward in appearance, these fish can cover short distances quickly. Fish or crustaceans are drawn into their gullets by the powerful suction created when they open their large mouths. Held securely by thousands of small, rasp-like teeth that cover the jaws, tongue and pallet, the prey is swallowed whole. Some are hermaphroditic, beginning life as females but changing to males with maturity.

Generally, their color and markings make them easy to distinguish on the reef. Several, however, have different appearing juveniles, such as the Leather Bass; others, like the Bacalao, have color phases. Most can, to some degree, change color intensity or markings which may cause confusion.

DISTINCTIVE FEATURES: 1. Row of large, white spots just above midbody.

DESCRIPTION: Dark yellow-brown to black upper body and forward half of tail; white belly; gold to yellow-brown head, dorsal fin, and rear half of tail fin.

ABUNDANCE & DISTRIBUTION: Common western Isabela, Fernandina; uncommon other islands. ENDEMIC.

HABITAT & BEHAVIOR: Inhabit deep reefs, rocky slopes and adjacent areas of sand. Most common in cool water below thermocline.

REACTION TO DIVERS: Tend to ignore divers. Can often be closely approached with slow, non-threatening movements.

DISTINCTIVE FEATURES: Shades of gray with numerous small dark spots; an uncommon phase is bright golden yellow.

DESCRIPTION: Gray phase may display faint body bars; belly lighter.

ABUNDANCE & DISTRIBUTION: Common entire archipelago. Malpelo, Cocos.

HABITAT & BEHAVIOR: Inhabit reefs and rocky, boulder strewn slopes.

REACTION TO DIVERS: Tend to ignore divers. Can often be closely approached with slow, non-threatening movements.

Barred Pattern

CAMOTILLO
Camotillo
Paralabrax albomaculatus
FAMILY:
Sea Bass – Serranidae

SIZE: 10-15 in., max. 20 in.
DEPTH: 70-250 ft.

BACALAO
Bacalao
Mycteroperca olfax
FAMILY:
Sea Bass – Serranidae

SIZE: 1-2 ft., max. 3 ft.
DEPTH: 15-125 ft.

Golden Yellow Phase, Known as GOLDEN GROUPER
Bacalao Rey

DISTINCTIVE FEATURES: 1. Large, dark bluish spot behind eye. 2. Nine to ten dark bars on body and base of tail.

DESCRIPTION: Bluish gray to gray and grayish brown; numerous orangish spots on head; fins dark.

ABUNDANCE & DISTRIBUTION: Common entire archipelago. North to Baja.

HABITAT & BEHAVIOR: Inhabit reefs and rocky, boulder strewn slopes.

REACTION TO DIVERS: Shy; rapidly retreat to protective crevice or hole when approached.

DISTINCTIVE FEATURES: 1. Large, white ovular blotches and small spots. 2. Black blotch upper base of tail.

DESCRIPTION: Olive to reddish brown.

ABUNDANCE & DISTRIBUTION: Abundant to common entire archipelago. Peru north to Baja.

HABITAT & BEHAVIOR: Inhabit rocky reefs, boulder strewn slopes and walls. Often rest on bottom. Most common 20-40 feet.

REACTION TO DIVERS: Tend to ignore divers. Can often be closely approached with slow, non-threatening movements.

DISTINCTIVE FEATURES: 1. Three, long prominent spines on foredorsal fin.

DESCRIPTION: Dark gray to silvery gray and brownish gray with faint dark bar markings; rear of tail fin dark; pectoral fins yellowish.

ABUNDANCE & DISTRIBUTION: Uncommon entire archipelago. South to northern Chile.

HABITAT & BEHAVIOR: Inhabit mangrove areas to shallow inlets and bays.

REACTION TO DIVERS: Tend to ignore divers. Can often be closely approached with slow, non-threatening movements.

PANAMIC GRAYSBY
Enjambre
Epinephelus panamensis
FAMILY:
Sea Bass – Serranidae

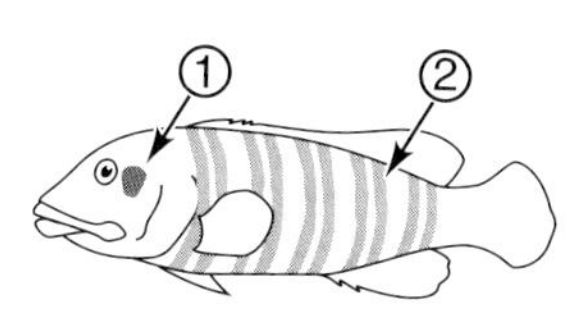

SIZE: 7-10 in., max. 1 ft.
DEPTH: 15-250 ft.

FLAG CABRILLA
Cabrilla
Epinephelus labriformis
FAMILY:
Sea Bass – Serranidae

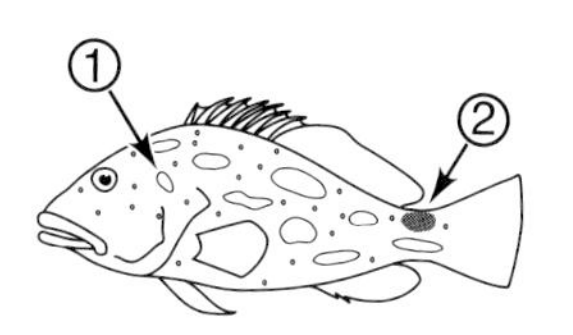

SIZE: 8-14 in., max. 1¾ ft.
DEPTH: 15-100 ft.

GRAY THREADFIN BASS
Plumero
Cratinus agassizii
FAMILY:
Sea Bass – Serranidae

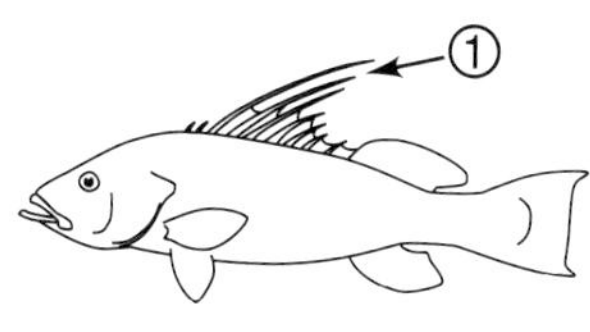

SIZE: 1-1½ ft., max. 2 ft.
DEPTH: 3-40 ft.

DISTINCTIVE FEATURES: 1. Numerous white blotches and small black spots on body. 2. Several dusky to dark gray to olive bars.

DESCRIPTION: Shades of light gray to olive, occasionally tinted with yellow (especially young adults); fins often bordered with yellow. Juveniles have alternating black and gray bars.

ABUNDANCE & DISTRIBUTION: Common entire archipelago. North to Baja.

HABITAT & BEHAVIOR: Inhabit reefs and rocky, boulder strewn slopes. Juveniles live in protection of Long Spine Urchin, *Diadema mexicanum*.

REACTION TO DIVERS: Wary; can occasionally be closely approached with slow, non-threatening movements.

Dark Color Phase with Yellow Markings

DISTINCTIVE FEATURES: 1. Three brilliant gold to yellow stripes.

DESCRIPTION: Bright red-brown stripe forehead to upper tail border; dark red-brown stripe midbody; red-brown of belly extends to lower tail border; yellow-gold markings on head.

ABUNDANCE & DISTRIBUTION: Uncommon entire archipelago. North to Baja.

HABITAT & BEHAVIOR: Inhabit deep walls and reefs; most common below 110 feet. Reclusive, lurk in cracks, crevices and under ledge overhangs.

REACTION TO DIVERS: Curious; peer out from hiding places. Can often be closely approached with slow, non-threatening movements.

NOTE: Also known as "Rainbow Basslet."

LEATHER BASS
Caga Leche
Dermatolepis dermatolepis
FAMILY:
Sea Bass – Serranidae

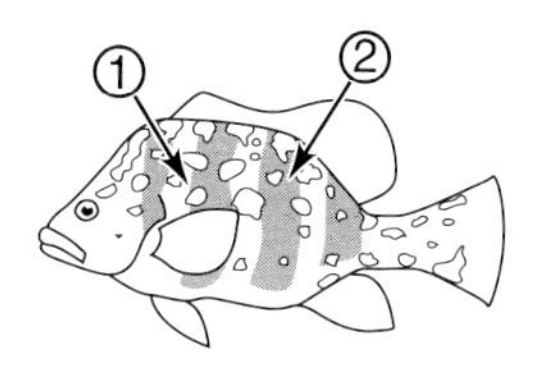

SIZE: 1-2 ft., max. 3 ft.
DEPTH: 15-125 ft.

Barred Juvenile in Protection of Long Spine Urchins

WRASSE ASS BASS
Cabrilla Rayada
Liopropoma fasciatum
FAMILY:
Sea Bass – Serranidae

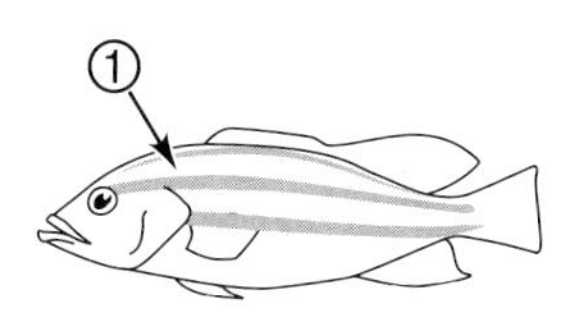

SIZE: 4-6 in., max. 7 in.
DEPTH: 80-250 ft.

DISTINCTIVE FEATURES: 1. Numerous small, whitish blotches and spots. 2. Red iris; pupil dark, often green.

DESCRIPTION: Mottled reddish brown with black speckles, often with indistinct dusky bars. Several indistinct bands on pectoral fins. Juveniles mottled red.

ABUNDANCE & DISTRIBUTION: Occasional entire archipelago. Peru north to Baja; also Caribbean.

HABITAT & BEHAVIOR: Inhabit reefs and rocky, boulder strewn slopes. Often rest on bottom, lurking in shaded areas.

REACTION TO DIVERS: Unafraid. Can be closely approached with slow, non-threatening movements.

VISUAL ID: Red. 1. White spots cover head, body, and dorsal, anal and tail fins.

DESCRIPTION: Vary from bright red to reddish brown; pectoral fins translucent with several indistinct bands formed by spots on fin rays; red iris; pupil dark, often green.

HABITAT & BEHAVIOR: Inhabit reefs and rocky, boulder strewn slopes. Often rest on bottom, lurking in shaded areas.

REACTION TO DIVERS: Unafraid. Can be closely approached with slow, non-threatening movements.

DISTINCTIVE FEATURES: 1. Four to five dark paired bars on back, may join to form a wide, irregular stripe. 2. Row of reddish brown squares below bars.

DESCRIPTION: Back gray to brown or yellow-brown; belly white; tail translucent with orangish spots.

ABUNDANCE & DISTRIBUTION: Abundant entire archipelago. Baja to Peru.

HABITAT & BEHAVIOR: Inhabit most marine environments from rocky reefs to areas of sand and rubble. Often rest on bottom, sitting on pectoral and anal fins.

REACTION TO DIVERS: Unafraid. Can be closely approached with slow, non-threatening movements.

MUTTON HAMLET
Guaseta
Alphestes afer
FAMILY:
Sea Bass – Serranidae

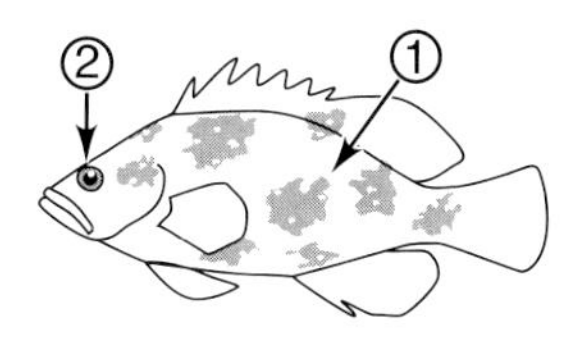

SIZE: 4-7 in., max. 10 in.
DEPTH: 15-100 ft.

Juvenile

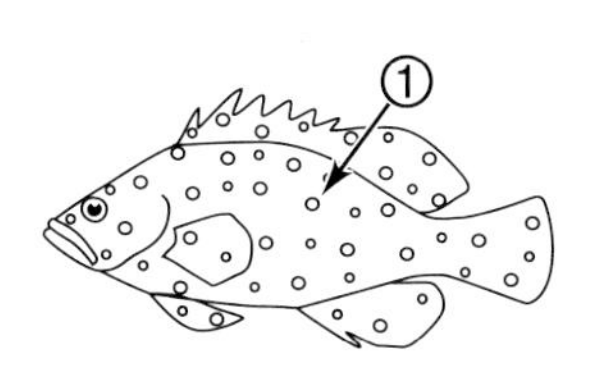

SIZE: 1½-3½ in.
DEPTH: 15-100 ft.

BARRED SERRANO
Serrano
Serranus fasciatus
FAMILY:
Sea Bass – Serranidae

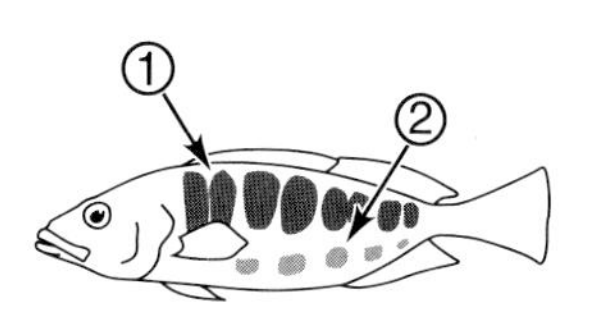

SIZE: 3-5 in., max. 7 in.
DEPTH: 20-200 ft.

DISTINCTIVE FEATURES: 1. Three to five white or dark spots on back and base of tail.

DESCRIPTION: Olive to gray or brownish red back; salmon belly. Eyes have black pupil, red iris. Forked tail. Juveniles yellow with blue markings under eye and red spot ringed in blue on pectoral fin. Intermediates salmon with dark spot ringed in blue on pectoral fin.

ABUNDANCE & DISTRIBUTION: Most abundant fish in entire archipelago. Peru north to Baja.

HABITAT & BEHAVIOR: During day form huge feeding aggregations in open water above reefs, rocky, boulder strewn slopes and along walls. Juveniles and intermediates stay near bottom, often hiding in cracks and small holes.

REACTION TO DIVERS: Unafraid. Can be closely approached with slow, non-threatening movements.

NOTE: Also known as "Five Spot Anthias."

Intermediate

CREOLE FISH
Gringo
Paranthias colonus
FAMILY:
Sea Bass – Serranidae

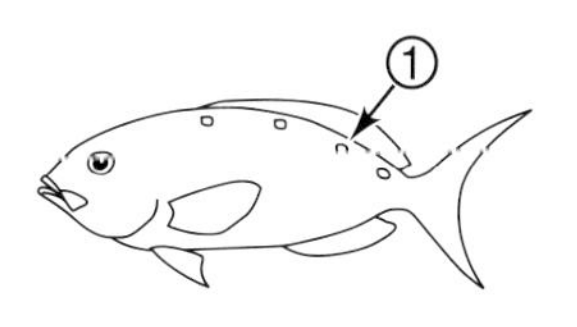

SIZE: 4-7 in., max. 14 in.
DEPTH: 10-200 ft.

Juvenile

IDENTIFICATION GROUP 6

Swim with Pectoral Fins/Obvious Scales

Parrotfish – Wrasse – Hogfish/Wrasse – Razorfish/Wrasse

This ID Group consists of fish that primarily use their pectoral fins to swim. (Other fish also use their pectoral fins, but not as conspicuously.) They have even rows of large, noticeable scales and beak-like mouths.

FAMILY: Parrotfish—Scaridae

5 Species Included

Parrotfish
(typical shape)

Parrotfish
(typical shape)

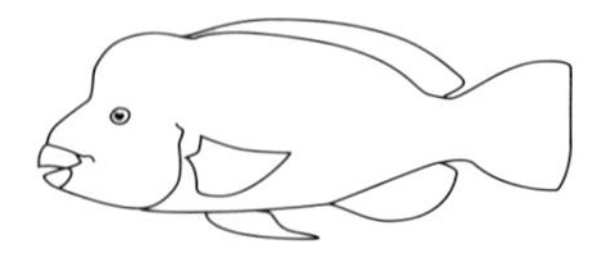

Bumphead Parrotfish

Powerful jaws, fused teeth or "beaks," and bright colors give parrotfish their common name. They are among the most common large fish seen on reefs. Sizes range from the two-and-a-half- foot Bumphead to the one-foot Loosetooth. Many are solitary, while others join loose aggregations that often mix with other species. Their stout, scaly bodies are colored in bizarre combinations of greens and blues highlighted with reds and yellows. They swim about the reefs using their pectoral fins; tails are only used for bursts of speed.

Their "beaks" are used to scrape algae and polyps from hard substrates. In the process, large amounts of hard material, such as barnacle shell and coral (limestone), are taken in and ground in their gullets to extract bits of polyp and algae. Clouds of the chalky residue are regularly excreted as the fish move about the reef, making parrotfish one of the major sources of sand. A few species secrete mucus bubbles that envelop their bodies at night while they sleep.

Identification of parrotfish is made difficult due to the dramatic changes in shape, color and markings that occur in most species as they mature. The phases include JUVENILE, ADULT, and SUPERMALE, which is the largest and most colorful. Some even have additional INTERMEDIATE phases. Adults include sexually mature females, and, in many species, immature males. Supermales are sexually mature males. Some parrotfish are hermaphroditic and go through a sex reversal to become supermales, while others simply mature, never changing their sex. Learning to identify parrotfish in all their phases can be quite a challenge.

FAMILY: Wrasse—Labridae
10 Species Included

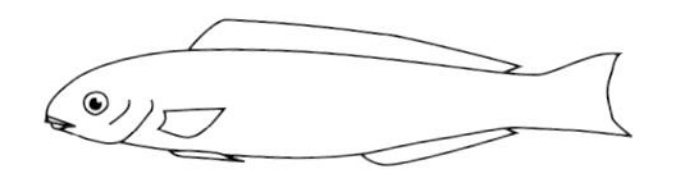
Wrasse
(typical shape)

Harlequin Wrasse

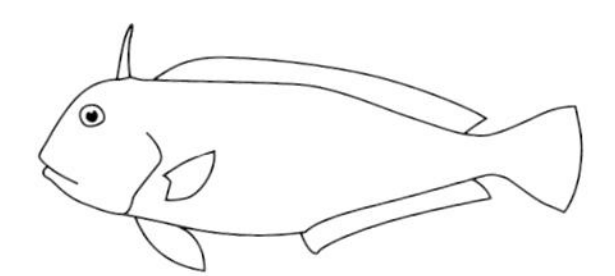
Wrasse/Razorfish

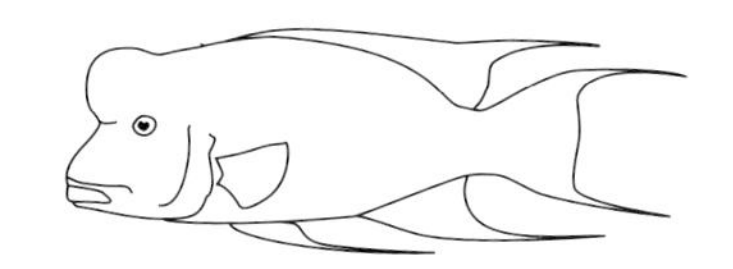
Streamer Hogfish
(supermale)

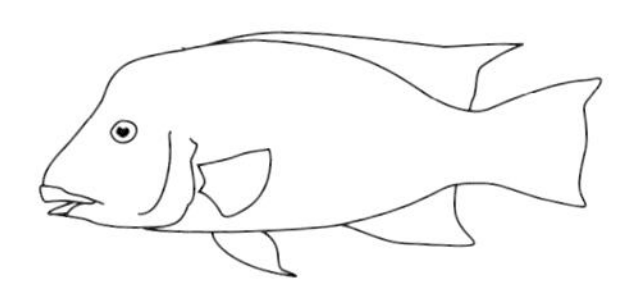
Goldspot Sheepshead

Wrasse are prolific reef inhabitants. They are closely related and similar to Parrotfish, but are generally much smaller and have more elongated "cigar" shapes. Sizes range from the two- and-a-half foot Goldspot Sheepshead to the six-inch Rainbow Wrasse. Greens, blues and yellows are the predominant colors of many species. All are scaly and have noticeable front teeth that give them a "bucktoothed" profile. The teeth are used to obtain food by crushing the shells of invertebrates, such as sea urchins.

By day, wrasse busily swim about the rocky reefs. Most are solitary or in small groups; the adult phase of Rainbow Wrasse, however, often come together in large schools to mate. At night, several species bury themselves in the sand.

The phases include JUVENILE, ADULT and SUPERMALE, the largest and most colorful. Some even have additional INTERMEDIATE phases. Adults include sexually mature females and, in many species, immature males and occasionally mature males with adult markings. Supermales are sexually mature males. Some wrasse are hermaphroditic and go through a sex reversal to become supermales, while others simply mature, never changing their sex. Identifying Wrasse in all their phases can be difficult.

Hogfish, Sheepshead and Razorfish are also members of the wrasse family.

DISTINCTIVE FEATURES: 1. Large, bulbous forehead. (Similar appearing supermale Streamer Hogfish [pg. 101] distinguished by yellow midbody bar.)

DESCRIPTION: Green to blue-green; fins generally more bluish; blue markings radiate from eye; blue bands around mouth. Only parrotfish with no substantial difference in color or markings between sexes. Size of bump on head increases with age.

ABUNDANCE & DISTRIBUTION: Occasional to common entire archipelago. Peru north to Baja.

HABITAT & BEHAVIOR: Inhabit rocky, boulder strewn reefs and slopes. Most common on reefs with reef building stony corals. Feed by scraping algae from rocks and corals. Solitary or in small groups.

REACTION TO DIVERS: Wary; usually move away, but can occasionally be closely approached with slow, non-threatening movements.

DISTINCTIVE FEATURES: 1. Conical head. (Similar Bicolor Parrotfish [next] has squared-off head.) **2. Blue markings under chin.**

DESCRIPTION: Green to blue-green; pink central stripe on dorsal and anal fins; blue markings around eye; area around pectoral fin and underside often yellowish to pinkish.

ABUNDANCE & DISTRIBUTION: Abundant to common entire archipelago. North to Baja; also tropical Indo-Pacific.

HABITAT & BEHAVIOR: Inhabit rocky, boulder strewn reefs and slopes. Most common on reefs with reef building stony corals. Feed by scraping algae from rocks and corals. Usually solitary.

REACTION TO DIVERS: Wary; usually move away, but can occasionally be closely approached with slow, non-threatening movements.

DISTINCTIVE FEATURES: 1. Five, somewhat uneven, blue bars on body and base of tail.

DESCRIPTION: Orangish to yellowish brown, pinkish brown or olive; blue markings under chin and around eye.

BUMPHEAD PARROTFISH
Loro Guacamaya
Scarus perrico
FAMILY:
Parrotfish – Scaridae

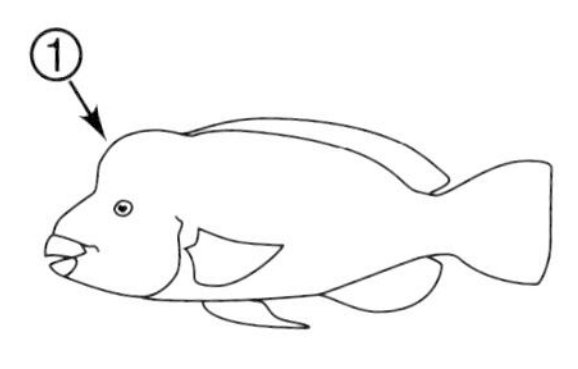

SIZE: 1-2 ft., max. 2½ ft.
DEPTH: 10-120 ft.

BLUE-CHIN PARROTFISH
Loro Barba Azul
Scarus ghobban
Supermale
FAMILY:
Parrotfish – Scaridae

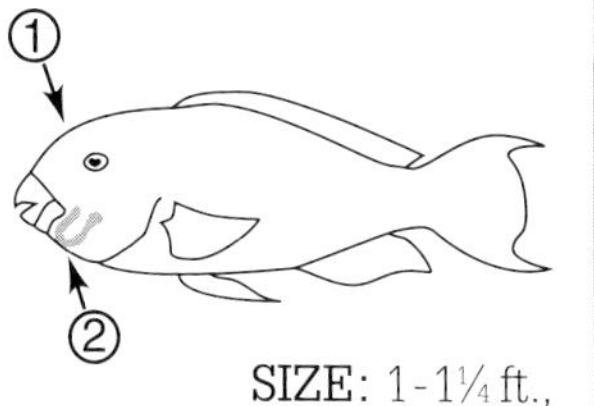

SIZE: 1-1¼ ft.,
max. 1½ ft.
DEPTH: 10-120 ft.

Adult

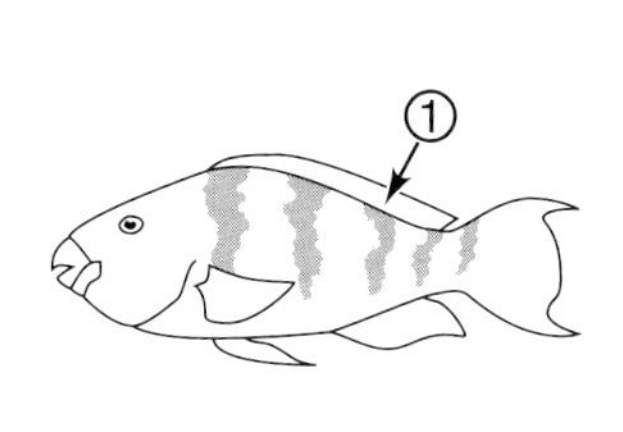

SIZE: ¾-1 ft.

DISTINCTIVE FEATURES: 1. Squared-off head. (Similar Blue-chin Parrotfish [previous] has conical head). **2. Blue and occasional pink markings under chin.**

DESCRIPTION: Green to blue-green; forebody often somewhat darker.

ABUNDANCE & DISTRIBUTION: Common to occasional entire archipelago. North to Baja; also tropical Indo-Pacific.

HABITAT & BEHAVIOR: Inhabit rocky, boulder strewn reefs and slopes. Most common on reefs with reef building stony corals. Feed by scraping algae from rocks and corals. Usually solitary.

REACTION TO DIVERS: Wary; usually move away, but can occasionally be closely approached with slow, non-threatening movements.

DISTINCTIVE FEATURES: 1. Dark reddish brown forebody, light reddish gray rear body.

DESCRIPTION: Tail reddish brown; scales of rear body often with thin, reddish line markings; underside of forebody and ventral fins occasionally red.

DISTINCTIVE FEATURES: 1. Bright green markings radiate from eye.

DESCRIPTION: Green; fins marked and shaded with blue and salmon. Adult females and males light blue to gray-blue and dusky blue. Juveniles reddish brown.

ABUNDANCE & DISTRIBUTION: Occasional entire archipelago. North to Baja.

HABITAT & BEHAVIOR: Inhabit rocky, boulder strewn reefs and slopes. Most common on reefs with reef building stony corals. Feed by scraping algae from rocks and corals. Usually solitary.

REACTION TO DIVERS: Wary; usually move away, but can occasionally be closely approached with slow, non-threatening movements.

BICOLOR PARROTFISH
Loro Bicolor
Scarus rubroviolaceus
Supermale

FAMILY:
Parrotfish – Scaridae

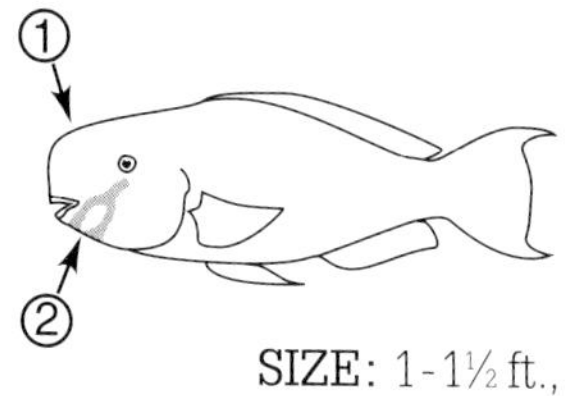

SIZE: 1-1½ ft., max. 1½ ft.
DEPTH: 10-120 ft.

Adult

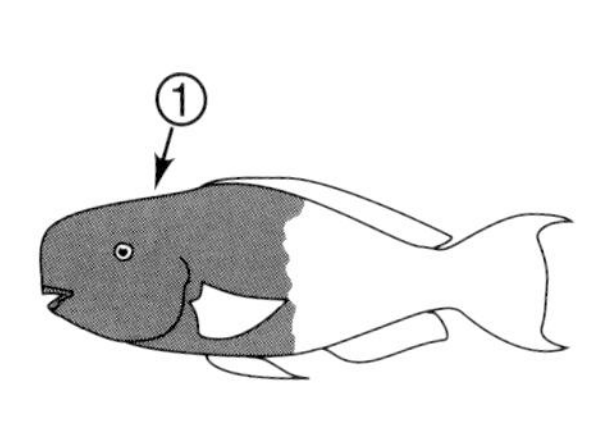

SIZE: ¾-1 ft.

AZURE PARROTFISH
Loro Verdeazul
Scarus compressus
Supermale

FAMILY:
Parrotfish – Scaridae

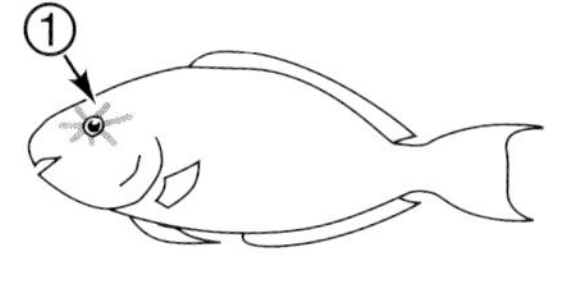

SIZE: 1-1½ ft., max. 2 ft.
DEPTH: 10-80 ft.

DISTINCTIVE FEATURES: Drab shades of brown, often mottled. No distinctive markings.

DESCRIPTION: Smallest parrotfish in eastern Pacific; resembles a wrasse. Teeth are not completely coalesced into a beak as those of most parrotfish. Can change color and markings to blend with background.

ABUNDANCE & DISTRIBUTION: Uncommon entire archipelago. Peru north to Baja.

HABITAT & BEHAVIOR: Prefer shallow water habitats in areas with algal growth. May be solitary or swim in loose schools.

REACTION TO DIVERS: Wary; usually move away, but can occasionally be closely approached with slow, non-threatening movements.

DISTINCTIVE FEATURES: 1. Wide yellow saddle patch behind head and above pectoral fin. 2. Blue to purple head.

DESCRIPTION: Body varies from violet to reddish green; blue dorsal, anal and tail fins.

ABUNDANCE & DISTRIBUTION: Abundant entire archipelago. North to Baja, including shore islands.

HABITAT & BEHAVIOR: Inhabit rocky reefs and slopes. Solitary, mate one-on-one with females (compare group spawning adult phase [next]). Constantly swim about reef with rapid movements and frequent changes of direction. Supermales can be either matured adult males or sex reversed females.

REACTION TO DIVERS: Wary; usually move away, but can occasionally be closely approached by moving into direction of travel.

DISTINCTIVE FEATURES: 1. Bright yellow midbody stripe.

DESCRIPTION: Dark back, may display a second yellow stripe below dorsal fin. Red to maroon stripe from base of pectoral fin through lower base of tail; belly white.

HABITAT & BEHAVIOR: Both sexually mature females and males cluster in large aggregations near reef tops. Most common between 10-40 feet. Spawn in large groups by suddenly rushing upward and coming together in a tight ball to mate — then with equal speed dissipate and return to reef top. Small juveniles have same color and markings and may be observed cleaning other fish.

REACTION TO DIVERS: Wary; usually move away, but can occasionally be closely approached by moving into direction of travel.

LOOSETOOTH PARROTFISH
Loro Pez Loro de Diente Flojo
Nicholsina denticulata
FAMILY:
Parrotfish – Scaridae

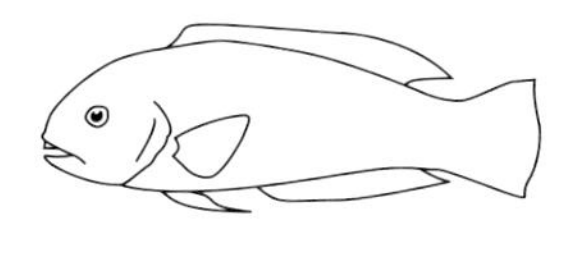

SIZE: 6 - 10 in., max. 12 in.
DEPTH: 3 - 35 ft.

RAINBOW WRASSE
Vieja Arco Iris
Thalassoma lucasanum
Supermale
FAMILY:
Wrasse – Labridae

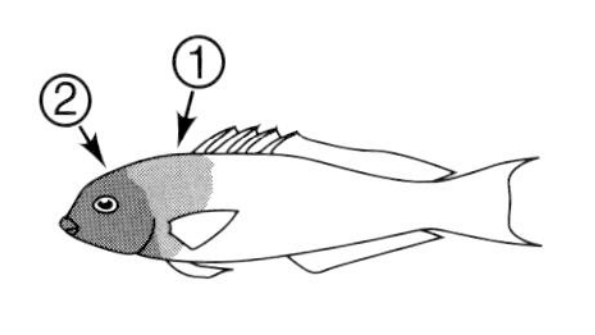

SIZE: 4 - 5 in., max. 6 in.
DEPTH: 10 - 160 ft.

Adult Females and Males

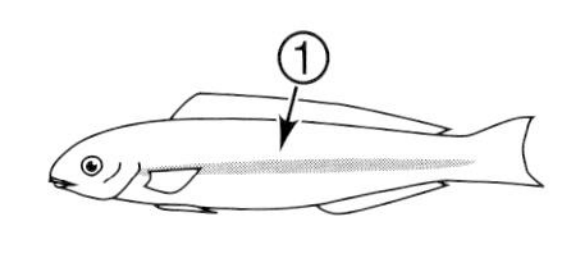

SIZE: 2½ - 4 in.

DISTINCTIVE FEATURES: 1. Small green to blue spot above pectoral fin.

DESCRIPTION: Can change colors rapidly and dramatically. Head shades of salmon changing to shades of blue-green on body; bright bluish line markings on head often continue as thin stripes on body. Adults light reddish brown to bluish white. Dark spot above pectoral fin, another on middorsal fin and an additional one on base of tail. Yellowish white midbody stripe and another below dorsal fin. Can rapidly change color and may or may not display spots and stripes.

ABUNDANCE & DISTRIBUTION: Abundant to common entire archipelago. North to Baja, including offshore islands; tropical Indo-Pacific.

HABITAT & BEHAVIOR: Inhabit rocky reefs and slopes. Solitary. Constantly swim about reef with rapid movements and frequent changes of direction.

REACTION TO DIVERS: Wary; usually move away, but can occasionally be closely approached by moving into direction of travel.

White Phase without Stripes and Displaying Only One Spot; Background Specimen Displaying Stripe below Dorsal Fin

DISTINCTIVE FEATURES: 1. Pink to violet head with green wavy band markings.

DESCRIPTION: Green to blue-green body. Color and shades quite variable and do not easily distinguish adult females and males. Young adults more yellow-green to green with orangish head. Juveniles yellow to yellow-brown with a dark maroon to black lateral stripe ending in a black spot at base of tail fin.

ABUNDANCE & DISTRIBUTION: Common entire archipelago, more abundant Darwin and Wolf. North to Baja, including offshore islands.

HABITAT & BEHAVIOR: Inhabit rocky, boulder strewn reefs and slopes. Solitary. Constantly swim about reef with rapid movements and frequent changes of direction.

REACTION TO DIVERS: Wary; usually move away, but can occasionally be closely approached by moving into direction of travel.

NOTE: Often incorrectly reported as *T. lutescens*, found in the tropical Indo-Pacific.

CHAMELEON WRASSE
Vieja Camaleón
Halichoeres dispilus
FAMILY:
Wrasse – Labridae

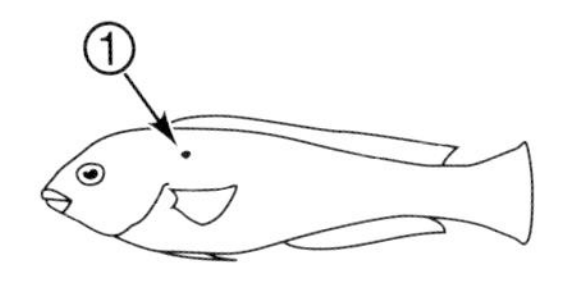

SIZE: 4 - 6 in., max. 8 in.
DEPTH: 10 - 250 ft.

Reddish Brown Phase and Displaying Midbody Stripe and Two Spots

SUNSET WRASSE
Vieja Atardecer
Thalassoma grammaticum
FAMILY:
Wrasse – Labridae

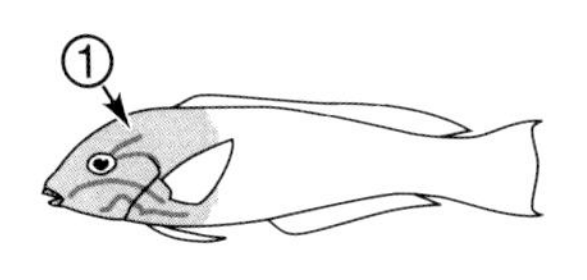

SIZE: 4 - 6 in., max. 8 in.
DEPTH: 10 - 100 ft.

DISTINCTIVE FEATURES: 1. Yellow spot or blotch just above and behind pectoral fin. 2. Wide black bar behind spot.

DESCRIPTION: Green to blue-green; belly lighter; dorsal and tail fins have rows of small blue spots.

ABUNDANCE & DISTRIBUTION: Common entire archipelago. North to Baja and offshore islands.

HABITAT & BEHAVIOR: Inhabit rocky reefs and slopes. Most common between 15-45 feet.

REACTION TO DIVERS: Wary; usually move away, but can occasionally be closely approached by moving into direction of travel.

DISTINCTIVE FEATURES: 1. Black stripe midbody. 2. Wide black bar from dorsal fin to midbody stripe.

DESCRIPTION: Light gray head and forebody; yellowish rear body and tail.

DISTINCTIVE FEATURES: 1. Large, dark ocellated spot fore-soft dorsal fin.

DESCRIPTION: Light yellow to yellow-brown with dark blotches.

HABITAT & BEHAVIOR: Inhabit shallow rocky reefs.

SPINSTER WRASSE
Vieja Soltera
Halichoeres nicholsi
Male

FAMILY:
Wrasse – Labridae

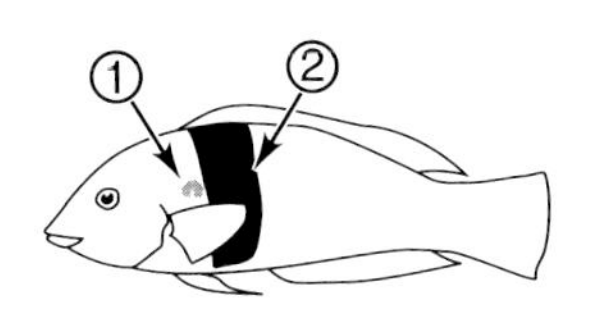

SIZE: 7-12 in., max. 15 in.
DEPTH: 10-250 ft.

Adult Female

SIZE: 6-10 in.

Juvenile

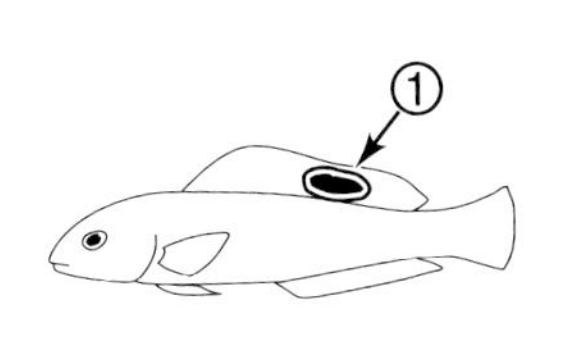

SIZE: 2-4 in.

DISTINCTIVE FEATURES: 1. Yellow midbody bar. 2. Long, streaming filamentous tips on dorsal, anal and lobes of tail fin.

DESCRIPTION: Gray, tinted red to reddish brown or green to blue-green. Large bulbous bump develops on head with age. Young supermales lack bump and have pointed snout [see bottom left page].

ABUNDANCE & DISTRIBUTION: Abundant entire archipelago. Chile north to Baja, including offshore islands.

HABITAT & BEHAVIOR: Inhabit rocky reefs, slopes and mixed areas of boulders and sand. Most common between 15-65 feet. Juveniles may act as cleaners.

REACTION TO DIVERS: Tend to ignore divers. Can often be closely approached with slow, non-threatening movements.

NOTE: Also commonly known as "Mexican Hogfish."

DISTINCTIVE FEATURES: 1. Two black stripes from eye to tail.

DESCRIPTION: Red-brown; rear body and tail often yellow. Juveniles also have two black stripes, but are yellow overall [below right page].

Young Supermale, Note Lack of Bulbous Bump on Head, Pointed Snout and Bright Yellow Bar

STREAMER HOGFISH
Veija Ribeteada
Bodianus diplotaenia
Supermale

FAMILY:
Wrasse/Hogfish – Labridae

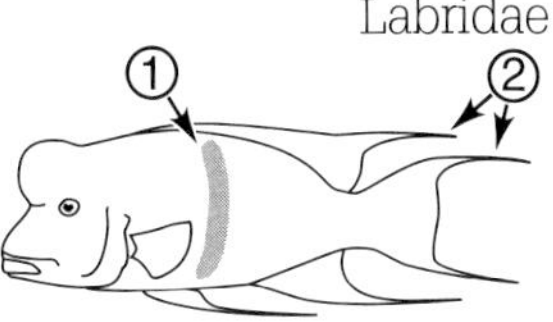

SIZE: 1-1¾ ft., max. 2½ in.
DEPTH: 10-250 ft.

Adult Female

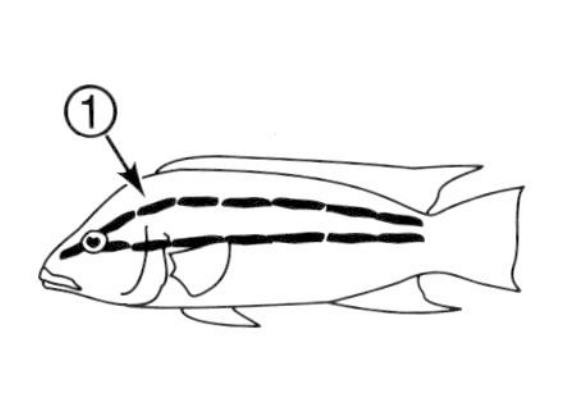

SIZE: 5-10 in.

Juvenile

DISTINCTIVE FEATURES: Harlequin designs of orange, black and white. Apparently no two fish are alike, and any of the three colors may predominate, although orange is most common. **1. Black spot base of pectoral fin.**

DESCRIPTION: Often have distinctive bump on forehead. Males and females not distinguished by color, patterns or physical appearance. Young have more pointed snouts and may lack black spot at base of pectoral fin.

ABUNDANCE & DISTRIBUTION: Common southern islands, western Isabela, Fernandina; occasional balance of archipelago. Ecuador to central Chile.

HABITAT & BEHAVIOR: Prefer cold water. Inhabit rocky reefs, slopes and areas of boulders and sand.

REACTION TO DIVERS: Wary; usually move away, but can occasionally be closely approached with slow, non-threatening movements.

NOTE: Also commonly known as "Galapagos Hogfish." Once thought to be endemic to Galapagos.

Young, Note Pointed Snout

DISTINCTIVE FEATURES: 1. Large whitish to yellow spot above pectoral fin.

DESCRIPTION: Maroon to red-brown, gray and pale gray.

ABUNDANCE & DISTRIBUTION: Occasional southern islands, western Isabela, Fernandina; uncommon balance of archipelago; absent Wolf and Darwin. South to Chile.

HABITAT & BEHAVIOR: Prefer cold water. Inhabit deeper rocky reefs, slopes and mixed areas of boulders and sand.

REACTION TO DIVERS: Wary; usually move away, but can occasionally be closely approached with slow, non-threatening movements.

NOTE: Also commonly known as "Galapagos Sheepshead."

HARLEQUIN WRASSE
Vieja Arlequín
Bodianus eclancheri
FAMILY:
Wrasse – Labridae

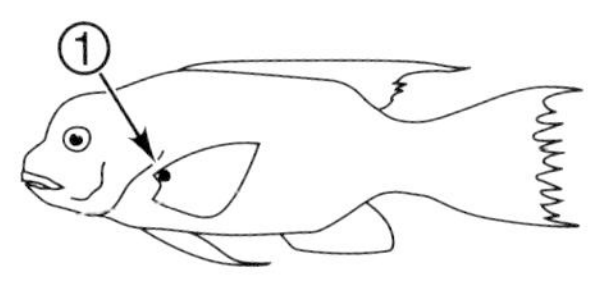

SIZE: 1-1½ ft., max. 2 ft.
DEPTH: 15-150 ft.

Color Variety

GOLDSPOT SHEEPSHEAD
Vieja Mancha Dorada
Semicossyphus darwini
FAMILY:
Wrasse – Labridae

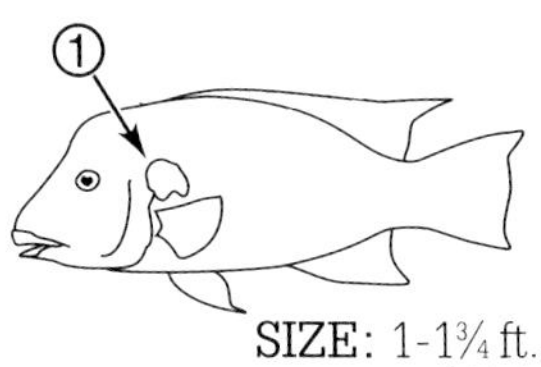

SIZE: 1-1¾ ft., max. 2½ ft.
DEPTH: 20-250 ft.

DISTINCTIVE FEATURES: 1. Distinctive white area at center of each scale. 2. White band foretail.

DESCRIPTION: Red-brown to gray body; head pale with four or five lines radiating from eye.

ABUNDANCE & DISTRIBUTION: Uncommon entire archipelago. North to Baja; also tropical Indo-Pacific and Hawaii.

HABITAT & BEHAVIOR: Prefer warmer water. Inhabit rocky reefs, slopes, gravel beds and mixed areas of boulders and sand.

REACTION TO DIVERS: Shy; move away, but can occasionally be closely approached with slow, non-threatening movements.

NOTE: Also commonly known as "Reindeer Wrasse", "Rockmover Wrasse", "Clown Razorfish," and "Pearlscale Razorfish."

DISTINCTIVE FEATURES: 1. First two spines of dorsal fin extremely long and antler-like. 2. Four rows of large white spots or rectangles on body.

DESCRIPTION: Maroon to greenish brown, dark brown and gray. Three bold, reddish brown to green bars on body extend onto dorsal and anal fins; fins generally translucent except for rays; lines and white markings radiate from eye.

HABITAT & BEHAVIOR: Inhabit shallow protected places on reefs and rocky, boulder strewn areas. Blend with background; occasionally mix in with leafy blades of algal growth.

REACTION TO DIVERS: Wary; but tend to remain still upon approach, apparently relying on camouflage.

NOTE: Juveniles are so different in appearance from adults that for years they were classified as separate species.

DISTINCTIVE FEATURES: 1. First two dorsal spines form a sharp spike. 2. Head blunt, squared-off.

DESCRIPTION: Pale gray with somewhat indistinct darker bands. Banding in juveniles brown to olive [pictured].

ABUNDANCE & DISTRIBUTION: Uncommon entire archipelago. North to Baja; also Hawaii.

HABITAT & BEHAVIOR: Prefer warmer water. Inhabit sandy areas near rocky reefs. Can point spike forward to ward off predators or can escape by diving into and moving under sand.

REACTION TO DIVERS: Wary; usually keep a safe distance, but can occasionally be closely approached with slow, non-threatening movements.

DRAGON WRASSE
Vieja Dragón
Novaculichthys taeniourus
FAMILY: Wrasse/Razorfish – Labridae

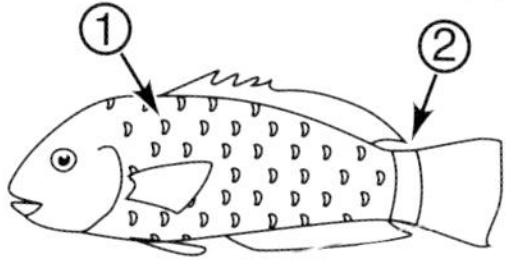

SIZE: 6 - 10 in., max. 12 in.
DEPTH: 15 - 100 ft.

Juvenile

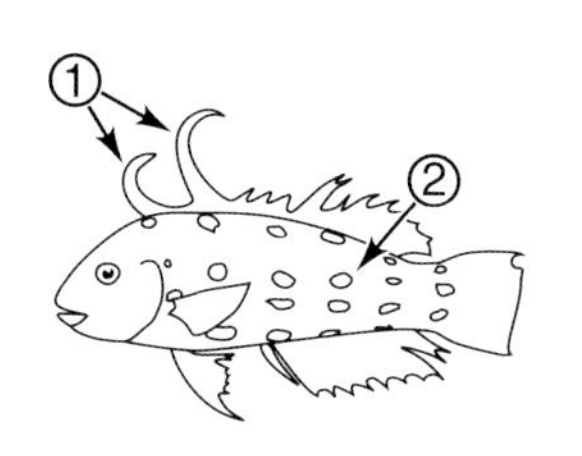

SIZE: 1¼ - 3¼ in.

PACIFIC RAZORFISH
Viejita del Pacífico
Xyrichthys pavo
FAMILY: Wrasse/Razorfish – Labridae

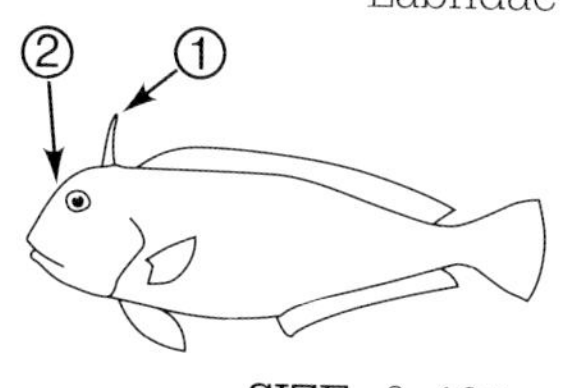

SIZE: 6 - 10 in., max. 15 in.
DEPTH: 15 - 100 ft.

IDENTIFICATION GROUP 7

Reddish/Big Eyes

Squirrelfish-Bigeye-Cardinalfish

This ID Group consists of fish that range in color from pale red to reddish-brown and have large eyes. They are generally nocturnal feeders, and usually hide in dark recesses during the day.

FAMILY: Squirrelfish- Holocentridae

3 Species Included

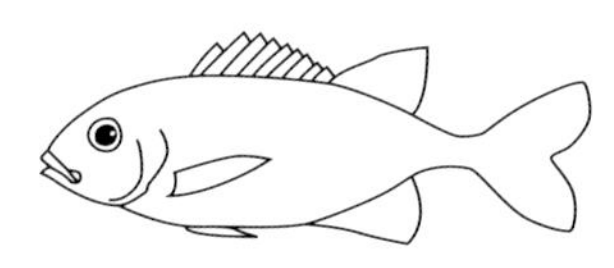

Squirrelfish
(typical shape)

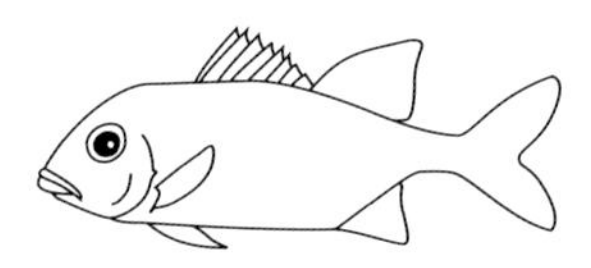

Bigscale Soldierfish

This family of reddish fish with large "squirrel-like" eyes is among the most striking on the reef. Its members often have white, silver and yellow-gold body markings. Another distinctive family characteristic is their pronounced rear dorsal fins.

During the day, they lurk in crevices, recesses, under ledge overhangs and other shaded areas. At night, they feed on invertebrates, in the open near the bottom.

The species are similar in appearance, but each has distinctive features that make identification easy. Juvenile squirrelfish are thin, silvery pelagics and are seldom seen.

FAMILY: Bigeye - Priancanthidae

2 Species Included

Glasseye

Popeye Catalufa

Bigeyes, also known as catalufas, are reddish fish with compressed bodies and small, rough scales. Body shape and markings make them easy to identify.

At night, their huge eyes and color make them effective, virtually invisible predators. During the day, they lurk in crevices, deep recesses, under ledge overhangs and other protected areas.

FAMILY: Cardinalfish - Apogonidae

2 Species Included

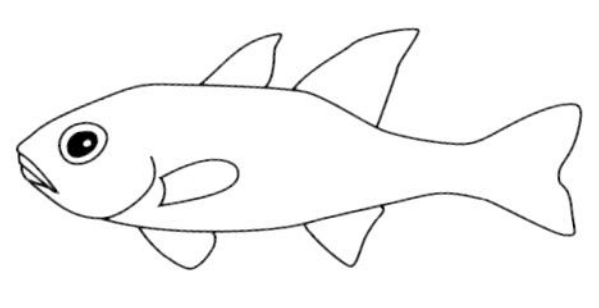

Cardinalfish
(typical shape)

Cardinalfish are named for their reddish color. They are quite small (1-3 inches), have large eyes, relatively short snouts, and two separate dorsal fins.

Although common reef inhabitants, they are seldom spotted by divers because they hide during the day. These small fish are most often seen hovering just inside dark recesses. Large groups of cardinalfish are occasionally found inside caves. At night they feed in the open, on tiny fish and crustaceans.

Black spots, dark body bars and eye markings are the keys to species identification.

DISTINCTIVE FEATURES: 1. Black diagonal band across rear of gill plate.

DESCRIPTION: Red; yellow to orange outer half of foredorsal fin; thin, white leading edges on rear dorsal, ventral, anal and tail fins. Large obvious scales.

ABUNDANCE & DISTRIBUTION: Occasional Darwin and Wolf; occasional to uncommon other islands. Tropical Indo-Pacific and tropical eastern Pacific.

HABITAT & BEHAVIOR: Drift in cracks, crevices, small caves and under ledge overhangs. May mix with Panamic Soldierfish and Tinsel Soldierfish [next]. Most common between 20-40 feet.

REACTION TO DIVERS: Wary; when approached, retreat deep into hiding place, but after short time will return to peer out entrance.

DISTINCTIVE FEATURES: Red. No distinctive markings.

DESCRIPTION: Eye has dark pupil, bright red iris.

ABUNDANCE & DISTRIBUTION: Common entire archipelago. Southern Baja to Ecuador.

HABITAT & BEHAVIOR: During day drift in cracks, crevices, small caves and under ledge overhangs. May mix with Bigscale Soldierfish [previous] and Tinsel Squirrelfish [next]. Feed in open at night. Most common between 15-40 feet.

REACTION TO DIVERS: Wary; when approached retreat deep into hiding place, but after short time will return to peer out entrance.

DISTINCTIVE FEATURES: Reddish silver. No distinctive markings.

DESCRIPTION: Prominent spines on gill plate and long second anal fin spine.

ABUNDANCE & DISTRIBUTION: Occasional entire archipelago. Central Baja to Ecuador.

HABITAT & BEHAVIOR: During day drift in cracks, crevices, small caves and under ledge overhangs. May mix with Bigscale Soldierfish and Panamic Soldierfish [previous]. Feed in open at night. Most common between 15-40 feet.

REACTION TO DIVERS: Wary; when approached retreat deep into hiding place, but after short time will return to peer out entrance.

BIGSCALE SOLDIERFISH
Soldado Escama Grande
Myripristis berndti
FAMILY:
Squirrelfish – Holocentridae

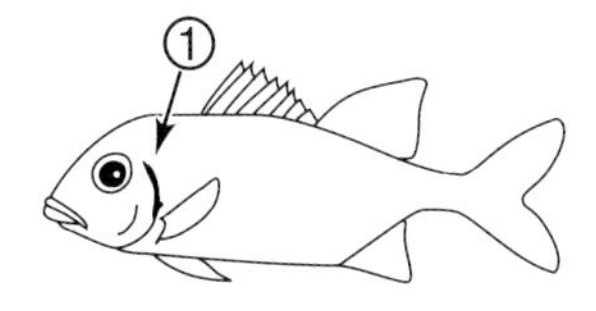

SIZE: 5-8 in., max. 1 ft.
DEPTH: 15-80 ft.

PANAMIC SOLDIERFISH
Soldado Panamico
Myripristis leiognathos
FAMILY:
Squirrelfish – Holocentridae

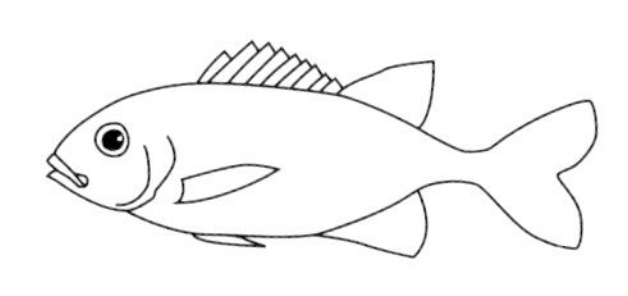

SIZE: 4½-6 in., max. 7 in.
DEPTH: 10-80 ft.

TINSEL SQUIRRELFISH
Candil
Adioryx suborbitalis
FAMILY:
Squirrelfish – Holocentridae

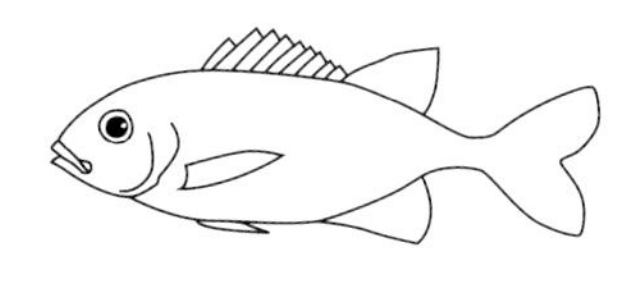

SIZE: 5-7 in., max. 10 in.
DEPTH: 10-80 ft.

Bigeye

DISTINCTIVE FEATURES: 1. Large mouth, sharply angled upward. 2. Large eye.

DESCRIPTION: Vary from bright red to silvery red and orange; rear dorsal, tail and anal fins often bordered in black. Compressed, saucer-shaped body.

ABUNDANCE & DISTRIBUTION: Occasional western Isabela, uncommon to absent balance of archipelago. Peru north to central California.

HABITAT & BEHAVIOR: Reclusive during day, hiding in dark protected recesses. Forage in open at night for small fish, crustaceans and polychaete worms on reefs and over sand flats.

REACTION TO DIVERS: On night dives, when mesmerized by underwater light, allow close approach.

DISTINCTIVE FEATURES: 1. Silver bars on back (occasionally obscure).

DESCRIPTION: Vary from solid to mottled red to silvery red, copper and pink, occasionally with yellow tints. Dorsal, tail and anal fins vary, reddish silver to pink to brownish yellow to bright yellow.

ABUNDANCE & DISTRIBUTION: Occasional Darwin, Wolf; uncommon to rare balance of archipelago. Circumtropical.

HABITAT & BEHAVIOR: During day drift under ledge overhangs and other shaded areas on rocky reefs and slopes. Feed in open at night.

REACTION TO DIVERS: Wary; may allow close approach with slow, non-threatening movements.

NOTE: Commonly known as "Glasseye Snapper" in Caribbean.

Bars on Back Obscure

POPEYE CATALUFA
Catalufa
Pseudopriacanthus serrula
FAMILY:
Bigeye – Priacanthidae

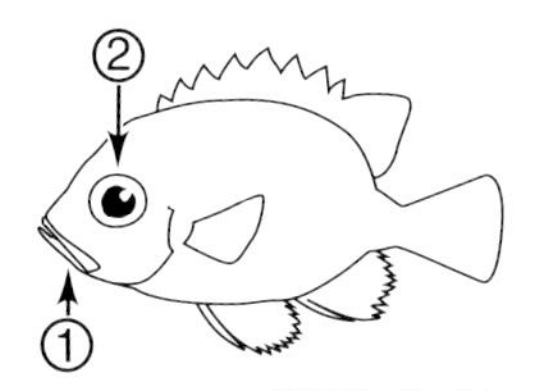

SIZE: 3-8 in.,
max. 1 ft.
DEPTH: 40-250 ft.

GLASSEYE
Semáforo
Heteropriacanthus cruentatus
FAMILY:
Bigeye – Priacanthidae

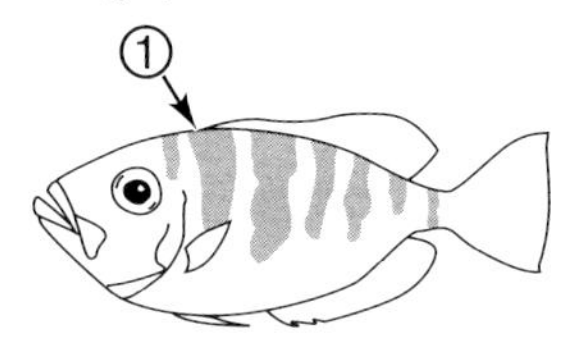

SIZE: 7-10 in.,
max. 1 ft.
DEPTH: 15-60 ft.

Displaying Bright Yellow Fins; Bars on Back Obscure

DISTINCTIVE FEATURES: 1. Black tip on rear dorsal fin.

DESCRIPTION: Red to copper and pink; tips of forked tail often dusky or black. Large dark eye.

ABUNDANCE & DISTRIBUTION: Abundant entire archipelago. ENDEMIC to Galapagos, Cocos and Malpelo.

HABITAT & BEHAVIOR: During day drift under ledge overhangs and other shaded areas on rocky reefs and slopes. Feed in open at night.

REACTION TO DIVERS: Tend to ignore divers. Allow close approach with slow, non-threatening movements.

SIMILAR SPECIES: Tail Spot Cardinalfish, *A. dovii*, black spot on base of tail, may have stripe through eye. This and several other cardinalfish are rarely observed except at night.

DISTINCTIVE FEATURES: 1. Black bar below second dorsal fin to midbody.

DESCRIPTION: Red to orange and copper; black stripe with thin gold outlined from snout through eyes.

ABUNDANCE & DISTRIBUTION: Occasional entire archipelago. Peru north to Baja, including offshore islands.

HABITAT & BEHAVIOR: During day drift under ledge overhangs and other shaded, reclusive areas on rocky reefs and slopes. Feed in open at night. Often mix with other cardinalfish. (Note Blacktip Cardinalfish in photograph.)

REACTION TO DIVERS: Tend to ignore divers. Allow close approach with slow, non-threatening movements.

NOTE: Also commonly known as "Barspot Cardinalfish."

BLACKTIP CARDINALFISH
Cardenal Punta Negra
Apogon atradorsatus
FAMILY:
Cardinalfish –
Apogonidae

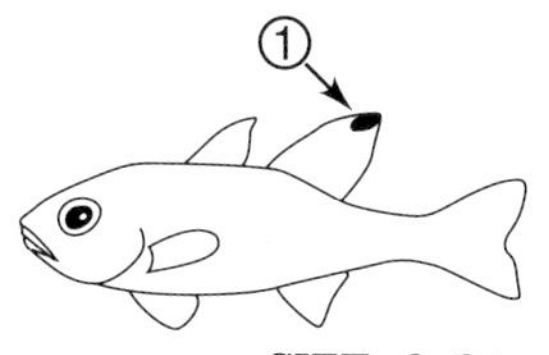

SIZE: 2 - 3 in.,
max. 3½ in.
DEPTH: 10 - 150 ft.

PINK CARDINALFISH
Cardenal Rosado
Apogon pacifici
FAMILY:
Cardinalfish –
Apogonidae

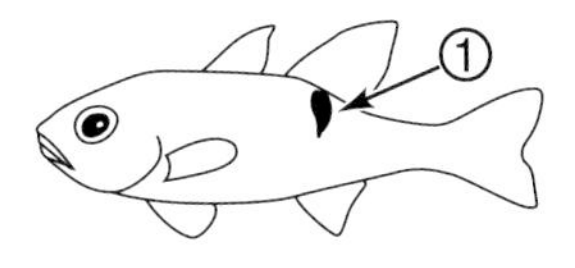

SIZE: 1½ - 2 in.,
max. 2¼ in.
DEPTH: 0 - 100 ft.

IDENTIFICATION GROUP 8

Small, Elongated Bottom - Dwellers
Blenny - Goby

This ID Group consists of small fish that generally grow to no more than three inches. All have long, cylindrical bodies and spend most of their time perched on the bottom or in small holes with only their heads protruding.

GROUP: Blenny - Labrisomidae, Tripterygiidae, Blenniidae & Chaenopsidae

10 Species Included

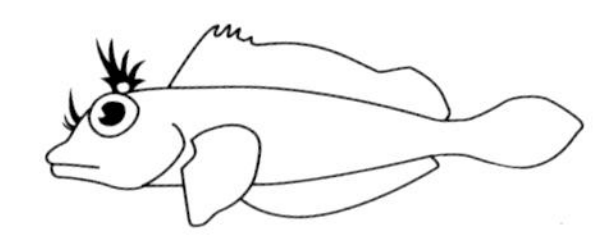

Scaled Blenny
(typical shape)

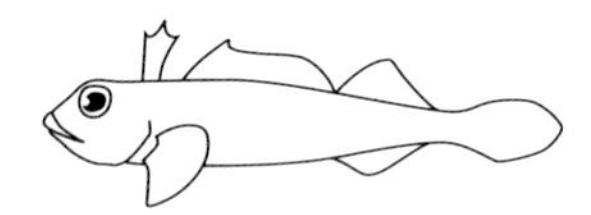

Triplefin Blenny
(typical shape)

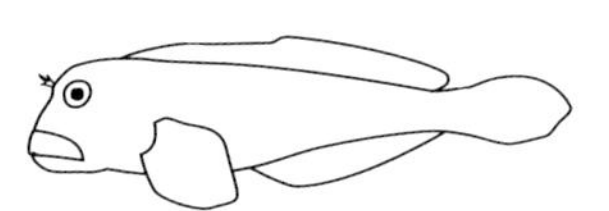

Scaleless Blenny
(typical shape)

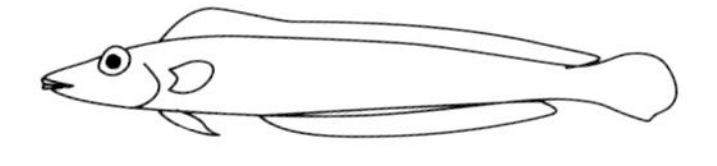

Pike Blenny
(typical shape)

Most blennies are small (1½-3 inches) and have long, thin ventral fins which they use to perch on the bottom. While resting and swimming, blennies tend to curve and flex their bodies, in contrast to the gobies that hold their bodies stiff and straight. Most blennies have fleshy appendages, called cirri, growing above their eyes. Often there are additional cirri on the snout and nape.

Because of their small size and ability to change colors and markings to blend with the background, they often go unnoticed. Several species live in holes and are only seen with their heads exposed. Occasionally, they dart out for a few seconds to nab a particle of food.

Many blennies are similar in appearance and difficult to distinguish. Adding to the confusion, males and females of several species are dramatically different from one another in appearance. Careful attention to detail, however, makes underwater identification possible in most cases.

Four scientific families, all sharing a common ancestor, comprise the common group known as blennies. Observable differences for the diver are: scaleless blennies, Blenniidae - no scales and a single dorsal fin; scaled blennies, Labrisomidae - noticeable scales and a single dorsal fin; pikeblennies, Chaenopsidae - elongated snout and body and absence of cirri; triplefins, Tripterygiidae - noticeable scales and three separate dorsal fins.

FAMILY: Goby - Gobiidae

3 Species Included

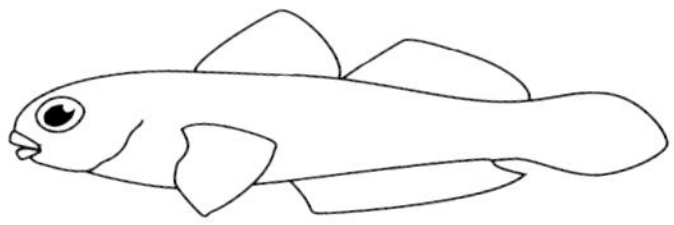

Goby
(typical shape)

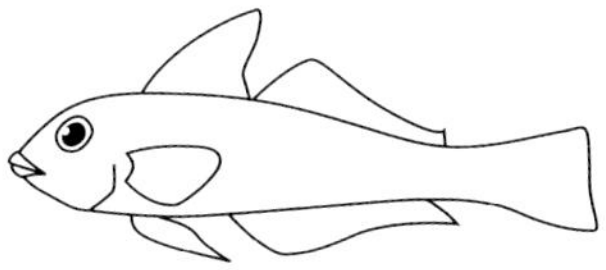

Goby
(typical shape)

Gobies are quite small (generally 1-2 inches, with only a few species ever exceeding 2½ inches). In fact, some of the world's smallest known vertebrates are in this family. Often they are brightly colored with bold markings. Most are carnivorous and many species are cleaners. They rest on their pectoral and ventral fins. In surge or current, a small suction disc is formed between their ventral fins, anchoring them in place. Their color and markings usually make them easy to identify.

Gobies and blennies are often confused, but can easily be distinguished by their dorsal fins. Gobies have two, while most blennies have one long, continuous fin, and a few species have three. Another observable difference is the tendency of gobies to rest in a stiff, straight position, while blennies are more flexed and curved. The same can be said for their swimming movements.

DISTINCTIVE FEATURES: 1. Olive to brown head with large "goggle" eyes bordered with an orange to yellow or white crescent and unbranched cirri above. 2. White lower jaw and throat, often with yellow spots.

DESCRIPTION: Head blunt with large lips and unbranched cirri above eyes. Fine blue spots on upper head; yellow spots on throat. Olive to brown body; row of large white spots down back and another along midbody.

ABUNDANCE & DISTRIBUTION: Abundant to common entire archipelago. ENDEMIC.

HABITAT & BEHAVIOR: Inhabit empty barnacle shells. Often perch in opening with only head protruding [below right]. Dart out to nab bits of floating food. Most common between 20-40 feet.

REACTION TO DIVERS: Tend to ignore divers, but retreat into protection of shell if molested.

Red-spotted Barnacle Blennies Residing in Barnacle Shell

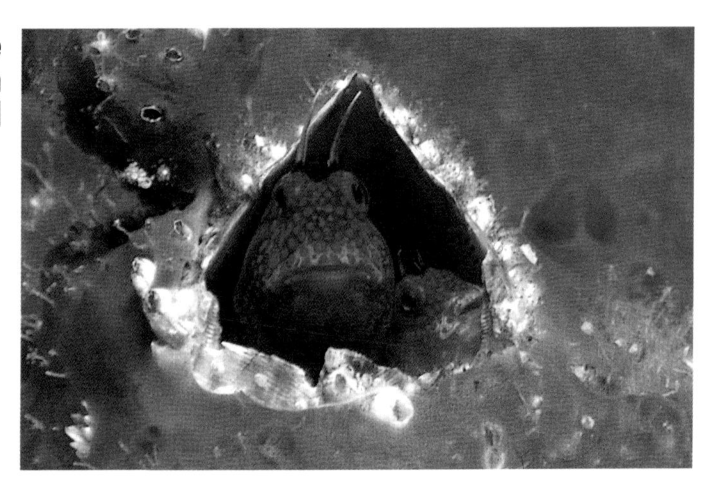

DISTINCTIVE FEATURES: 1. Numerous red spots on head. 2. Large "goggle" eyes with unbranched cirri above.

DESCRIPTION: Red-brown; row of large white spots with darkish centers down back and another along midbody. Head blunt with large lips.

ABUNDANCE & DISTRIBUTION: Occasional central and southern islands of archipelago. North to Baja.

HABITAT & BEHAVIOR: Inhabit empty barnacle shells. Often perch in opening with only head protruding [above left]. Dart out to nab bits of floating food. Most common between 5-20 feet.

REACTION TO DIVERS: Tend to ignore divers, but retreat into protection of shell if molested.

GALAPAGOS BARNACLE BLENNY
Trambollito Percebes de Galápagos
Acanthemblemaria castroi
FAMILY:
Blenny – Blennidae

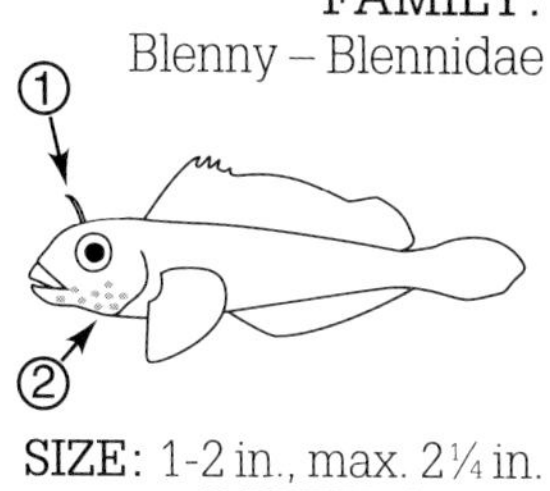

SIZE: 1-2 in., max. 2¼ in.
DEPTH: 3-75 ft.

Galapagos Barnacle Blenny Residing in Barnacle Shell

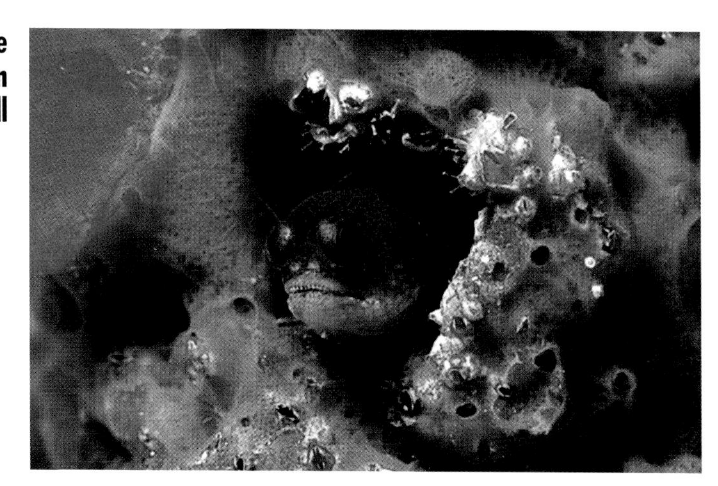

RED-SPOTTED BARNACLE BLENNY
Trambollito Percebes de Puntos Rojos
Hypsoblennius brevipinnis
FAMILY:
Blenny – Blennidae

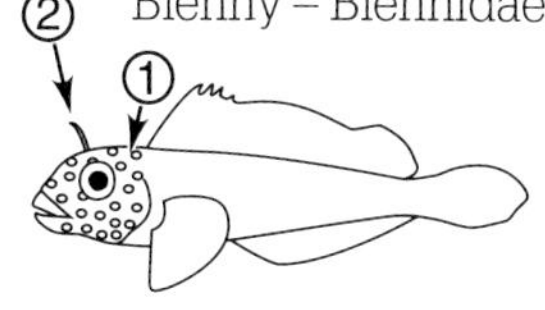

SIZE: 1-2 in., max. 2½ in.
DEPTH: 3-30 ft.

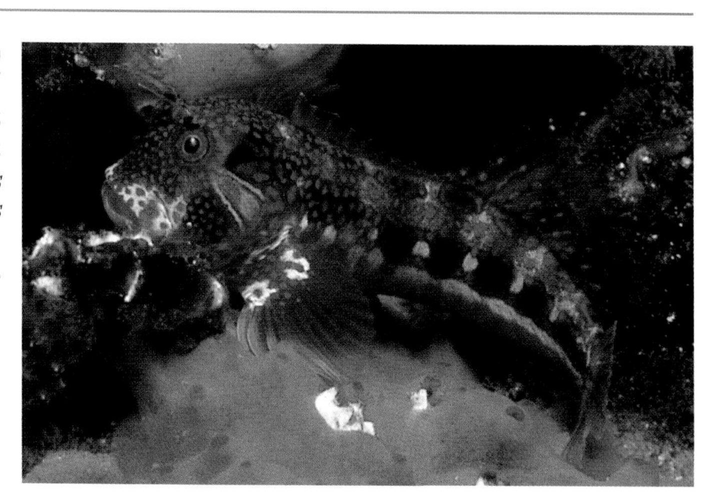

DISTINCTIVE FEATURES: 1. Black central stripe on back split by dorsal fin. 2. Black stripe runs from between eyes along midbody to tail. 3. Black stripe on upper lip runs to pectoral fin.

DESCRIPTION: White to reddish brown between black stripes; fins translucent to reddish brown. Small, multiple branched cirri above eyes.

ABUNDANCE & DISTRIBUTION: Rare San Cristobal. Additional distribution unknown.

HABITAT & BEHAVIOR: Inhabit rocky, surgey zones with barnacle growth.

REACTION TO DIVERS: Tend to ignore divers, but retreat into protective recess if closely approached.

NOTE: Pictured specimen is unidentified and possibly an undescribed species. Author has observed this species on several occasions off San Cristobal.

DISTINCTIVE FEATURES: 1. Dark ocellated spot behind eye. 2. Two or three wide, irregular bars behind spot.

DESCRIPTION: Olive to brown; reddish circle around eye. Two narrow bars from upper lip run to eye. Blunt head with large lips and obvious cirri. Juveniles lack bar markings.

ABUNDANCE & DISTRIBUTION: Abundant to common entire archipelago. Peru north to Baja, including offshore islands.

HABITAT & BEHAVIOR: Inhabit small holes and cracks on rocky slopes, especially in surge zones. Often perch in recesses blending with background.

REACTION TO DIVERS: Wary; usually retreat to protection of hole or other recess, but can occasionally be closely approached with slow non-threatening movements.

NOTE: Also commonly known as "Panamic Fanged Blenny," and "Trambollito Negro."

Adult

BLACKSTRIPED BLENNY
Trambollito Rayado Negro

FAMILY:
Blenny – Blennidae

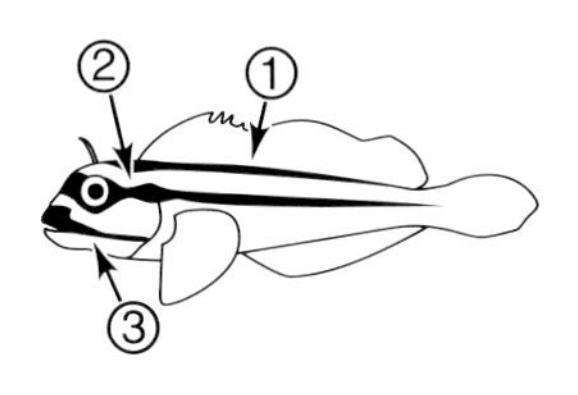

SIZE: 1¼-2 in.
DEPTH: 5-30 ft.

LARGE BANDED BLENNY
Chupa Piedra
Ophioblennius steindachneri

FAMILY:
Blenny – Blennidae

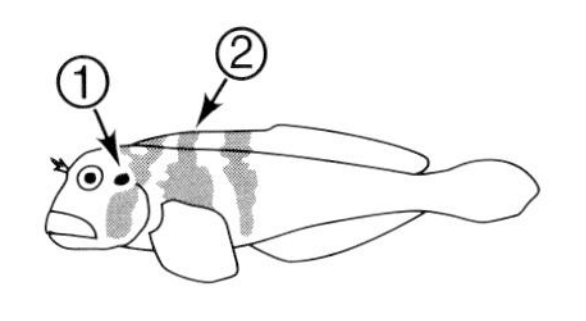

SIZE: 4-7 in., max. 9 in.
DEPTH: 1-60 ft.

Juvenile, Note Lack of Bar Markings

DISTINCTIVE FEATURES: 1. Two black stripes with yellow between on upper body. 2. Mouth underslung.

DESCRIPTION: Underside white to cream; tail whitish to translucent.

ABUNDANCE & DISTRIBUTION: Common entire archipelago. Peru north to Baja.

HABITAT & BEHAVIOR: Inhabit empty tube-worm snail shells, often extending head from opening. Feed by joining loose groups of look-alike Rainbow Wrasse [pg. 95]; dart out to nip at nearby fish, taking mucus and perhaps small bits of flesh.

REACTION TO DIVERS: Wary. Upon approach, usually retreat to protection of tube-worm snail shell, or, if in open, keep a safe distance; however, can occasionally be closely approached with slow non-threatening movements.

DISTINCTIVE FEATURES: 1. Four or five dark bars on back. 2. Series of diamond-shaped markings (belt) runs from below pectoral fin base to lower tail.

DESCRIPTION: Color highly variable earthtones. May have numerous dark spots; black spot behind eye; rows of dark spots on translucent fins. Can pale, darken and/or change color rapidly.

ABUNDANCE & DISTRIBUTION: Occasional entire archipelago. Peru north to Baja.

HABITAT & BEHAVIOR: Inhabit rocky, boulder strewn areas and walls. (Similar Belted Blenny [next] prefers tide pools and shallow water habitats.)

REACTION TO DIVERS: Unafraid; often somewhat curious. Allow close approach with slow non-threatening movements.

NOTE: Previously reported as *M. ajuerae*, a junior synonym.

DISTINCTIVE FEATURES: 1. Dark stripe, "belt," runs from above pectoral fin base to upper tail. (Similar Chameleon Clinid [previous] "belt" is below pectoral fin base.)

DESCRIPTION: Color highly variable earthtones. May have numerous dark spots; black spot behind eye; rows of dark spots on translucent fins. Can pale, darken and/or change color rapidly.

ABUNDANCE & DISTRIBUTION: Occasional entire archipelago. Peru north to Baja.

HABITAT & BEHAVIOR: Inhabit tide pools, shallow, rocky, boulder strewn areas and walls. (Similar Chameleon Clinid [above] prefer deeper water habitats.)

REACTION TO DIVERS: Unafraid; often somewhat curious. Allow close approach with slow non-threatening movements.

SABERTOOTH BLENNY
Cachudito Diente Sable
Plagiotremus azaleus
FAMILY:
Blenny – Blennidae

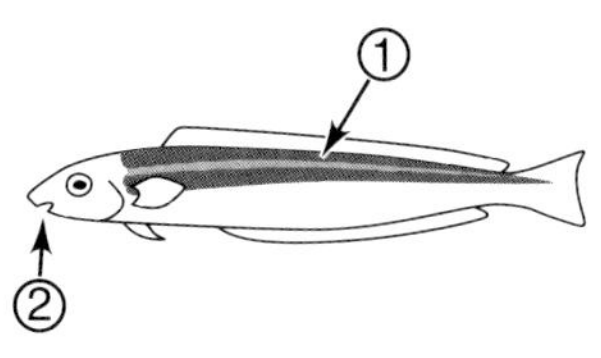

SIZE: 2-3½ in., max. 4 in.
DEPTH: 10-75 ft.

CHAMELEON CLINID
Clínido Camaleón
Malacoctenus tetranemus
FAMILY
Blenny – Labrisomidae

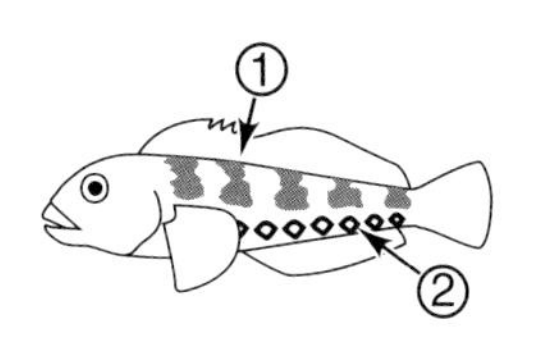

SIZE: 1¼-2½ in.
DEPTH: 20-75

BELTED BLENNY
Trambollito de Cintuón
Malacoctenus zonogaster
FAMILY
Blenny – Labrisomidae

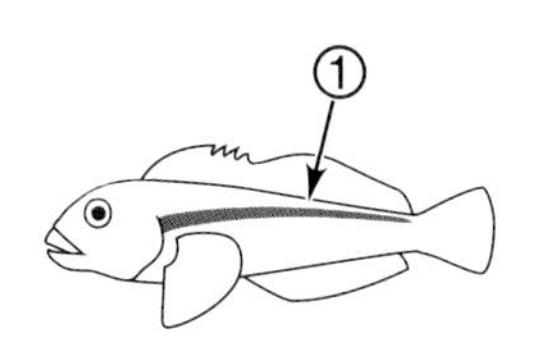

SIZE: 1¼-2½ in.
DEPTH: 0-15

DISTINCTIVE FEATURES: 1. Large spot on rear gill cover. 2. Large "goggle" eyes with two sets of large branched cirri above. 3. First three dorsal spines longer than those behind.

DESCRIPTION: Several dark bars on back. Color highly variable with full range of earthtones to white; large spot and markings on head may blend with body color or stand out in bright shades of green, red or yellow. Can pale, darken and/or change color rapidly. Breeding males white with black bars on back and yellow markings on head.

ABUNDANCE & DISTRIBUTION: Common entire archipelago. ENDEMIC to Galapagos and Malpelo.

HABITAT & BEHAVIOR: Wide range of habitats from boulder strewn slopes and reefs to ledges and undercuts along wall faces. Most common between 20-60 feet.

REACTION TO DIVERS: Unafraid; often somewhat curious. Allow close approach with slow non-threatening movements.

Juvenile

DISTINCTIVE FEATURES: 1. Interior of mouth bright yellow. 2. Alternating dusky and light bars on back from pectoral fin to tail.

DESCRIPTION: Elongated body with tall foredorsal fin. Tan to dirty white; can pale, darken and/or change color rapidly to blend with background. Occasionally a few white to bluish spots and streaks and dusky blotches.

ABUNDANCE & DISTRIBUTION: Occasional entire archipelago. ENDEMIC.

HABITAT & BEHAVIOR: Inhabit sandy areas mixed with rocks and gravel.

REACTION TO DIVERS: Unafraid; often somewhat curious. Allow close approach with slow non-threatening movements.

BRAVO CLINID
Trambollo Bravo
Labrisomus dendriticus
FAMILY:
Blenny – Labrisomidae

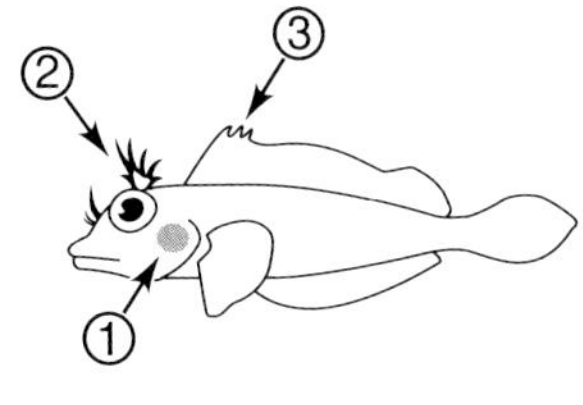

SIZE: 4-6 in., max. 7 in.
DEPTH: 3-75 ft.

Breeding Male, Note White Body with Black Bars and Yellow Markings on Head

YELLOW-MOUTH PIKEBLENNY
Trambollito Pico Boca Amarilla
Chaenopsis schmitti
FAMILY:
Blenny – Labrisomidae

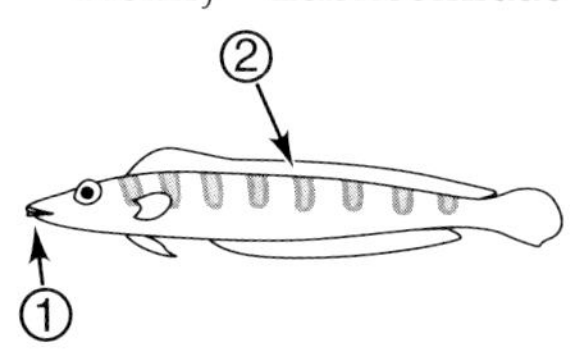

SIZE: 1¼-2½ in., max. 3 in.
DEPTH: 10-50 ft.

DISTINCTIVE FEATURES: 1. Black spot on base of tail 2. Three dorsal fins.

DESCRIPTION: Dark midbody stripe formed by four sets of paired spots. Dusky bars extend above and below spots. Reddish brown overall. First dorsal fin of breeding males becomes black with two bright gold spots; apparently (see note) non-breeding males have two pale spots [opposite] and females have reddish markings and/or shadings without spots. Two rear dorsal fins translucent with red spotted rays.

ABUNDANCE & DISTRIBUTION: Abundant to common entire archipelago. ENDEMIC.

HABITAT & BEHAVIOR: Inhabit rocky reefs, boulder strewn slopes and walls.

REACTION TO DIVERS: Unafraid; often somewhat curious. Allow close approach with slow non-threatening movements.

NOTE: Information concerning markings of breeding male has been scientifically confirmed; however, markings of non-breeding male and female have been observed, but not conclusively established.

Female, Note Reddish Markings on First Dorsal Fin

DISTINCTIVE FEATURES: 1. Dark spot on lower base of tail.

DESCRIPTION: Whitish translucent body with rows of reddish and occasional white and dark spots on body.

ABUNDANCE & DISTRIBUTION: Occasional entire archipelago. North to Baja, including offshore islands.

HABITAT & BEHAVIOR: Perch on sand bottoms, blending with background.

REACTION TO DIVERS: Tend to ignore divers, but retreat upon close approach.

GALAPAGOS TRIPLEFIN BLENNY
Trambollito Triple Aleta de Galápagos
Lepidonectes corallicola
FAMILY:
Blenny – Tripterygiidae

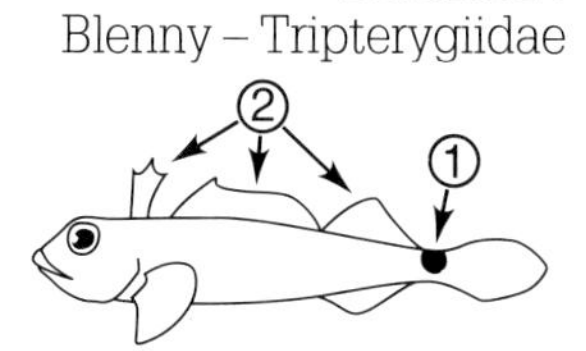

SIZE: 1½-2¾ in., max. 3¼ in.
DEPTH: 3-40 ft.

Mating Male, Note Two, Bright Yellow Spots on Black First Dorsal Fin

REDLIGHT GOBY
Gobio Luz Roja
Coryphopterus urospilus
FAMILY:
Goby – Gobiidae

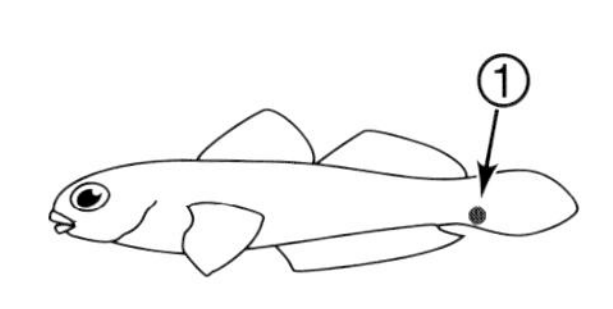

SIZE: 1¼-2 in., max. 2½ in.
DEPTH: 15-130 ft.

DISTINCTIVE FEATURES: 1. Bright red with 9 or 10 dark outlined blue bands.

DESCRIPTION: Blue markings on head; translucent fins. First spine of dorsal fin long.

ABUNDANCE & DISTRIBUTION: Abundant entire archipelago. ENDEMIC.

HABITAT & BEHAVIOR: Inhabit small recesses on rocky reefs, slopes and walls.

REACTION TO DIVERS: Tend to ignore divers, but retreat upon close approach.

DISTINCTIVE FEATURES: 1. Bright orange snout followed by three orange bars on head. 2. Ten orange to orange-brown bars from behind pectoral fin to base of tail; bars often fork near midbody.

DESCRIPTION: White background color; bars have brown outlines. Five diffuse gray squares along midbody. Pectoral and dorsal fins translucent.

ABUNDANCE & DISTRIBUTION: Occasional entire archipelago. ENDEMIC to Galapagos and Cocos (and possibly Malpelo).

HABITAT & BEHAVIOR: Inhabit small recesses on rocky reefs, slopes and walls, often under ledge overhangs. May be observed cleaning large fish.

REACTION TO DIVERS: Wary; retreat upon approach. Occasionally can be closely observed with slow non-threatening movements.

GALAPAGOS BLUE-BANDED GOBY

Gobio de Bandas Azules de Galápagos

Lythrypnus gilberti

FAMILY:
Goby – Gobiidae

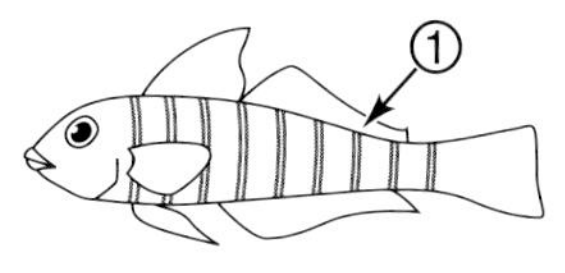

SIZE: ½-1 in., max. 1½ in.
DEPTH: 3-130 ft.

BANDED CLEANER GOBY

Gobio Barbero de Bandas

Elacatinus nesiotes

FAMILY:
Goby – Gobiidae

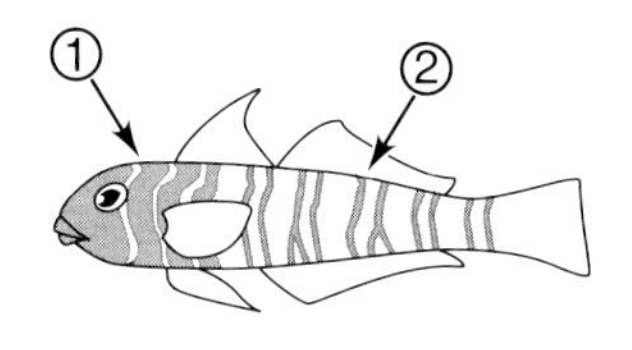

SIZE: ½-¾ in., max. 1 in.
DEPTH: 15-100 ft.

IDENTIFICATION GROUP 9

Odd-Shaped Bottom-Dwellers

Hawkfish - Scorpionfish - Flatfish - Frogfish - Others

This ID Group consists of bottom dwellers that do not have a typical fish-like shape. Most are experts at camouflage.

FAMILY: Hawkfish - Cirrhitidae

3 Species Included

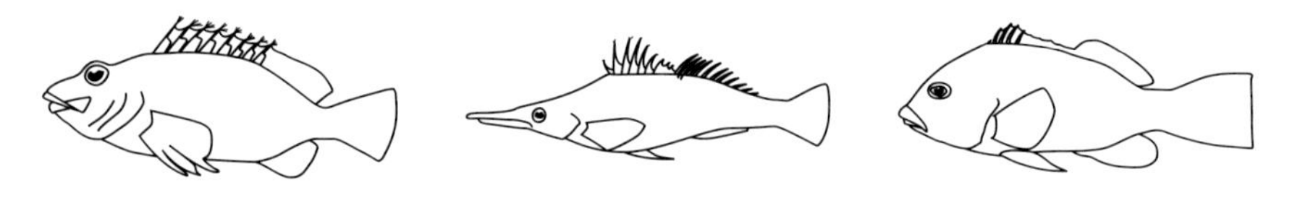

Coral Hawkfish — Longnosed Hawkfish — Hieroglyphic Hawkfish

Tassels (cirri) projecting from the tips of the dorsal fins, spines and paired cirri on the snout are distinguishing characteristics of the hawkfish family. Most have bright colors and bold markings, making them easy to identify.

Their avian name comes from their habit of perching in the branches of gorgonians, on coral heads and rocky outcroppings waiting to swoop down on unsuspecting prey, which include small fish and crustaceans.

FAMILY: Scorpionfish - Scorpaenidae

3 Species Included

Scorpionfish (typical shape)

Fleshy appendages, or flaps, help camouflage the large heads and stocky bodies of the scorpionfish. Their changeable mottled colors make them difficult to detect as they lie motionless on the bottom. Their pectoral fins are often brightly colored, but unseen unless spread. The spines of the dorsal fin are venomous and can cause a painful wound. Although species are similar at first glance, they are not difficult to distinguish.

GROUP: Flatfish - Bothidae & Cynoglossidae

2 Species Included

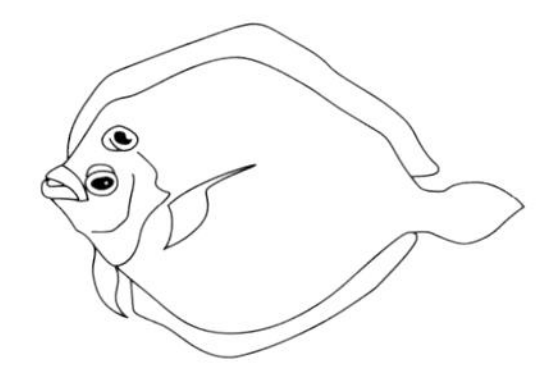

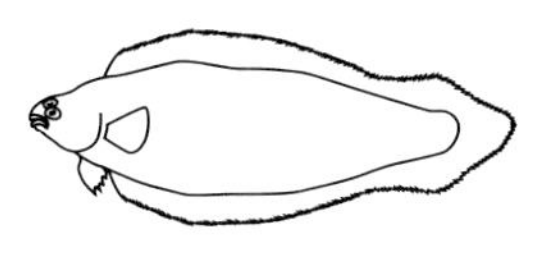

Flounder (typical shape)

Tonguefish

Flatfishes are highly compressed and uniquely lie on one side (not their stomachs as assumed by many). Within a few weeks of birth, the eye on the bottom slowly migrates to the exposed side. The eyes protrude noticeably, sometimes appearing to be on short stalks. If a pectoral fin is present, it is more like a dorsal fin, while the dorsal and anal fins almost ring the body. Flatfish can change, lighten or darken their colors to blend with the bottom. Many enhance their camouflage by partly burying themselves in sand or mud. They glide over the bottom with a slight wave-like motion. Many are difficult to distinguish, but with careful attention to subtle markings, they can be identified.

Four scientific families comprise the common group known as flatfish; however, only two are represented in Galapagos. Observable differences for the diver are: Bothidae - have a pectoral fin and distinct tail fin; Cynoglossidae - do not have pectoral fins and the dorsal, anal and tail fins merge into a continuous fin around the body. Members of both families lie on their left side.

FAMILY: Others

9 Species Included

Frogfish

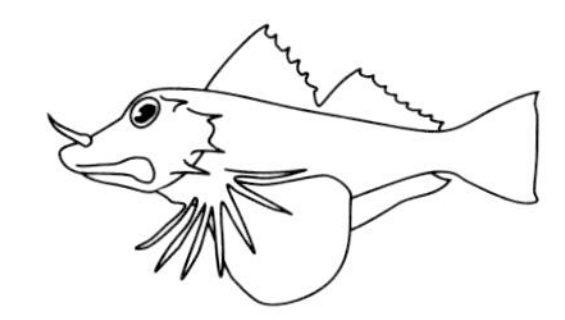

Searobin

Lizardfish

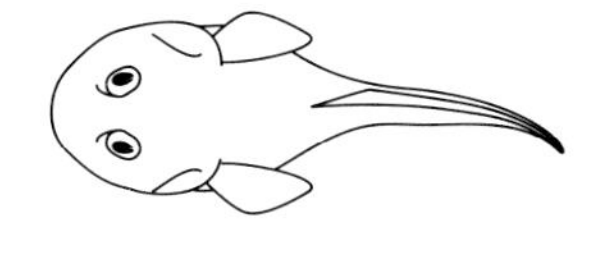

Clingfish

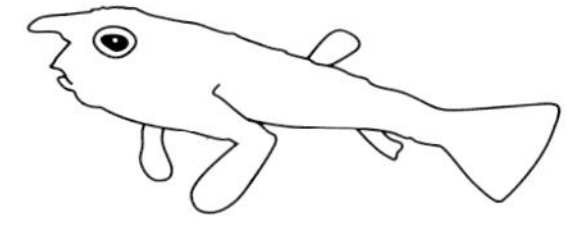

Batfish

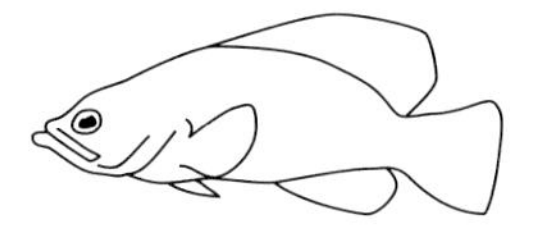

Soapfish

Frogfish

DISTINCTIVE FEATURES: 1. Eye has dark pupil; iris with radiating bands.

DESCRIPTION: Stout, lumpy body and head with upturned mouth. Long translucent filament, called a lure, on central forehead. Variety of blotched and mottled color phases include yellow, orange, red, violet, lavender, brown, tan and cream. Can change color, pale or darken to blend with background.

ABUNDANCE & DISTRIBUTION: Common (but rarely observed) entire archipelago. Peru north to Baja.

HABITAT & BEHAVIOR: Inhabit small recesses on rocky reefs and especially along walls. Blending almost perfectly with background, they appear like encrusting sponges.

REACTION TO DIVERS: Remain still, relying on camouflage. Move only when closely approached or molested.

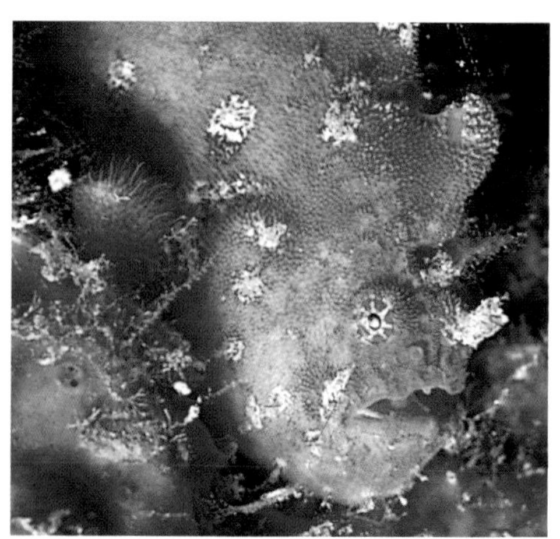

DISTINCTIVE FEATURES: 1. Pale band followed by dark band on base of tail.

DESCRIPTION: Stout, lumpy body and head with upturned mouth. Long, translucent filament, called a lure, on central forehead. Variety of line markings, blotched and mottled color phases include yellow, orange, red, violet, lavender, brown, tan and cream. Can change color, pale or darken to blend with background.

ABUNDANCE & DISTRIBUTION: Uncommon (rarely observed) entire archipelago. North to Baja.

HABITAT & BEHAVIOR: Inhabit small recesses on rocky reefs and especially along walls. Blending almost perfectly with background, they often take on the markings of tube-worm snails or appear to be encrusting sponges.

REACTION TO DIVERS: Remain still, relying on camouflage. Move only when closely approached or molested.

SANGUINE FROGFISH
Pez Sapo Sanguíneo
Antennatus sanguineus

FAMILY:
Frogfish – Antennariidae

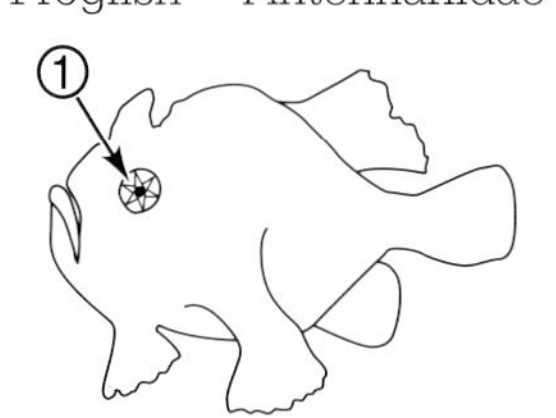

SIZE: 3½-4½ in., max. 5½ in.
DEPTH: 3-60 ft.

Color Varieties

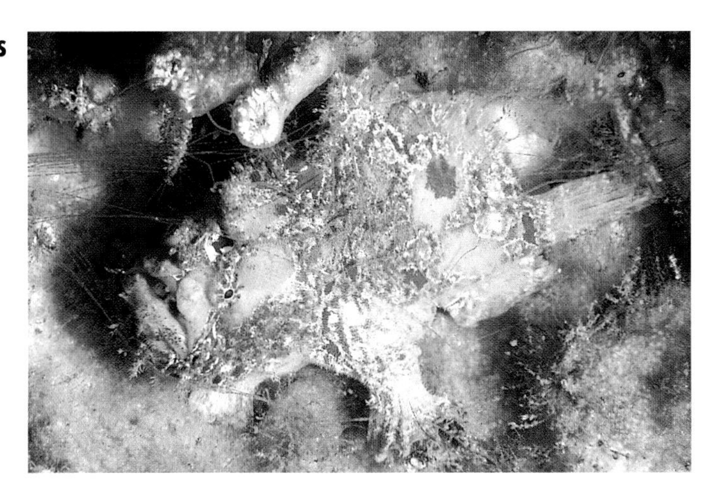

BANDTAIL FROGFISH
Pez Sapo Cola de Banda
Antennatus strigatus

FAMILY:
Frogfish – Antennariidae

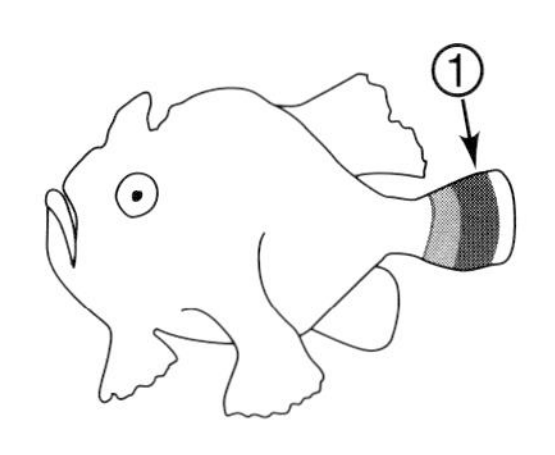

SIZE: 2-3½ in., max. 4 in.
DEPTH: 3-60 ft.

DISTINCTIVE FEATURES: 1. Bright red lips. 2. Dark unicorn-like spike extends from snout.

DESCRIPTION: Disk-shaped body with pectoral and ventral fins appearing more as legs; circular gill opening behind pectoral fins. Brown to tan or gray upper body; underside cream to white.

ABUNDANCE & DISTRIBUTION: Common entire archipelago. South to Peru. When first described in 1958, thought to be endemic.

HABITAT & BEHAVIOR: Inhabit sand areas. Rest on bottom, perched on fins. Move about with hop-like motion; occasionally swim short distances by spreading pectoral fins as wings and making broad sideways strokes with their tail.

REACTION TO DIVERS: Do not move unless very closely approached or molested.

DISTINCTIVE FEATURES: 1. Dark, large, rounded wing-like pectoral fins with white margin.

DESCRIPTION: Mottled brown body and fins with several darkish bands and spots on body and tail. White margin on rear of tail.

ABUNDANCE & DISTRIBUTION: Occasional entire archipelago. North to Baja.

HABITAT & BEHAVIOR: Inhabit sandy bottoms. May bury in sand during day. "Walk" about on spines of ventral fins.

REACTION TO DIVERS: Tend to ignore divers, but if molested move away or bury.

SIMILAR SPECIES: There are three additional species in Galapagos that are difficult to distinguish without close examination. One deep water species, Galapagos Searobin, *P. miles*, is endemic.

DISTINCTIVE FEATURES: Flatfish lying on their right side. **1. Alternating dark and light bands on joined dorsal, tail and anal fins.**

DESCRIPTION: Elongated oval-shaped with obvious scales; close-set, tiny spherical eyes on left (upper) side above twisted mouth; single, small ventral fin below gill plate opening; no pectoral fins. Shades of brown to reddish brown and greenish brown with some dusky banding.

ABUNDANCE & DISTRIBUTION: Common to occasional entire archipelago. Peru north to Panama and Revillagigedo.

HABITAT & BEHAVIOR: Lie on bottom in areas of rubble, sand or mud. Actively feed at night on tiny invertebrates; usually bury below surface during day.

REACTION TO DIVERS: Remain still, relying on camouflage. Move only when closely approached or molested.

RED-LIPPED BATFISH
Pez Murciélago Labio Rojo
Ogcocephalus darwini
FAMILY:
Batfish – Ogcocephalidae

SIZE: 3½-5 in., max. 6 in.
DEPTH: 10 - 250 ft.

WHITE-MARGINED SEAROBIN
Gallineta Margen Blanco
Prionotus albirostris
FAMILY:
Searobin – Triglidae

SIZE: 1½ -3 in., max. 4 in.
DEPTH: 3 - 100 ft.

RAINBOW TONGUEFISH
Lengua Arco Iris
Symphurus atramentatus
FAMILY:
Tonguefish – Cynoglossidae

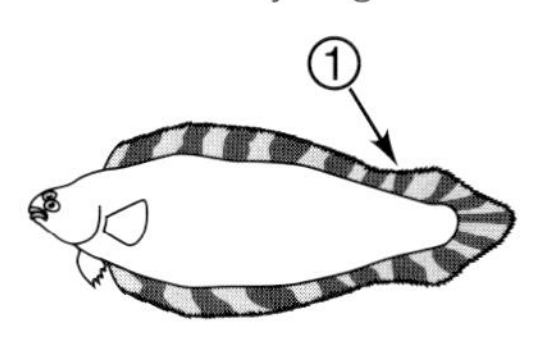

SIZE: 1½ -2½ in., max. 3¾ in.
DEPTH: 10 -70 ft.

DISTINCTIVE FEATURES: Flatfish lying on their right side. **1. White to blue doughnut-shaped "eye" markings and spots with dark borders. 2. Usually a diffuse, dusky blotch near midback** (often a second blotch just behind pectoral fin).

DESCRIPTION: Doughnut-shaped markings may be somewhat irregular and incomplete. Background tan to brown or gray with numerous dark spots. Elongated oval-shaped with eyes on left (upper side); single, long pectoral fin behind head; broad brush-shaped tail. Can pale, darken or change color to blend with background.

ABUNDANCE & DISTRIBUTION: Occasional entire archipelago. Tropical Indo-Pacific, including Red Sea and Hawaii.

HABITAT & BEHAVIOR: Inhabit sandy bottoms and rocky, boulder and gravel strewn slopes. When moving, glide over bottom with wave-like motion.

REACTION TO DIVERS: Remain still, relying on camouflage. Move only when closely approached.

NOTE: Previously reported as *B. pantherinus*, a junior synonym.

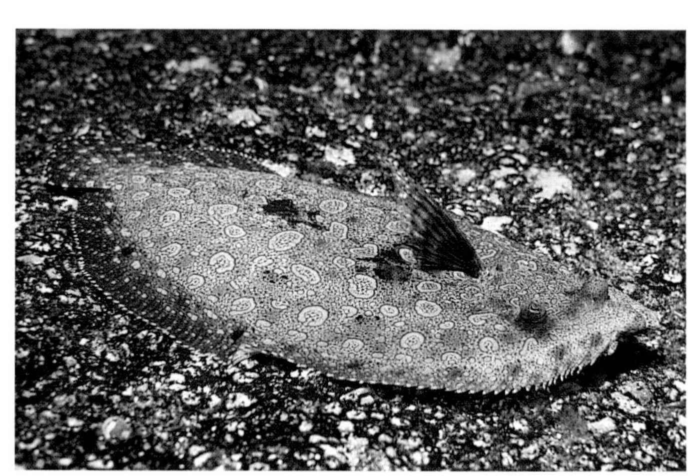

Displaying Blue Markings

DISTINCTIVE FEATURES: Pinkish.

DESCRIPTION: Frying pan shape. Mottled, pinkish brown with tiny blue spots.

ABUNDANCE & DISTRIBUTION: Occasional entire archipelago. ENDEMIC.

HABITAT & BEHAVIOR: Inhabit small recesses on rocky reefs, slopes and walls, clinging to rocky substrates.

REACTION TO DIVERS: Remain still, relying on camouflage. Move only when closely approached or molested.

SIMILAR SPECIES: *Tomicodon petersi* and *T. chilensis* both distinguished by more slender bodies, and shades of brown (never pinkish) with black spots. Neither are endemic.

LEOPARD FLOUNDER
Lenguado Ojo Leopardo
Bothus leopardinus
FAMILY:
Lefteye Flounder – Bothidae

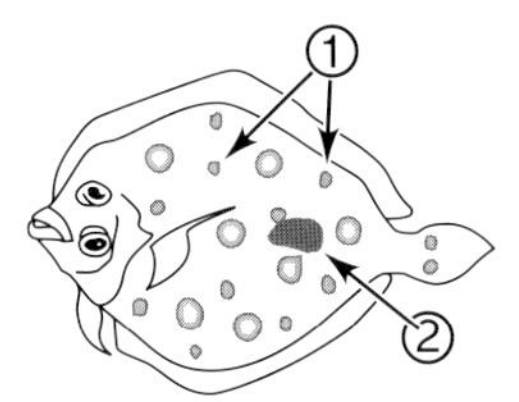

SIZE: 6 - 8 in., max. 10 in.
DEPTH: 10 - 350 ft.

Gray Phase

GALAPAGOS CLINGFISH
Pez Prendedor de Galápagos
Arcos poecilophthalmus
FAMILY:
Clingfish – Gobiesocidae

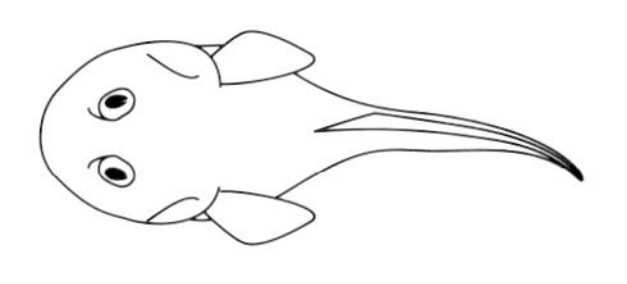

SIZE: 1 - 1¾ in., max. 2 in.
DEPTH: 15 - 100 ft.

DISTINCTIVE FEATURES: 1. Red and white stripes on first dorsal fin.

DESCRIPTION: Cylindrical, elongated body with pointed head. Color and patterns extremely variable, shades of red to brown overall, or white with five red to brown bars formed by diamond-shaped blotches. Can change color and patterns rapidly to blend with background.

ABUNDANCE & DISTRIBUTION: Occasional entire archipelago. North to Baja.

HABITAT & BEHAVIOR: Perch motionless on pectoral fins in a wide range of habitats. Most common on sandy bottoms or sand patches around rocky reefs, and boulder/ gravel strewn slopes. Active at night, may bury in sand with only eyes and mouth protruding during day.

REACTION TO DIVERS: Remain still, relying on camouflage. Move only when closely approached.

DISTINCTIVE FEATURES: 1. Few scattered spots on translucent first dorsal fin. (Similar Night Lizardfish [previous] distinguished by stripes on dorsal fin.)

DESCRIPTION: Cylindrical, elongated body with pointed head. Color and patterns extremely variable, shades of red to brown overall or white with five red to brown bars formed by diamond-shaped blotches. Can change color and patterns rapidly to blend with background.

ABUNDANCE & DISTRIBUTION: Occasional entire archipelago. North to San Francisco, California.

HABITAT & BEHAVIOR: Perch motionless on pectoral fins in a wide range of habitats. Most common on sandy bottoms or sand patches around rocky reefs, and boulder/ gravel strewn slopes. Active during day. May bury in sand with only eyes and mouth protruding.

REACTION TO DIVERS: Remain still, relying on camouflage. Move only when closely approached.

DISTINCTIVE FEATURES: 1. Prominent dark spot on lower rear edge of gill plate.

DESCRIPTION: Mottled and blotched in shades of red to reddish brown and white. Can pale, darken or change color to blend with background. No barbels under mouth.

ABUNDANCE & DISTRIBUTION: Common entire archipelago. Peru north to Southern California, including offshore islands.

HABITAT & BEHAVIOR: Inhabit cracks, crevices, under ledge overhangs and other recesses on rocky reefs, steep slopes, and especially on walls. Small individuals often near protective spines of Long Spined Urchin, *Diadema mexicanum.*

REACTION TO DIVERS: Remain still, relying on camouflage. Move only when closely approached or molested. The spines of the dorsal fin are venomous and can cause a painful wound.

NIGHT LIZARDFISH
Pez Lagartija Noche
Synodus lacertinus

FAMILY:

Lizardfish – Synodontidae

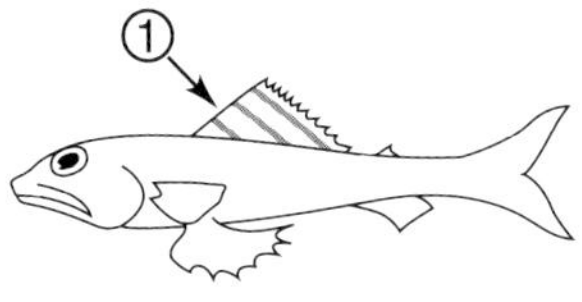

SIZE: 5 - 8 in., max. 10 in.
DEPTH: 10 - 80 ft.

CALIFORNIA LIZARDFISH
Pez Lagartija de California
Synodus lucioceps

FAMILY:
Lizardfish – Synodontidae

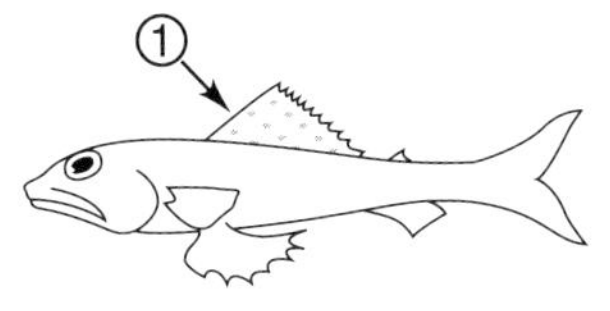

SIZE: 5 - 12 in., max. 24 in.
DEPTH: 5 - 750 ft.

RAINBOW SCORPIONFISH
Brujo Arco Iris
Scorpaenodes xyris

FAMILY:
Scorpionfish – Scorpaenidae

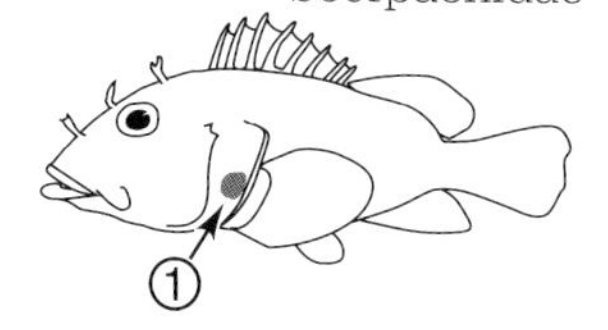

SIZE: 1 - 4½ in., max. 6 in.
DEPTH: 0 - 100 ft.

Scorpionfish

DISTINCTIVE FEATURES: 1. Numerous barbels under mouth. 2. Pectoral fin rays forked.

DESCRIPTION: Heavy, stout head and body, often with numerous skin flaps. Mottled with blotches in earthtones, and occasional shades of red and lavender. Can pale, darken or change color to blend with background.

ABUNDANCE & DISTRIBUTION: Common entire archipelago. North to Southern California.

HABITAT & BEHAVIOR: Inhabit rocky, boulder and gravel strewn slopes and on ledges along walls.

REACTION TO DIVERS: Remain still, relying on camouflage. Move only when closely approached or molested. The spines of the dorsal fin are venomous and can cause a painful wound.

NOTE: Also commonly known as "Spotted Scorpionfish."

DISTINCTIVE FEATURES: 1. Rays of pectoral fins not forked. (Rays of genus *Scorpaena* [above] branched.)

DESCRIPTION: Heavy, stout head and body, often with numerous skin flaps and branched cirri above eye. Mottled with blotches in earthtones. Tail fin banded.

ABUNDANCE & DISTRIBUTION: Occasional western Isabela. Additional distribution unknown.

HABITAT & BEHAVIOR: Inhabit sandy bottoms in protected bays and coves.

REACTION TO DIVERS: Remain still; move or bury in sand only when closely approached or molested. The spines of the dorsal fin are venomous and can cause a painful wound.

NOTE: Pictured specimen is unidentified and possibly an undescribed species. Author has observed this species on several occasions in Tagus Cove at night.

STONE SCORPIONFISH
Brujo
Scorpaena plumieri mystes
FAMILY:
Scorpionfish – Scorpaenidae

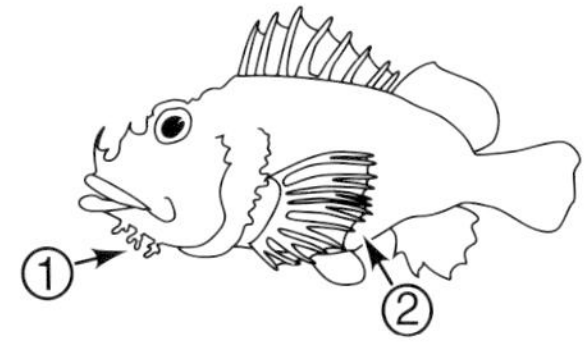

SIZE: 8 - 14 in., max. 1½ ft.
DEPTH: 1 - 100 ft.

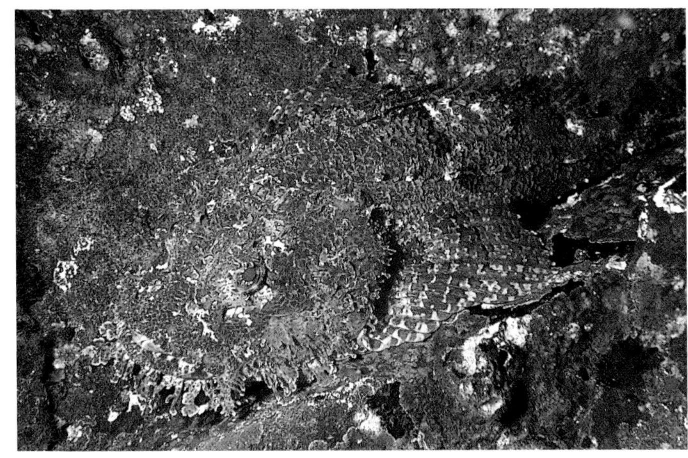

Color Varieties

RED SCORPIONFISH
Brujo Rojo
Pontinus sp.
FAMILY:
Scorpionfish – Scorpaenidae

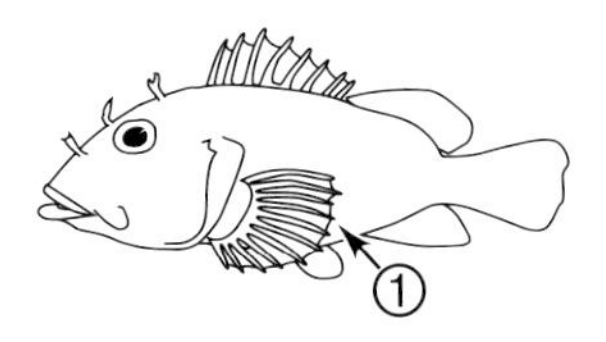

SIZE: 1-4 in.
DEPTH: 30-80 ft.

Hawkfish

DISTINCTIVE FEATURES: 1. Large red to pink, reddish gold and gold spots on whitish head and body.

DESCRIPTION: Short pointed snout. Tassels on tips of dorsal fin spines.

ABUNDANCE & DISTRIBUTION: Common entire Archipelago. North to Baja, including offshore islands; also tropical Indo-Pacific.

HABITAT & BEHAVIOR: Remain still, perched on pectoral fins, usually in shaded, slightly recessed areas. Inhabit rocky reefs, boulder strewn slopes and on walls.

REACTION TO DIVERS: Tend to ignore divers; remain still, moving away only when closely approached.

DISTINCTIVE FEATURES: 1. Long pointed snout. 2. Red rectangular pattern on whitish body.

DESCRIPTION: Tassels on tips of dorsal fin spines.

ABUNDANCE & DISTRIBUTION: Occasional entire archipelago. North to Baja, including offshore islands; also tropical Indo-Pacific.

HABITAT & BEHAVIOR: Remain still, perched on pectoral fins, usually on branches of black coral or sea fans. Inhabit rocky reefs, boulder strewn slopes and on walls.

REACTION TO DIVERS: Shy; move away, but can occasionally be closely approached with very slow, non-threatening movements.

DISTINCTIVE FEATURES: 1. Dark olive to brown bands and markings outlined in bright blue to blue-green. 2. Two white to pale spots below rear dorsal fin.

DESCRIPTION: Medium to light olive to brown. Large, fat lips; tassels on tips of dorsal fin spines.

ABUNDANCE & DISTRIBUTION: Common entire archipelago. North to Upper Baja, including offshore islands.

HABITAT & BEHAVIOR: Remain still, perched on pectoral fins, blending with background, usually in shaded, somewhat recessed areas. Inhabit rocky reefs, boulder strewn slopes and on walls.

REACTION TO DIVERS: Seem curious, often moving out of recess to watch divers. Wary, however; dart away when closely approached.

NOTE: Also commonly known as "Giant Hawkfish," "Chino Mero" and "Halcón Jeroglífico."

CORAL HAWKFISH
Halcón de Coral
Cirrhitichthys oxycephalus
FAMILY:
Hawkfish – Cirrhitidae

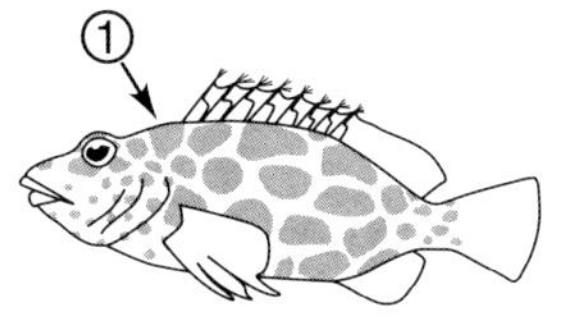

SIZE: 1½-2½ in., max. 3 in.
DEPTH: 10-75 ft.

LONGNOSED HAWKFISH
Halcón de Nariz Puntuda
Oxycirrhites typus
FAMILY:
Hawkfish – Cirrhitidae

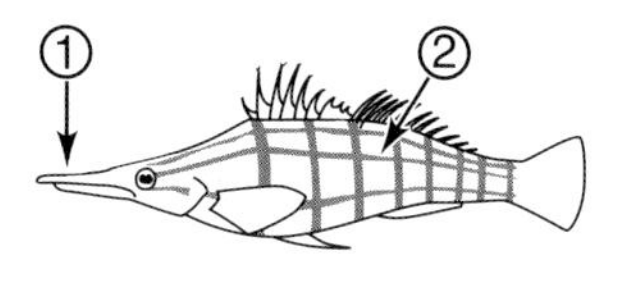

SIZE: 1½-3 in., max. 3½ in.
DEPTH: 40-150 ft.

HIEROGLYPHIC HAWKFISH
Carabalí
Cirrhitus rivulatus
FAMILY:
Hawkfish – Cirrhitidae

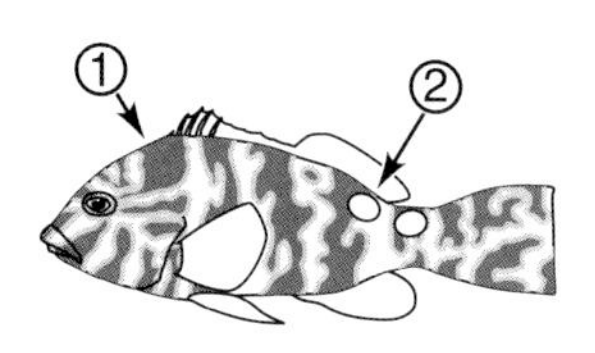

SIZE: 10-16 in., max. 21 in.
DEPTH: 15-75 ft.

IDENTIFICATION GROUP 10

Odd-Shaped Swimmers

Puffer—Triggerfish & Filefish—Others

This ID Group consists of swimming fish that do not have a typical fish-like shape.

FAMILY: Smooth & Spiny Puffers—Tetraodontidae & Diodontidae

8 Species Included

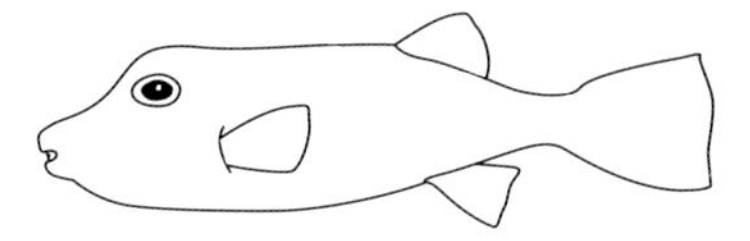

Smooth Puffer
(typical shape)

Spiny Puffer
(typical shape)

Most scientists classify puffers in two families, but some feel they should be combined into one — Tetraodontidae. Puffers have the unique ability to draw in water, which greatly inflates their bodies. This defense dissuades most predators. They all have fused teeth and powerful jaws which are used to crush hard-shelled invertebrates. Smooth puffers have smooth skin; spiny puffers have a covering of stout spines, and are sub-divided into two groups: porcupinefish, spines become erect as the body inflates; burrfish, spines are always erect.

FAMILY: Triggerfish & Filefish—Balistidae & Monacanthidae

6 Species Included

Triggerfish
(typical shape)

Filefish
(typical shape)

Triggerfish and filefish are regarded as two separate families by most scientists, although a few classify them together as Balistidae. The front dorsal fins of both families have evolved into an elongated front spine that can be raised or lowered. Triggerfish can lock their spine into place with a second spine, called a "trigger." Filefish cannot lock their file-shaped spine into place. Both have thin bodies.

The body profile of triggerfish resembles a football. Rear dorsal and anal fins are pronounced, and undulated for swimming. The outer tips of the tail fin are elongated and pointed.

The body profiles of filefish are irregular. They have elongated snouts with small mouths and protruding lips, extendible belly appendages and broom-like tails.

FAMILY: Pipefish & Seahorse—Syngnathidae

2 Species Included

Pipefish

Seahorse

These strange little fish all have trumpet-like snouts and small mouths. Their bodies are encased in protective bony rings which are quite apparent. Seahorses are vertically oriented, and have a cocked head. Their finless elongated tail is often coiled around a holdfast. Pipefish are elongated and snake-like. Both are slow swimmers.

FAMILY: Others

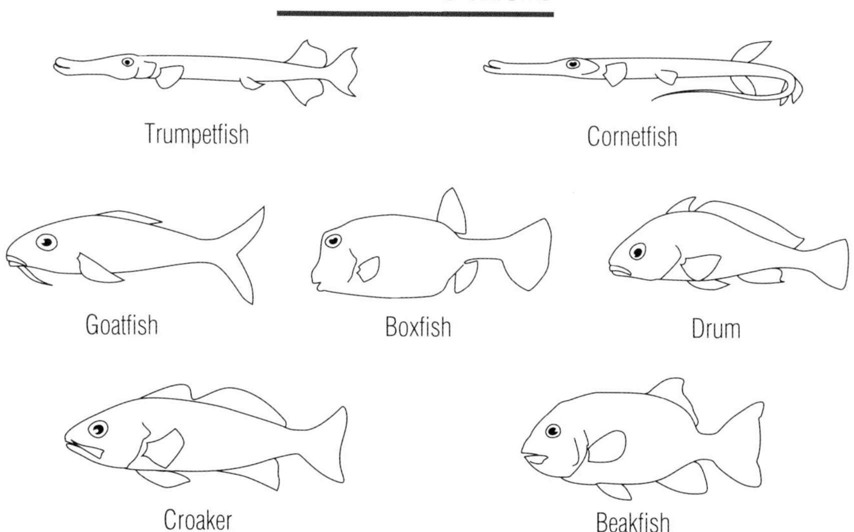

Trumpetfish

Cornetfish

Goatfish

Boxfish

Drum

Croaker

Beakfish

Smooth Puffer

DISTINCTIVE FEATURES: 1. Pattern of concentric circles on back.

DESCRIPTION: Upper head and body shades of brown to gray, pale gray or white; underside pale. Often numerous small dark spots.

ABUNDANCE & DISTRIBUTION: Abundant entire archipelago. Peru north to Southern California, including offshore islands; also tropical Pacific.

HABITAT & BEHAVIOR: Scavenge in open water over shallow sandy areas. Bury in sand at night.

REACTION TO DIVERS: Seem to ignore divers, but tend to keep their distance.

NOTE: Also commonly known as "Concentric Puffer."

DISTINCTIVE FEATURES: Greenish gray with white spots.

DESCRIPTION: White and dusky ring markings around pectoral fin base; belly pale with dusky stripes; dorsal, anal and tail fins whitish translucent.

ABUNDANCE & DISTRIBUTION: Rare entire archipelago. North to Baja, including offshore islands; also tropical Indo-Pacific, including Hawaii.

HABITAT & BEHAVIOR: Inhabit rocky reefs, boulder strewn slopes and along walls.

REACTION TO DIVERS: Seem curious and unafraid; often allow close approach with slow, non-threatening movements.

NOTE: Also commonly known as "Striped-belly Puffer," "White Spotted Puffer," "Deadly Death Puffer," "Stars & Stripes Puffer" and "Miki Maki."

DISTINCTIVE FEATURES: No distinctive markings. **1. Green opal-like pupil and orange/gold iris.**

DESCRIPTION: Upper head and body indistinctly mottled in shades of olive to brown and gray; underside pale.

ABUNDANCE & DISTRIBUTION: Occasional to uncommon entire archipelago. ENDEMIC.

HABITAT & BEHAVIOR: Hover just above bottom in mixed areas of sand, gravel and boulders. Bury in sand at night.

REACTION TO DIVERS: Seem curious and unafraid; often allow close approach with slow, non-threatening movements.

BULLSEYE PUFFER
Tambulero
Sphoeroides annulatus
FAMILY:
Smooth Puffer –
Tetraodontidae

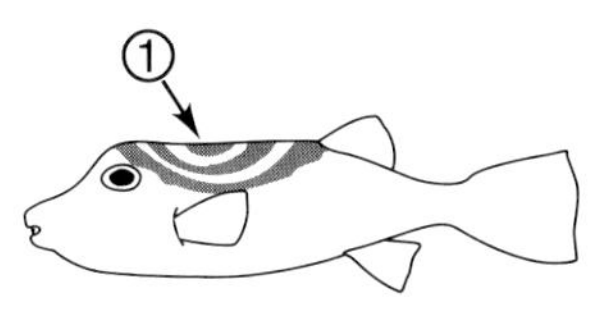

SIZE: 8-12 in., max. 16 in.
DEPTH: 0-35 ft.

SPOTTED GREEN PUFFER
Tamboril Verde de Puntos Blancos
Arothron hispidus
FAMILY:
Smooth Puffer –
Tetraodontidae

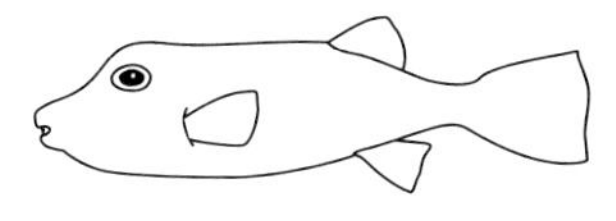

SIZE: 6-10 in., max. 12 in.
DEPTH: 10-80 ft.

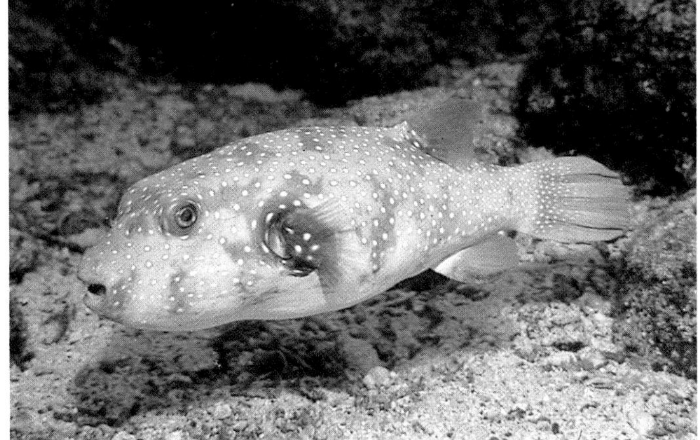

GALAPAGOS PUFFER
Tambulero de Galápagos
Sphoeroides angusticeps
FAMILY:
Smooth Puffer –
Tetraodontidae

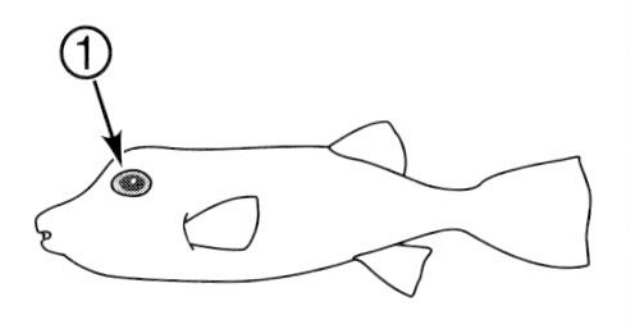

SIZE: 6-10 in., max. 12 in.
DEPTH: 15-60 ft.

Smooth Puffer

DISTINCTIVE FEATURES: Spotted Phase: **1. black to dark purple with white spots.** Golden Phase: gold to yellow.

DESCRIPTION: Spotted Phase: dorsal, anal and tail fins bordered in light purplish gray to white. Golden phase: whitish belly; may have some dark spotting and whitish blotches.

ABUNDANCE & DISTRIBUTION: Common entire archipelago. North to Baja; also tropical Pacific.

HABITAT & BEHAVIOR: Inhabit rocky reefs, boulder strewn slopes and along walls. Often hover near recesses and other shaded areas.

REACTION TO DIVERS: Seem curious and unafraid; often allow close approach with slow, non-threatening movements.

Changing Color Phases

DISTINCTIVE FEATURES: Whitish spots cover body. **1. Pointed snout.**

DESCRIPTION: Whitish spots often tinted yellowish to bluish; head and body reddish brown to gray and greenish gray; no spots on fins; pectoral, dorsal and anal fins translucent.

ABUNDANCE & DISTRIBUTION: Common northern archipelago; occasional central and southern archipelago. North to Baja, including offshore islands.

HABITAT & BEHAVIOR: Lurk in shaded, protective recesses in rocky reefs, boulder strewn slopes and along walls.

REACTION TO DIVERS: Seem curious and unafraid; often allow close approach with slow, non-threatening movements.

GUINEAFOWL PUFFER
Tamboril Negro
Arothron meleagris
Spotted Phase

FAMILY:
Smooth Puffer –
Tetraodontidae

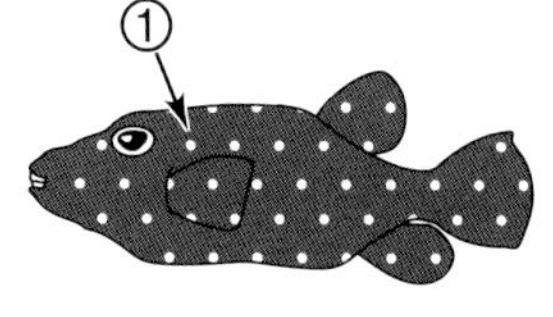

SIZE: 6 -10 in., max. 12 in.
DEPTH: 10 - 80 ft.

Golden Phase,
Tamboril Amarillo

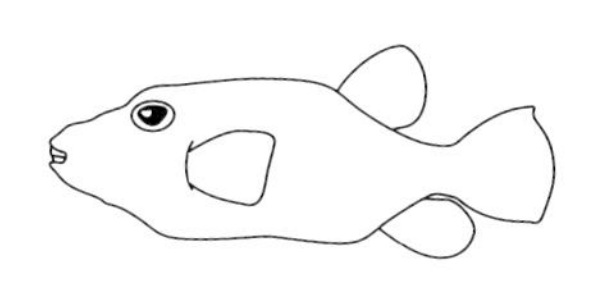

SPOTTED SHARPNOSE PUFFER
Tamboril Punteado Nariz Aguda
Canthigaster punctatissima

FAMILY:
Smooth Puffer –
Tetraodontidae

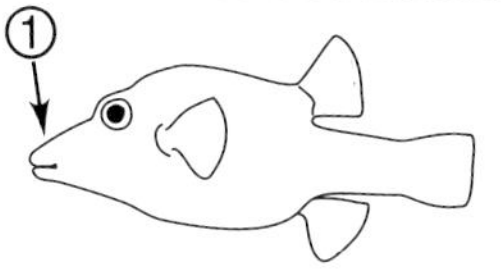

SIZE: 2-3 ½ in., max. 4 in.
DEPTH: 10 -70 ft.

Porcupinefish

DISTINCTIVE FEATURES: Small, dark spots over entire body. **1. Spots on fins.**

DESCRIPTION: Olive to brown or gray back, fading to whitish belly. Can pale or darken. Long spines are erect only when body is inflated.

ABUNDANCE & DISTRIBUTION: Occasional entire archipelago. Northern Chile north to southern California; circumtropical.

HABITAT & BEHAVIOR: Lurk in shaded, protective recesses in rocky reefs, boulder strewn slopes and along walls.

REACTION TO DIVERS: Shy; retreat into protective recess if approached. Often return to peer out entrance where they can be closely observed. Inflate if molested.

DISTINCTIVE FEATURES: 1.Long spines on head. Small dark spots on body. No spots on fins.

DESCRIPTION: Olive to brown. Dusky band runs from eye to eye. May have dusky blotches or bands on back. Iris is yellow; pupil has iridescent blue-green specks. Spines usually lowered, but may become erect without inflation.

ABUNDANCE & DISTRIBUTION: Occasional entire archipelago. Peru north to Southern California; circumtropical.

HABITAT & BEHAVIOR: Lurk in shaded, protective recesses in rocky reefs, boulder strewn slopes and along walls.

REACTION TO DIVERS: Shy; retreat to protective recess if approached. Often return to peer out entrance where they can be closely observed. Inflate if molested.

NOTE: Also commonly known as "Barred Porcupinefish."

DISTINCTIVE FEATURES: 1. Short, triangular, erect spines on body. Dark spots on body and fins.

DESCRIPTION: Bluish gray back, tan or light gray sides, shading to white belly. Dusky band under eyes and another forward of pectoral fin.

ABUNDANCE & DISTRIBUTION: Occasional entire archipelago. North to Southern California; tropical and subtropical Indo-Pacific.

HABITAT & BEHAVIOR: Lurk in shaded, protective recesses in rocky reefs, boulder strewn slopes and along walls.

REACTION TO DIVERS: Shy; retreat to protective recess if approached. Often return to peer out entrance where they can be closely observed. Inflate if molested.

NOTE: Also commonly known as "Spotted Burrfish" and "Spottedfin Burrfish."

SPOTTED PORCUPINEFISH
Pez Erizo Punteado
Diodon hystrix
FAMILY:
Porcupinefish – Diodontidae

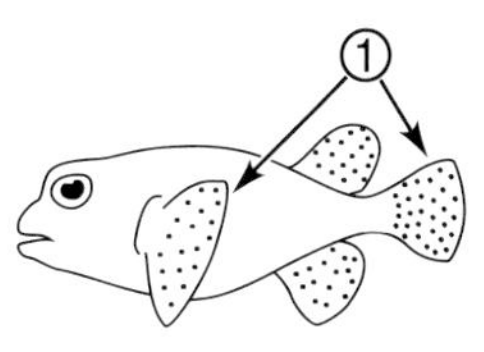

SIZE: 1-2 ft., max. 3 ft.
DEPTH: 10-60 ft.

BALLOONFISH
Pez Erizo Balón
Diodon holocanthus
FAMILY:
Porcupinefish – Diodontidae

SIZE: 8-14 in., max. 20 in.
DEPTH: 10-50 ft.

PACIFIC BURRFISH
Pez Erizo del Pacífico
Chilomycterus affinis
FAMILY:
Porcupinefish – Diodontidae

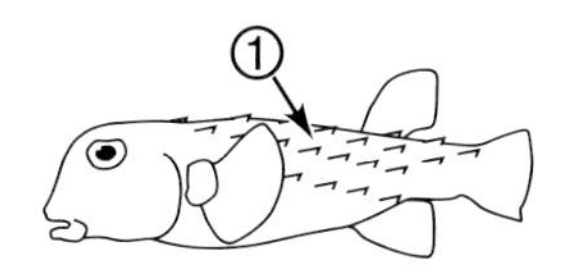

SIZE: 10-16 in., max. 20 in.
DEPTH: 10-90 ft.

DISTINCTIVE FEATURES: 1. Conspicuous gold to light yellow spot at base of short, triangular, erect spines.

DESCRIPTION: Shades of light to dark brown. Wide pale bar under eyes; pale snout.

ABUNDANCE & DISTRIBUTION: Rare entire archipelago. Tropical Indo-Pacific, including Red Sea and Hong Kong.

HABITAT & BEHAVIOR: Habitat variable from sandy areas to rocky reefs. During day often lurk in shaded areas, under ledge overhangs, in caves and other dark recesses.

REACTION TO DIVERS: Shy; retreat to protective recess if approached. Often return to peer out where they can be closely approached with slow, non-threatening movements. Inflate if molested.

NOTE: Formally classified in the genus *Chilomycterus.*

DISTINCTIVE FEATURES: 1. Gold and/or dark spots on blue sides. 2. Bright white spots on back.

DESCRIPTION: Box-like exoskeleton. Often gold band between eyes; back black to reddish brown or gold; no spots on head.

ABUNDANCE & DISTRIBUTION: Occasional northern archipelago; uncommon other islands. North to Baja; also tropical Indo-Pacific.

HABITAT & BEHAVIOR: Lurk in shaded, protective recesses in rocky reefs, boulder strewn slopes and along walls.

REACTION TO DIVERS: Shy; retreat to protective recess if approached. Often return to peer out of entrance where they can be closely observed.

NOTE: Commonly known as "Spotted Trunkfish" and "Blue Boxfish."

DISTINCTIVE FEATURES: 1. White spots cover entire body and head.

DESCRIPTION: Box-like exoskeleton. Navy blue to medium blue. No spots on fins, except foretail.

SPOT-BASE BURRFISH
Pez Erizo Base de Punto
Cyclichthys spilostylus
FAMILY:
Porcupinefish – Diodontidae

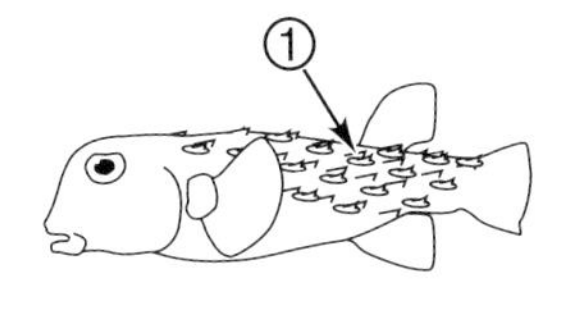

SIZE: 6 - 10 in., max. 12 in.
DEPTH: 30 - 280 ft.

PACIFIC BOXFISH
Pez Caja del Pacífico
Ostracion meleagris
Male
FAMILY:
Boxfish – Ostraciidae

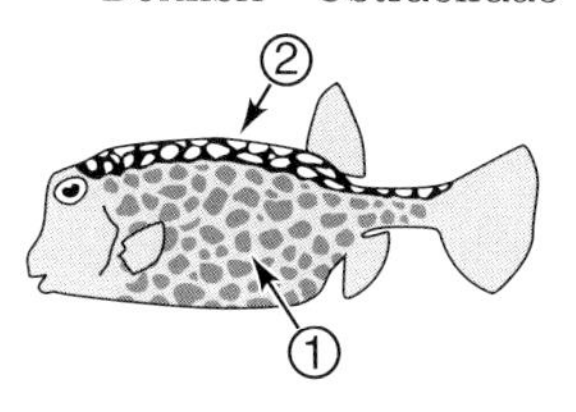

SIZE: 4 - 6 in., max. 7 in.
DEPTH: 10 - 50 ft.

Female

DISTINCTIVE FEATURES: 1. Male, red tail; female, yellow tail. 2. Dorsal and anal fins trimmed in brilliant yellow-gold.

DESCRIPTION: Gold body with dark outlines on scales; blue line markings on head below eyes; bluish sub-border on tail.

ABUNDANCE & DISTRIBUTION: Common Darwin and Wolf; occasional Roca Redonda; rare balance of archipelago. North to Southern California, including offshore islands; also tropical Indo-Pacific, including Japan, Hawaii and Easter Island.

HABITAT & BEHAVIOR: Swim in open water above rocky reefs, boulder strewn slopes and along walls.

REACTION TO DIVERS: Wary; tend to keep their distance and retreat upon approach.

DISTINCTIVE FEATURES: 1. Yellow to orange belly.

DESCRIPTION: Drab shades of gray to brown-gray and olive-brown; yellow to orange stripe runs from under chin toward pectoral fin. Can pale or darken and change color of belly to match background.

ABUNDANCE & DISTRIBUTION: Common entire archipelago. Northern Peru north to Baja, including offshore islands.

HABITAT & BEHAVIOR: Inhabit rocky reefs, boulder strewn slopes and adjacent areas of sand. Feed on sea urchins, small crustaceans and mollusks, often blowing into sand to uncover prey or turn over urchins.

REACTION TO DIVERS: Very shy; keep their distance and rapidly retreat into small recesses upon approach. Can lock themselves in place by raising their triggers.

NOTE: Also commonly known as "Orangeside Triggerfish."

Dark Belly Color Phase

RED-TAILED TRIGGERFISH
Cachudo Cola Roja
Xanthichthys mento
FAMILY:
Triggerfish – Balistidae

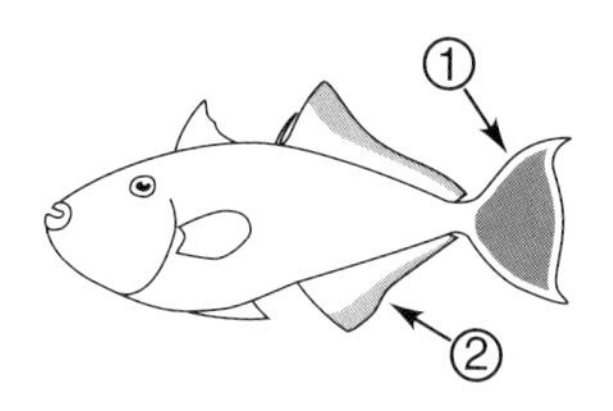

SIZE: 6 - 8 in., max. 10 in.
DEPTH: 10 - 80 ft.

YELLOW-BELLIED TRIGGERFISH
Cachudo Panza Amarilla
Sufflamen verres
FAMILY:
Triggerfish – Balistidae

SIZE: 8 -12 in., max. 16 in.
DEPTH: 10 -120 ft.

Juvenile

Triggerfish

DISTINCTIVE FEATURES: Black body. **1. Pale blue lines along base of dorsal and anal fins.**

DESCRIPTION: May have bluish to greenish cast. Above eye, head may be blue, and below, orange or yellow. Scales have pale diamond outline. Can change color, and pale or darken.

ABUNDANCE & DISTRIBUTION: Common Darwin and Wolf; occasional balance of archipelago. North to Southern California, including offshore islands; circumtropical.

HABITAT & BEHAVIOR: Swim in open water above rocky reefs, boulder strewn slopes and along walls.

REACTION TO DIVERS: Tend to ignore divers, but wary, keeping a safe distance and retreating upon approach.

NOTE: Also commonly known as "Black Durgon."

DISTINCTIVE FEATURES: 1. Three or four dark bars on body, occasionally indistinct. 2. Blunt (slightly concave), prominent forehead (nape).

DESCRIPTION: Shades of bluish gray to gray and brownish gray with fine line markings. Can pale or darken and change intensity of banding.

ABUNDANCE & DISTRIBUTION: Occasional entire archipelago. North to Baja, including offshore islands; circumtropical.

HABITAT & BEHAVIOR: Inhabit rocky reefs, boulder strewn slopes and adjacent areas of sand. Feed on sea urchins, small crustaceans and mollusks, often blowing into sand to uncover prey or turn over urchins.

REACTION TO DIVERS: Tend to ignore divers, but keep their distance and retreat upon approach. Slow, non-threatening movements may allow close view.

DISTINCTIVE FEATURES: No distinctive markings.

DESCRIPTION: Drab shades of bluish gray to gray and brownish gray; belly generally lighter shade. Can pale or darken to match background. Small, fine scales on deep, rounded body.

ABUNDANCE & DISTRIBUTION: Occasional to uncommon entire archipelago. Northern Chile north to northern California, including offshore islands.

HABITAT & BEHAVIOR: Inhabit rocky reefs, boulder strewn slopes and adjacent areas of sand. Feed on sea urchins, small crustaceans and mollusks.

REACTION TO DIVERS: Tend to ignore divers and are occasionally somewhat curious, but keep their distance and retreat upon approach. Slow, non-threatening movements may allow close view.

BLACK TRIGGERFISH
Cachudo Negro
Melichthys niger
FAMILY:
Triggerfish – Balistidae

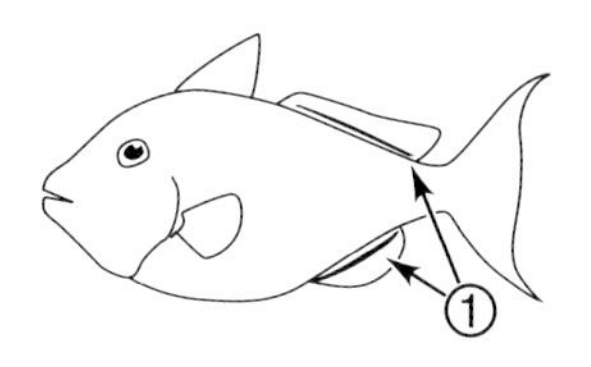

SIZE: 6 - 12 in., max. 20 in.
DEPTH: 10 - 80 ft.

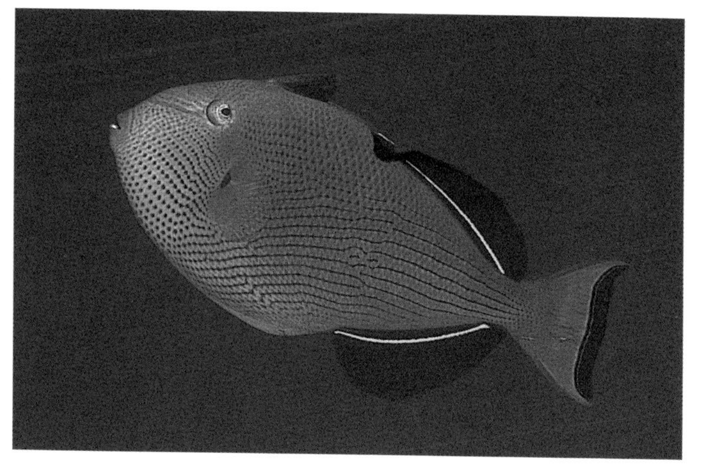

BLUNTHEAD TRIGGERFISH
Cachudo de Piedra
Pseudobalistes naufragium
FAMILY:
Triggerfish – Balistidae

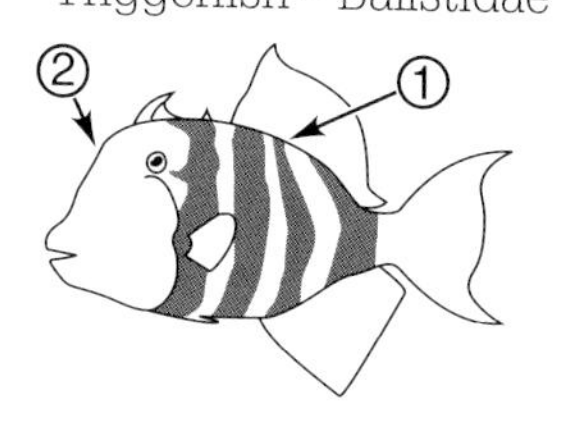

SIZE: 1 - 2 ft., max. 3 ft.
DEPTH: 10 - 120 ft.

FINESCALE TRIGGERFISH
Cachudo Escama Fina
Balistes polylepis
FAMILY:
Triggerfish – Balistidae

SIZE: 1-2 ft., max. 2 ½ ft.
DEPTH: 10-120 ft.

DISTINCTIVE FEATURES: 1. Numerous blue, broken stripes formed of dashes and dots. 2. Numerous black spots.

DESCRIPTION: Shades of gray to tan, brown and olive; translucent dorsal and anal fins. Elongated body with long, brush-like tail. Can pale or darken to blend with background.

ABUNDANCE & DISTRIBUTION: Uncommon entire archipelago. North to Baja, including offshore islands; circumtropical.

HABITAT & BEHAVIOR: Swim in open water above rocky reefs, boulder strewn slopes and adjacent areas of sand.

REACTION TO DIVERS: Tend to ignore divers; are occasionally somewhat curious, but keep their distance and retreat upon approach. Slow, non-threatening movements may allow close view.

DISTINCTIVE FEATURES: 1. Two yellow-gold recurved spines on base of tail. 2. Eyes have dark pupil and yellow-gold iris.

DESCRIPTION: Shades of gray to tan, brown and olive, with several indistinct bars on side, and pale lips. (Often confused with surgeonfish because of recurved spines.)

ABUNDANCE & DISTRIBUTION: Uncommon Darwin, Wolf and Roca Redonda; not reported balance of archipelago. North to Baja, including offshore islands; also tropical Indo-Pacific.

HABITAT & BEHAVIOR: In open water above rocky reefs and boulder strewn slopes.

REACTION TO DIVERS: Tend to ignore divers; are occasionally somewhat curious, but keep their distance and retreat upon approach. Slow, non-threatening movements may allow close view.

NOTE: Also commonly known as "Gray Filefish."

DISTINCTIVE FEATURES: 1. Numerous pale yellow to white spots on back.

DESCRIPTION: Relatively short pointed head with beak-like mouth; wide triangular tail. Belly pale.

ABUNDANCE & DISTRIBUTION: Common western Isabela, Fernandina and southern sides of Floreana and Espanola; rare to absent balance of archipelago. South to Chile.

HABITAT & BEHAVIOR: Constantly swim about rocky reefs, boulder strewn slopes and along walls. More common in shallow water.

REACTION TO DIVERS: Tend to ignore divers; however, keep their distance and retreat upon approach. May swim close by if remain still and non-threatening.

NOTE: Also known as "Spotted Dick" and "Pejerizo Chiquito."

SCRAWLED FILEFISH
Pez Lija Puntiazul
Alutera scripta
FAMILY:
Filefish – Monacanthidae

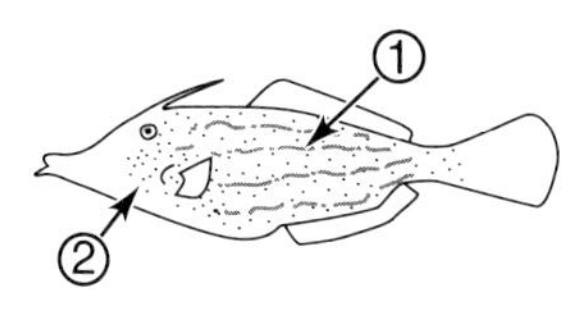

SIZE: 1-2 ft., max. 3 ft.
DEPTH: 10 - 50 ft.

VAGABOND FILEFISH
Pez Lija Vagabundo
Cantherhines dumerilii
FAMILY:
Filefish – Monacanthidae

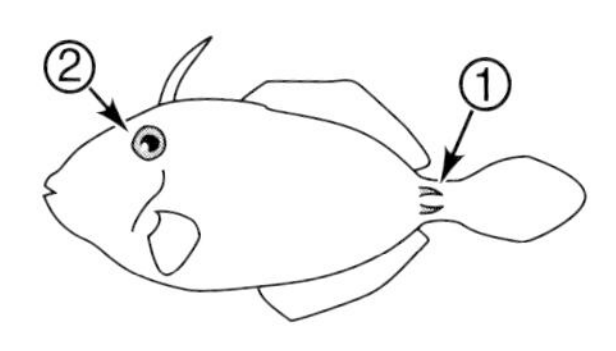

SIZE: 7 - 10 in., max. 12 in.
DEPTH: 10 - 50 ft.

PACIFIC BEAKFISH
Tigris
Oplegnathus insignis
FAMILY:
Beakfish – Oplegnathidae

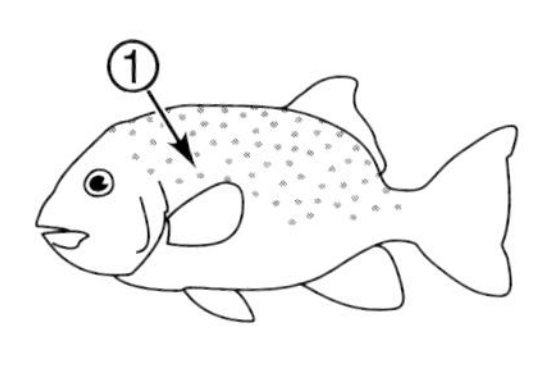

SIZE: 12 - 20 in., max. 2 ft.
DEPTH: 10 - 100 ft.

DISTINCTIVE FEATURES: 1. Dark area from lips extends between eyes and onto the nape where it blends into body coloration. (Similar Mottled Soapfish [next] lack this marking.) **2. Lower jaw rounded.**

DESCRIPTION: Somewhat flattened body with distinctly rounded ends on dorsal, anal and tail fins. Mottled shades of dark brown to black (Mottled Soapfish generally lighter color). Pale, often yellowish, spots extending on fins and cheeks (spots rarely join to form blotches or patches as Mottled Soapfish). Large spots on adults often have dark centers. Juveniles to young adults have narrow, cream stripe running from lips onto nape.

ABUNDANCE & DISTRIBUTION: Uncommon entire archipelago. Peru north to Baja.

HABITAT & BEHAVIOR: Lie motionless, often on side, hidden in dark recesses on rocky reefs and along walls during day. Actively hunt at night, preying on small fish.

REACTION TO DIVERS: Remain still, relying on camouflage. Move only when closely approached.

NOTE: Also commonly known as "Blackfin Soapfish."

DISTINCTIVE FEATURES: 1. Lower jaw pointed.

DESCRIPTION: Somewhat flattened body with distinctly rounded ends on dorsal, anal and tail fins. Mottled shades of tan to brown. (Similar Twice-spotted Soapfish [previous] generally darker color.) Cream, often yellowish, small spots often join to form blotches or patches and extend onto dorsal and tail fins (but not on cheeks). The spots of young adults have dark centers. Juveniles to young adults have narrow, cream stripe running from lips onto nape.

ABUNDANCE & DISTRIBUTION: Occasional entire archipelago. Peru north to Baja, including offshore islands (except Revillagigedo).

HABITAT & BEHAVIOR: Lie motionless, often on side, hidden in dark recesses on rocky reefs and along walls during day. Actively hunt at night, preying on small fish.

REACTION TO DIVERS: Remain still, relying on camouflage. Move only when closely approached.

NOTE: Also commonly known as "Cortez Soapfish."

DISTINCTIVE FEATURES: 1. Wavy, narrow, brown stripes below lateral line. 2. Fine, brown lines above lateral line, diagonal upward on forebody, becoming horizontal and extending to tail on rear body.

DESCRIPTION: Silvery bronze to brown; head darker; fins dusky gray. Blunt snout; squared off tail.

ABUNDANCE & DISTRIBUTION: Uncommon entire archipelago. ENDEMIC.

HABITAT & BEHAVIOR: Prefer shallow water. Often above rocky, small boulder strewn slopes covered with leafy blade algae. Often in large schools or loose aggregations.

REACTION TO DIVERS: Wary; usually retreat upon approach, often taking refuge in small recesses between boulders.

SIMILAR SPECIES: There are four similar species. *Umbrina galapagorum* and *Larimus pacificus* are easily distinguished by their chin barbels. They are silvery gray with only faint striping, which coloration and markings also distinguish *Cynoscion phoxocephalus*. *Pareques perissa* easily distinguished by a rounded tail.

TWICE-SPOTTED SOAPFISH
Jabonero Doble Punteado
Rypticus nigripinnis
FAMILY:
Soapfish – Grammistidae

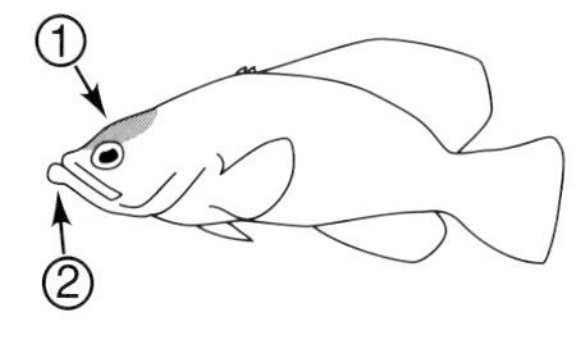

SIZE: 5 - 7 in., max. 8 in.
DEPTH: 10 - 200 ft.

MOTTLED SOAPFISH
Jabonero Moteado
Rypticus bicolor
FAMILY:
Soapfish – Grammistidae

SIZE: 6 - 9 in., max. 11 in.
DEPTH: 10 - 225 ft.

BRONZE CROAKER
Corvina Bronce
Odontoscion eurymesops
FAMILY:
Croaker – Scianidae

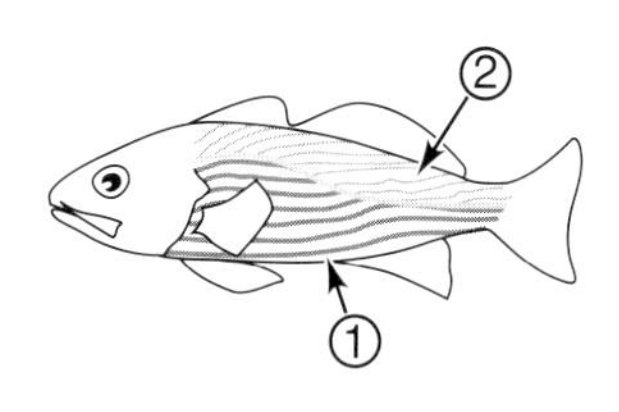

SIZE: 4 - 7 in.
DEPTH: 10 - 100 ft.

DISTINCTIVE FEATURES: 1. Tall foredorsal fin.

DESCRIPTION: Drab, dark gray to brown, with numerous thin, indistinct stripes.

ABUNDANCE & DISTRIBUTION: Occasional (but rarely observed) entire archipelago. ENDEMIC

HABITAT & BEHAVIOR: Cryptic; hide in dark recesses, cracks, crevices and under ledge overhangs during day. Forage about reef at night.

REACTION TO DIVERS: Wary; usually retreat deep into recess upon approach. A short quiet, non-threatening wait near entrance, however, is often rewarded by return and curious peering out of recess.

DISTINCTIVE FEATURES: 1. Tall foredorsal fin. 2. Black cross in eye.

DESCRIPTION: Orange to pale yellow. Wide, black bar from foredorsal fin to behind ventral fins; black midbody stripe; and several additional black markings. Reddish ventral fins.

DISTINCTIVE FEATURES: 1. Yellowish borders on tail.

DESCRIPTION: Elongated, heavy body with smallish mouth. Back slivery light gray to brown; belly white; may have some bluish tinting. Fins often yellowish and may have bluish stripes.

ABUNDANCE & DISTRIBUTION: Occasional western Isabela and Fernandina; rare balance of archipelago. Peru north to Vancouver, Canada.

HABITAT & BEHAVIOR: Inhabit soft sand and mud bottoms. Dig in bottom for food. Most common between 80 and 180 feet. Solitary.

REACTION TO DIVERS: Tend to ignore divers, but move away when approached. Slow, non-threatening movements may allow close approach.

GALAPAGOS DRUM
Gungo de Galápagos
Pareques perissa
FAMILY:
Croaker – Scianidae

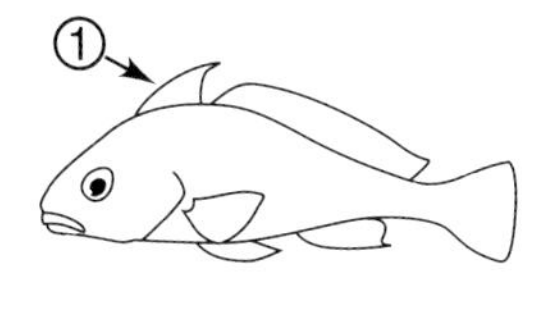

SIZE: 4 - 8 in., max. 10 in.
DEPTH: 10 - 120 ft.

Juvenile

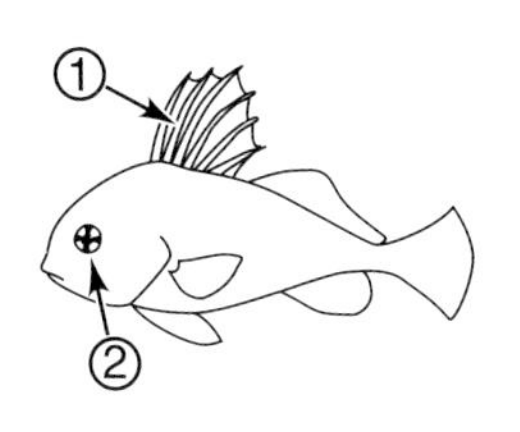

SIZE: ¾ - 2 in.

OCEAN WHITEFISH
Blanquillo
Caulolatilus princeps
FAMILY:
Tilefish – Branchiostegidae

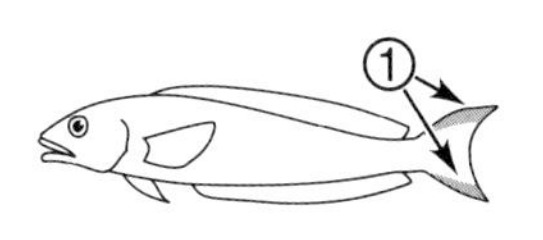

SIZE: 8 - 15 in., max. 1½ ft.
DEPTH: 35 - 300 ft.

DISTINCTIVE FEATURES: 1. Bright yellow midbody stripe. 2. Bright yellow tail.

DESCRIPTION: White head and body, often with some bluish tinting and fine markings. Two barbels under chin.

ABUNDANCE & DISTRIBUTION: Common entire archipelago. Peru north to Southern California, including offshore islands.

HABITAT & BEHAVIOR: Inhabit sandy areas. May be solitary, but often in small groups to large aggregations, and occasionally form large polarized schools. Feed by digging in sand with barbels. At night rest on bottom, dramatically changing both color and daytime pattern to reddish blotches.

REACTION TO DIVERS: Wary; tend to move away, but when busy digging in sand can often be closely approached with slow, non-threatening movements.

NOTE: Also commonly known as "Mexican Goatfish."

DISTINCTIVE FEATURES: Long, thin body. **1. Trumpet-like mouth.**

DESCRIPTION: Adept at color change. Most common phase is shades of brown to reddish brown; can be blue-gray, bright yellow or gold. Have pale thin lines and scattered, small black spots; several prominent white or dark spots extreme rear body; three whitish bands base of tail. May display darkish stripes or bands. Small barbel under chin.

ABUNDANCE & DISTRIBUTION: Common entire Archipelago. Costa Rica, Panama and offshore islands; also tropical Indo-Pacific, Red Sea, Japan, Hawaii and Easter Island.

HABITAT & BEHAVIOR: Inhabit rocky reefs and boulder strewn slopes. Their bodies change color and position to blend with background. Often drift in vertical position, head down.

REACTION TO DIVERS: Generally remain still to maintain camouflage. Move away when obviously detected or closely approached.

Banded Phase

YELLOW-TAILED GOATFISH
Salmonete Barbón Cola Amarilla
Mulloidichthys dentatus

FAMILY:
Goatfish – Mullidae

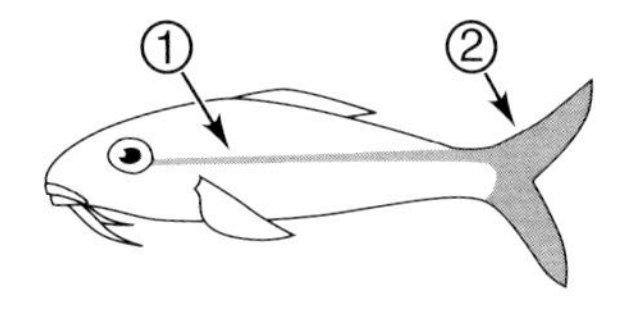

SIZE: 6-9 in., max. 12 in.
DEPTH: 10-150 ft.

TRUMPETFISH
Pez Trompeta
Aulostomus chinensis

FAMILY:
Trumpetfish – Aulostomidae

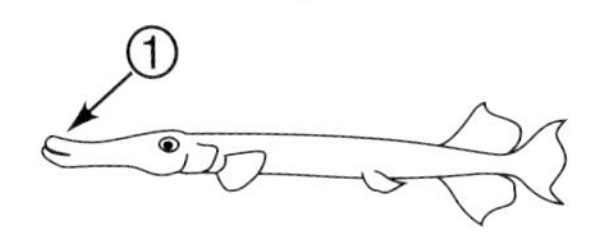

SIZE: 1-2 ft., max. 2½ ft.
DEPTH: 10-120 ft.

Golden Color Phase

DISTINCTIVE FEATURES: Long, thin head and body. **1. Long tail filament.**

DESCRIPTION: Silvery with blue to blue-green to green tints on back; silvery white belly. Two thin blue stripes on back and sides.

ABUNDANCE & DISTRIBUTION: Common entire Archipelago. North to Baja, including offshore islands; also tropical Indo-Pacific.

HABITAT & BEHAVIOR: Alternately hover and swim above rocky reefs and boulder strewn slopes; occasionally just below surface.

REACTION TO DIVERS: Tend to ignore divers, but move away when approached. Occasionally, if diver remains motionless, become curious and will approach for close look.

DISTINCTIVE FEATURES: 1. Numerous fine, light and dark line markings radiate from eye and on body.

DESCRIPTION: Colors highly variable, including shades of gray, brown, yellow and gold.

ABUNDANCE & DISTRIBUTION: Occasional (but rarely observed) entire archipelago. Peru north to Southern California. Only seahorse in eastern Pacific.

HABITAT & BEHAVIOR: Curl tail around branches of gorgonians and black coral trees, camouflaging within their branches. Occasionally float free or lie on bottom.

REACTION TO DIVERS: Allow close approach and rarely move, but tuck their heads and turn away.

DISTINCTIVE FEATURES: 1. Orange to yellow spots on fan-like tail.

DESCRIPTION: Shades of brown to black elongated body with trumpet-like mouth.

ABUNDANCE & DISTRIBUTION: Occasional (but rarely observed) entire archipelago. North to Baja, including offshore islands; also Indo-Pacific.

HABITAT & BEHAVIOR: Cryptic; inhabit small cracks, crevices, recesses and under ledge overhangs.

REACTION TO DIVERS: Wary; however, can often be closely approached with slow, non-threatening movements.

SIMILAR SPECIES: Sailor Pipefish, Pez Pipa Velero, *Bryx veleronis*, shades of tan with white markings on gill plate. Spotjaw Pipefish, Pez Pipa Manchado, *Bryx coccineus*, tan to brown, lower jaw and throat dark with a series of regular white blotches.

REEF CORNETFISH
Pez Corneta de Arrecife
Fistularia commersonii
FAMILY:
Trumpetfish – Aulostomidae

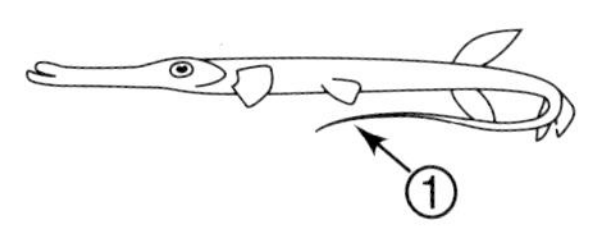

SIZE: 1½-3 ft., max. 4 ft.
DEPTH: 0-80 ft.

PACIFIC SEAHORSE
Caballito de Mar del Pacífico
Hippocampus ingens
FAMILY:
Pipefish & Seahorse – Syngathidae

SIZE: 4-8 in., max. 12 in.
DEPTH: 10-60 ft.

FANTAIL PIPEFISH
Piz Pipa Chica
Doryrhamphus excisus
FAMILY:
Pipefish & Seahorse – Syngathidae

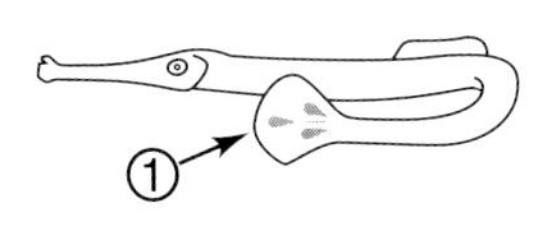

SIZE: 1½-2½ in., max. 3 in.
DEPTH: 10-60 ft.

IDENTIFICATION GROUP 11

Eels

Moray—Conger Eel—Snake Eel

This ID Group consists of fish with long, snake-like bodies. They are generally found on the bottom in dark reef recesses, or in sand.

FAMILY: Moray—Muraenidae

9 Species Included

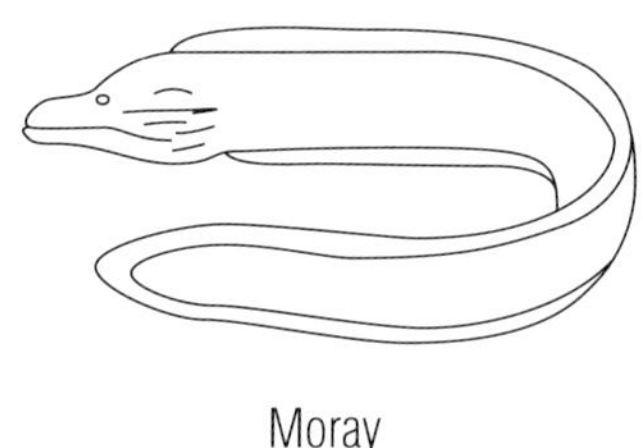

Moray
(typical shape)

Moray eels have no pectoral or ventral fins. Their dorsal, tail and anal fins are continuous. They have heavy bodies and smooth, scaleless skin. Morays constantly open and close their mouths, which is often perceived as a threat but, in reality, this behavior is necessary to move water through their gills for respiration. They are not aggressive, although they can inflict a nasty bite if molested. During the day, they are reclusive and tend to hide in dark recesses. Occasionally they are seen with their heads extended from holes. They forage in the open on the reefs at night. Many morays are similar in appearance and difficult to distinguish; however, with careful attention to spot patterns and other markings they can be identified.

FAMILY: Conger—Congridae

2 Species Included

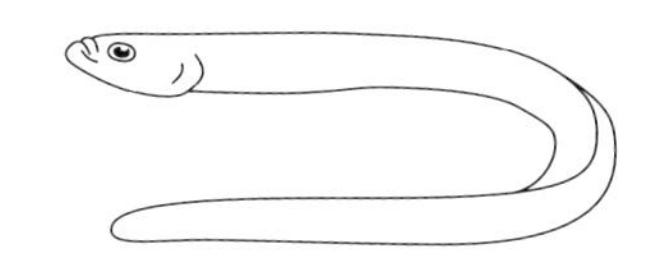

Conger Eel
(typical shape)

Conger eels have dorsal, anal and tail fins that are continuous like morays, but unlike morays, they have pectoral fins. They are thin and elongated, with dull colors and few markings. Because they often bury themselves in the sand or hide in deep recesses, divers rarely encounter these eels. An exception is the garden eel, which lives in colonies in sand around reefs.

FAMILY: Snake Eel—Ophichthidae

2 Species Included

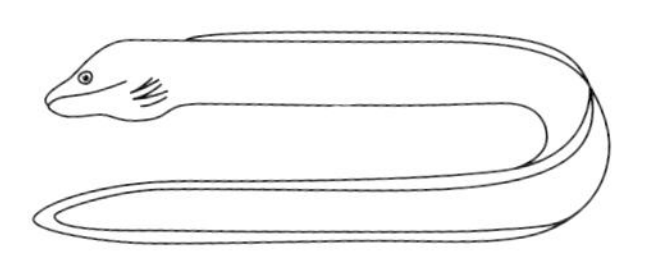

Snake Eel
(typical shape)

Snake eels are virtually without fins and strongly resemble snakes. In fact, when first encountered, uninformed divers think they are seeing a sea snake. Extremely shy and reclusive fish, these eels hide in dark recesses or burrow under sand during the day. Often they are seen with only their heads extended from the sand. They come out at night to forage about the reefs. Although similar in appearance, the size and pattern of their spots are distinctive, making identification possible.

DISTINCTIVE FEATURES: Snake-like body with blunt snout. **1. Row of white spots along lateral line.**

DESCRIPTION: Dark to light gray to brown; occasionally with some white blotches and/or mottling. White spot around dark base of pectoral fin.

ABUNDANCE & DISTRIBUTION: Common central and southern islands. ENDEMIC.

HABITAT & BEHAVIOR: Inhabit sand flats, especially in areas of current. Live in burrows, extending head and upper body six inches or more to nab bits of food floating by in current. Often form large colonies of 100 or more individuals.

REACTION TO DIVERS: Shy; retreat into burrow upon approach, especially sensitive to bubble noise.

DISTINCTIVE FEATURES: Snake-like body with blunt snout. **1. Upper edge of gill opening about even with center of pectoral fin base.** (See note.)

DESCRIPTION: Dark to light gray to brown, may show some iridescence. Fins transparent to translucent.

ABUNDANCE & DISTRIBUTION: Occasional entire archipelago. North to Baja.

HABITAT & BEHAVIOR: Inhabit sand flats, often in protected bays and coves. Can bury and move about beneath sand. Often bury during day, and forage in open at night.

REACTION TO DIVERS: Shy; bury in sand upon approach.

NOTE: Similar *Paraconger* Eel's upper edge of gill opening about even with upper edge of pectoral fin base.

DISTINCTIVE FEATURES: 1. Dorsal, tail and anal fins join to form a single fin around body that is translucent with dark border. 2. Four long white barbels under chin.

DESCRIPTION: Elongated; somewhat compressed body; ventral fins absent. Shades of gray to brown; can pale or darken.

ABUNDANCE & DISTRIBUTION: Uncommon entire archipelago. ENDEMIC.

HABITAT & BEHAVIOR: Inhabit sandy areas. Nocturnal, move about in open digging in sand with barbels. Can bury and move about beneath the sand.

REACTION TO DIVERS: Tend to ignore divers, but move away or bury if molested.

NOTE: At date of publication, this species was scientifically undescribed.

GALAPAGOS GARDEN EEL
Anguila Jardín de Galápagos
Taenioconger klausewitzi
FAMILY:
Conger Eel – Congridae

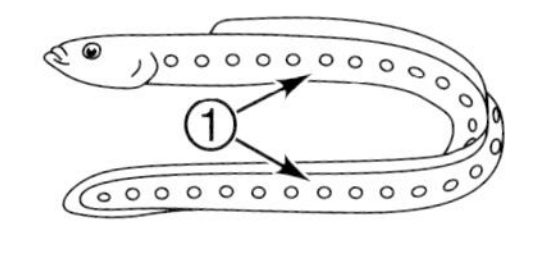

SIZE: 8 -14 in., max. 25 in.
DEPTH: 15 -180 ft.

PANAMIC CONGER EEL
Anguila Congrio Panámica
Ariosoma gilberti
FAMILY:
Conger Eel – Congridae

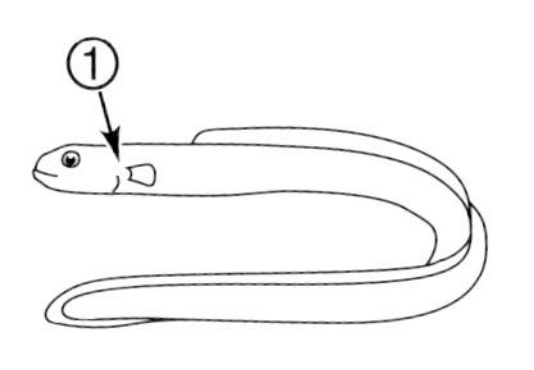

SIZE: 6 -9 in., max. 11 in.
DEPTH: 3 -300 ft.

GALAPAGOS CUSK-EEL
Lengua de Galápagos
Ophidion sp.
FAMILY:
Cusk-eel – Ophidiidae

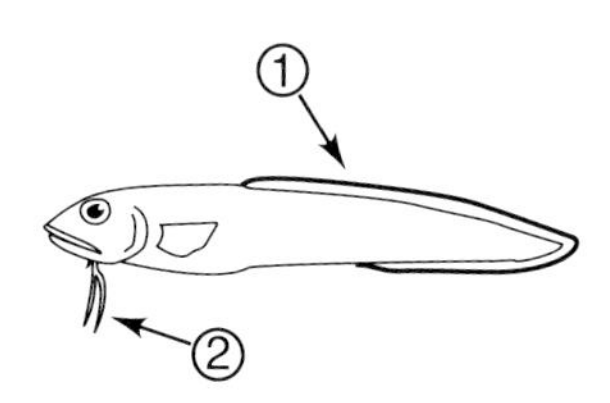

SIZE: 3½-5½ in.
DEPTH: 10-60 ft.

DISTINCTIVE FEATURES: 1. Two rows of large, dark, somewhat oval spots on each side.

DESCRIPTION: Tan, often with whitish, reddish or grayish tinting; border of dorsal fin dusky. Golden eye with dark pupil. Tubular nostrils and small pectoral fins.

ABUNDANCE & DISTRIBUTION: Occasional entire archipelago. Peru north to Baja, including Malpelo and Cocos.

HABITAT & BEHAVIOR: Inhabit sand flats and rocky areas with boulders and gravel rubble. Can bury and move beneath sand or gravel rubble.

REACTION TO DIVERS: Shy; retreat into sand or gravel upon approach. Occasionally slow, non-threatening movements will allow close observation.

DISTINCTIVE FEATURES: 1. Numerous dark spots on head. 2. Numerous dark spots form alternating, ragged, diamond-shaped areas of large compacted spots and areas of smaller, more widely spaced spots.

DESCRIPTION: White, occasionally with some grayish tinting. Golden eye with dark pupil. Tubular nostrils and small pectoral fins.

ABUNDANCE & DISTRIBUTION: Occasional entire archipelago. ENDEMIC.

HABITAT & BEHAVIOR: Inhabit sand flats and rocky areas mixed with boulders, gravel rubble and sand. Can bury and move beneath sand or gravel rubble.

REACTION TO DIVERS: Shy; retreat into sand or gravel upon approach. Occasionally slow, non-threatening movements will allow close observation.

DISTINCTIVE FEATURES: 1. Numerous white to bluish white rings encircle head and body.

DESCRIPTION: Black to dark brown and purplish brown. Blunt head; pair of tubular nostrils above mouth.

ABUNDANCE & DISTRIBUTION: Uncommon entire archipelago. North to Baja; also tropical Indo-Pacific.

HABITAT & BEHAVIOR: Inhabit rocky, boulder strewn areas. Reclusive, hide in holes, crevices and dark recesses. Constantly open and close mouth, an action required for respiration — not a threat. Feed on shelled crustaceans and mollusks, primarily crabs.

REACTION TO DIVERS: Shy; retreat into dark recess upon approach. Occasionally slow, non-threatening movements will allow close observation.

TIGER SNAKE EEL
Anguila Tigre
Myrichthys tigrinus
FAMILY:
Snake Eel – Ophichthidae

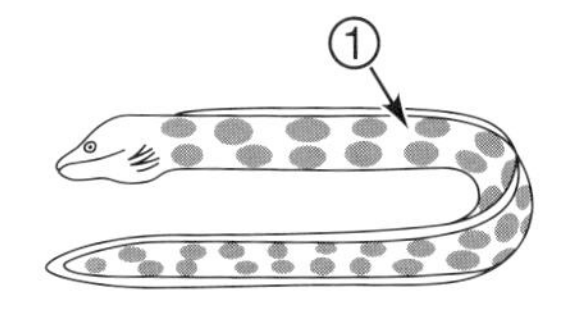

SIZE: 8 -15 in., max. 29 in.
DEPTH: 10 - 200 ft.

GALAPAGOS SNAKE EEL
Anguila de Galápagos
Quassiremus evionthas
FAMILY:
Snake Eel – Ophichthidae

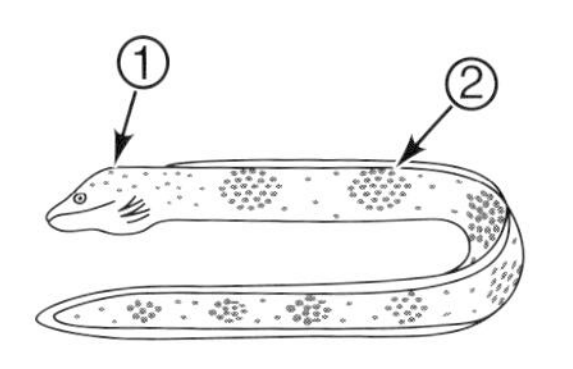

SIZE: 8 -15 in., max. 28 in.
DEPTH: 10 - 100 ft.

ZEBRA MORAY
Morena Zebra
Gymnomuraena zebra
FAMILY:
Moray – Muraenidae

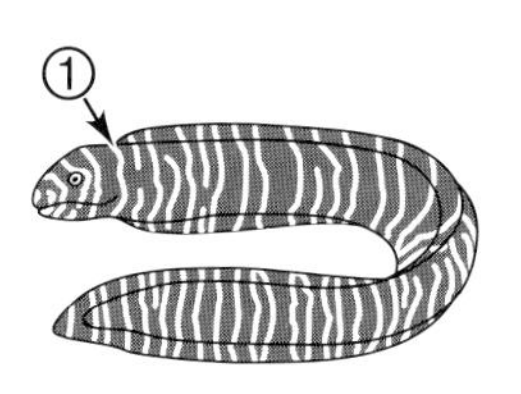

SIZE: 14 -24 in., max. 30 in.
DEPTH: 15 - 80 ft.

DISTINCTIVE FEATURES: 1. Long, slender arched jaws.

DESCRIPTION: Shades of brown. Numerous exposed fang-like teeth. Slender body.

ABUNDANCE & DISTRIBUTION: Rare entire archipelago. North to Baja.

HABITAT & BEHAVIOR: Inhabit rocky, boulder strewn areas and walls. Lurk in holes, crevices and dark recesses during day; forage in open at night. Constantly open and close mouth, an action required for respiration — not a threat.

REACTION TO DIVERS: Curious; often peer out from hole or crack with head and forebody exposed, retreating only if molested.

DISTINCTIVE FEATURES: Unmarked green to dark brown head and forebody.

DESCRIPTION: Occasionally have fine white to yellow spots or flecks on rear body and dorsal fin.

ABUNDANCE & DISTRIBUTION: Uncommon entire archipelago. North to Baja.

HABITAT & BEHAVIOR: Inhabit rocky, boulder strewn areas and walls. Lurk in holes, crevices and dark recesses during day; forage in open at night. Constantly open and close mouth, an action required for respiration — not a threat.

REACTION TO DIVERS: Curious; often peer out from hole or crack with head and forebody exposed, retreating only if molested.

DISTINCTIVE FEATURES: 1. Numerous white spots on body and dorsal fin.

DESCRIPTION: Olive to dark brown and black.

ABUNDANCE & DISTRIBUTION: Common entire archipelago. Pacific coast Panama and Colombia.

HABITAT & BEHAVIOR: Inhabit rocky, boulder strewn areas and walls. Lurk in holes, crevices and dark recesses. Constantly open and close mouth, an action required for respiration — not a threat.

REACTION TO DIVERS: Curious; often peer out from hole or crack with head and forebody exposed, retreating only if molested.

SLENDERJAW MORAY
Morena Kuijada Esbelto
Enchelycore octaviana
FAMILY:
Moray – Muraenidae

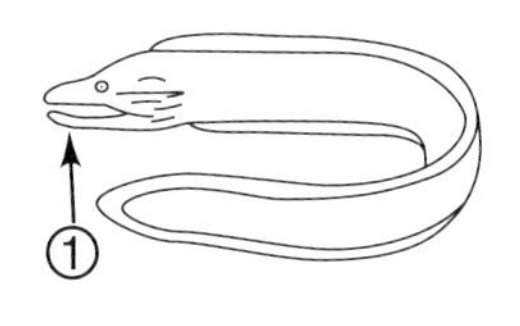

SIZE: 1½-2½ ft., max. 3 ft.
DEPTH: 10-120 ft.

PANAMIC GREEN MORAY
Morena Verde
Gymnothorax castaneus
FAMILY:
Moray – Muraenidae

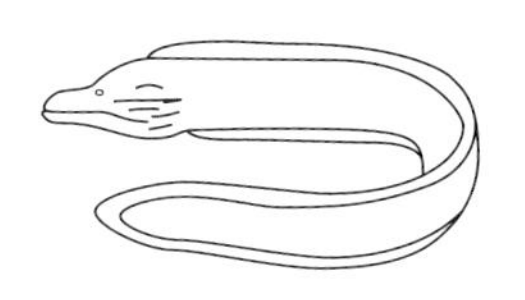

SIZE: 2½-3½ ft., max. 4¾ ft.
DEPTH: 10-120 ft.

FINE SPOTTED MORAY
Morena Puntofino
Gymnothorax dovii
FAMILY:
Moray – Muraenidae

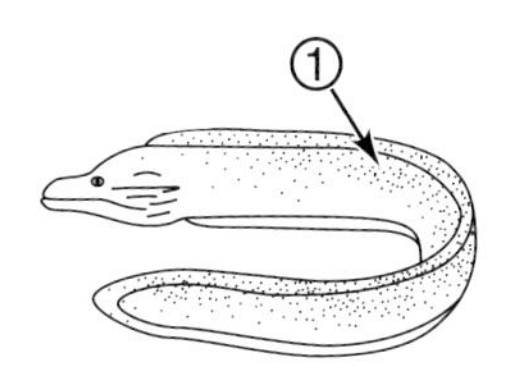

SIZE: 3-4 ft., max. 5½ ft.
DEPTH: 10-120 ft.

DISTINCTIVE FEATURES: 1. Interior of mouth white. 2. Numerous white spots cover body and head.

DESCRIPTION: Shades of dark brown to reddish brown. Pair of nostrils above mouth and additional set between eyes.

ABUNDANCE & DISTRIBUTION: Rare entire archipelago. Tropical Indo-Pacific, including Hawaii.

HABITAT & BEHAVIOR: Inhabit rocky, boulder strewn areas and walls. Lurk in holes, crevices and dark recesses. Constantly open and close mouth, an action required for respiration — not a threat.

REACTION TO DIVERS: Curious; often peer out from hole or crack with head and forebody exposed, retreating only if molested.

DISTINCTIVE FEATURES: 1. Large, dark spot, bordered in white, around gill opening.

DESCRIPTION: Shades of gray to brown, somewhat mottled, and speckled with irregular light and dark spots on head, body and fins. Pair of tubular nostrils above mouth and another set between eyes.

ABUNDANCE & DISTRIBUTION: Occasional entire archipelago. Peru north to Baja, including offshore islands.

HABITAT & BEHAVIOR: Inhabit rocky, boulder strewn areas and walls. Lurk in holes, crevices and dark recesses. Constantly open and close mouth, an action required for respiration — not a threat.

REACTION TO DIVERS: Curious; often peer out from hole or crack with head and forebody exposed, retreating only if molested.

DISTINCTIVE FEATURES: 1. Numerous, dark-bordered white spots cover body. 2. Dark spot around gill opening.

DESCRIPTION: Shades of brown; back darker with distinctive light blotches. Eyes golden with black pupil. Pair of tubular nostrils above mouth and another set between eyes.

ABUNDANCE & DISTRIBUTION: Occasional entire archipelago. Peru north to Baja.

HABITAT & BEHAVIOR: Inhabit deep, rocky, boulder strewn areas and walls. Lurk in holes, crevices and dark recesses. Constantly open and close mouth, an action required for respiration — not a threat.

REACTION TO DIVERS: Curious; often peer out from hole or crack with head and forebody exposed, retreating only if molested.

WHITEMOUTH MORAY
Morena Boca Blanca
Gymnothorax meleagris
FAMILY:
Moray – Muraenidae

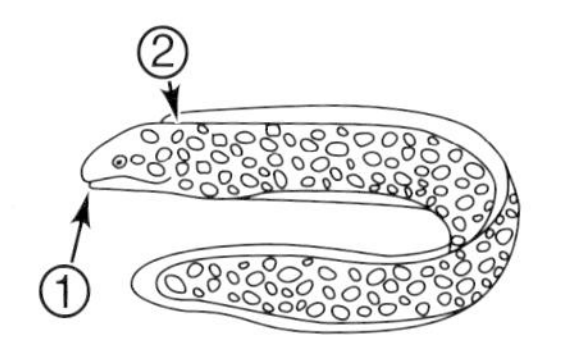

SIZE: 1½-2½ ft., max. 3 ft.
DEPTH: 15-80 ft.

BLACKSPOT MORAY
Morena Mancha Negra
Muraena clepsydra
FAMILY:
Moray – Muraenidae

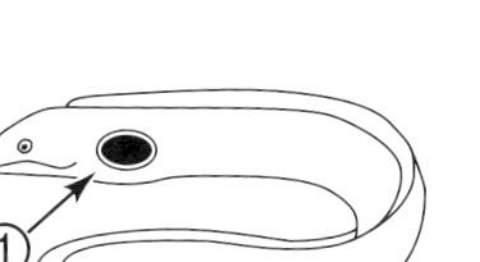

SIZE: 1½-2½ ft., max. 3 ft.
DEPTH: 15-80 ft.

STARRY MORAY
Morena Estrellada
Muraena argus
FAMILY:
Moray – Muraenidae

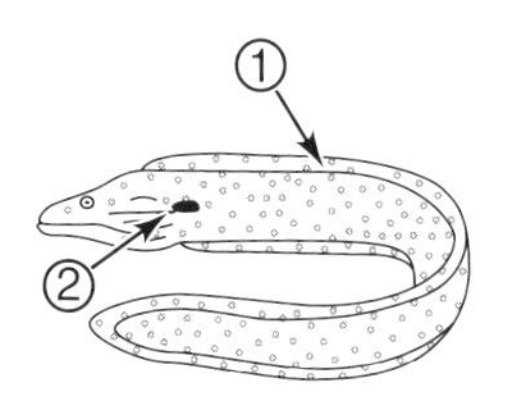

SIZE: 1½-2½ ft., max. 3 ft.
DEPTH: 60-200 ft.

DISTINCTIVE FEATURES: 1. Numerous gold to yellow or pale yellow spots with dark outline on body.

DESCRIPTION: Brown to light brown and yellowish tan; often with darkish markings and mottling. Pair of tubular nostrils above mouth and another set between eyes; dorsal fin starts immediately behind head.

ABUNDANCE & DISTRIBUTION: Common entire archipelago. Peru north to Baja; also tropical Indo-Pacific.

HABITAT & BEHAVIOR: Inhabit rocky, boulder strewn areas and walls. Lurk in holes, crevices and dark recesses. Constantly open and close mouth, an action required for respiration — not a threat.

REACTION TO DIVERS: Curious; often peer out from hole or crack with head and forebody exposed, retreating only if molested.

Brilliant Gold Spot Pattern

DISTINCTIVE FEATURES: 1. Patches, composed of small brownish gold spots, form mosaic pattern on head and body.

DESCRIPTION: Background color brown to dark brown and black.

ABUNDANCE & DISTRIBUTION: Rare entire archipelago. Japan.

HABITAT & BEHAVIOR: Inhabit rocky, boulder strewn areas and walls. Lurk in holes, crevices and dark recesses. Constantly open and close mouth, an action required for respiration — not a threat.

REACTION TO DIVERS: Curious; often peer out from hole or crack with head and forebody exposed, retreating only if molested.

JEWELED MORAY
Morena Pinta
Muraena lentiginosa
FAMILY:
Moray – Muraenidae

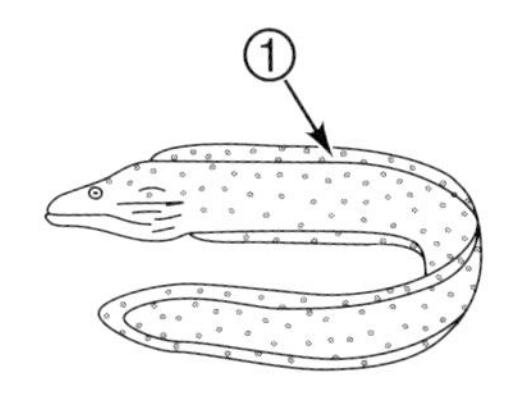

SIZE: 1-1½ ft., max. 2 ft.
DEPTH: 15-80 ft.

Mottled Pattern with Pale Yellow Spots

MOSAIC MORAY
Morena Mosaico
Enchelycore lichenosa
FAMILY:
Moray – Muraenidae

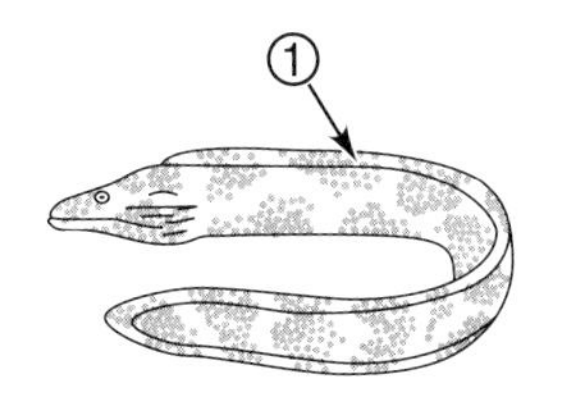

SIZE: 1½-2½ ft., max. 3 ft.
DEPTH: 15-80 ft.

IDENTIFICATION GROUP 12

Sharks & Rays

Whale Shark—Hammerhead—Pointed-Nose Shark—Ray

This ID Group consists of fish whose skeletons are composed of cartilage rather than bone. They are called cartilaginous fishes. All have small, hard scales that give them a rough, sandpapery feel. They are classified into numerous families which are often difficult to distinguish and remember. Consequently, they will be discussed more by general appearance than by family.

FAMILY: Whale Shark—Rhincodontidae

1 Species Included

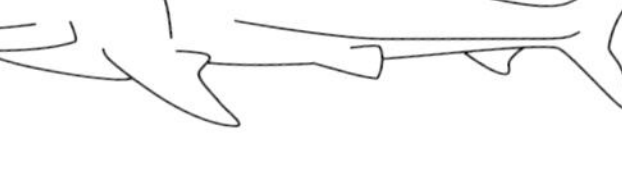

Whale Shark

The only member of this family is the Whale Shark — the world's largest fish. Maximum size is thought to be about 55 feet, although they are more commonly between 15-40 feet. They are circumglobal in tropical and temperate waters. Their size and white spotted pattern make identification unmistakable.

FAMILY: Hammerhead—Sphyrnidae

1 Species Included

Scalloped

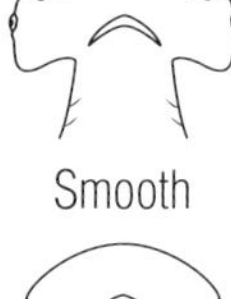

Smooth

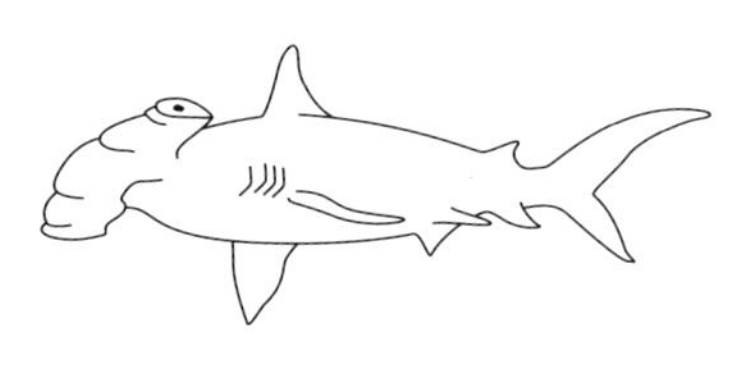

Scalloped Hammerhead

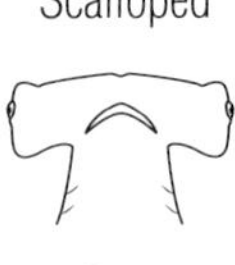

Great

Bonnethead

Hammerheads are distinctive sharks whose heads have evolved dramatically. The head is flattened and extended to either side, with the eyes set on the outer edges. The species can be distinguished by the shape of the leading edge of their hammer-shaped heads. Only the Scalloped Hammerhead is commonly observed in Galapagos.

Pointed-Nose Shark

4 Species Included

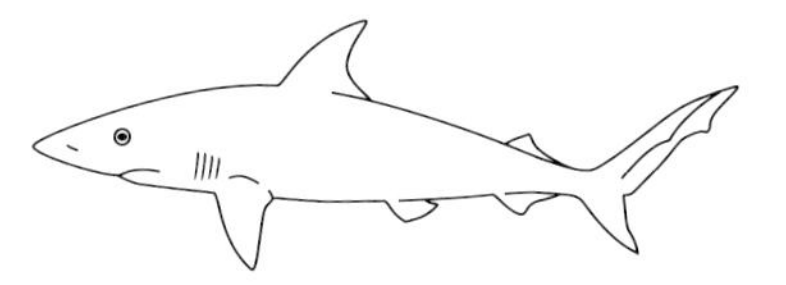

Pointed-Nose Shark (typical shape)

Sharks with more-or-less pointed noses are represented by numerous families within the archipelago; the most common family in this group is known as the Requiem Sharks. Identifying sharks underwater can be difficult; important clues include subtle shading on body and fins, general shape of the snout, placement of the dorsal fin in relation to the pectoral fin, and the shape and size of fins. Only a few sharks, including the Tiger, Blacktip and Whitetip, have distinctive markings. In Galapagos only two species, the Galapagos Shark and White-tipped Reef Shark, are commonly observed.

ORDER: Ray—Rajiformes

5 Species Included

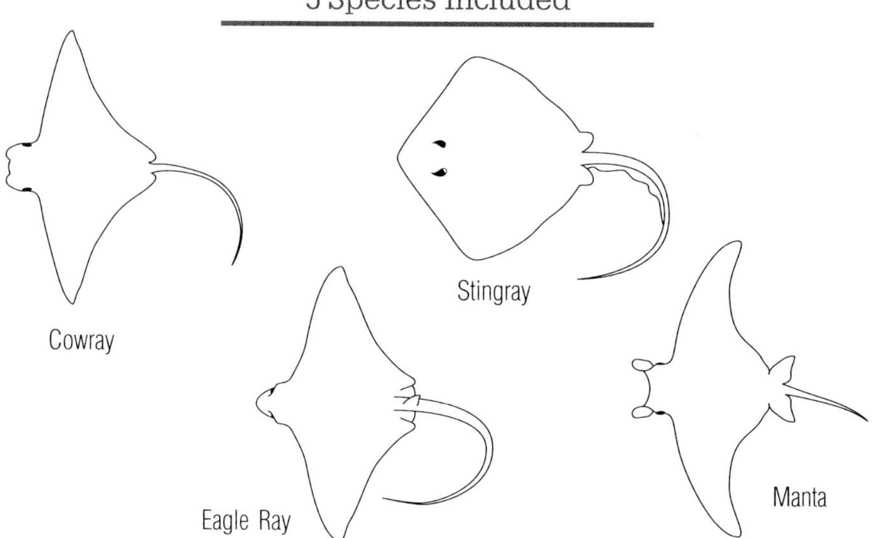

Rays are represented by four families within the archipelago. These fish have greatly enlarged pectoral fins which give them a basic disk-like shape. Swimming is accomplished as they move their pectoral fins in a fashion reminiscent of birds in flight. Thus, the fins are occasionally referred to as "wings."

Stingrays are bottom dwellers and have sharp spines on their elongated tails that may be used defensively. "Flying" rays include Eagle Rays, Golden Cowrays and Mantas. They spend most of their time swimming in open water. Keys to identification are head and body shape, and back markings.

DISTINCTIVE FEATURES: 1. Numerous dark spots cover head, body and fins. 2. A short spine just forward of each dorsal fin.

DESCRIPTION: Shades of gray to brown; white underside. Blunt, rectangular head.

ABUNDANCE & DISTRIBUTION: Uncommon western Isabela and Fernandina; rare balance of archipelago. South to Peru.

HABITAT & BEHAVIOR: Inhabit sand flats and rocky, boulder strewn reef areas with sand between outcroppings. Rest motionless on bottom. Docile, unaggressive; poor swimmer.

REACTION TO DIVERS: Ignore divers unless molested, which may cause them to move sluggishly away.

NOTE: Also commonly known as "Port Jackson Horn Shark."

DISTINCTIVE FEATURES: 1. Bold pattern of large, white spots cover body.

DESCRIPTION: Gray to gray-brown, fading to white underside; thin whitish lines join spots on back. Three ridges run on sides from head to base of tail; first dorsal fin more than halfway back on body. World's largest fish.

ABUNDANCE & DISTRIBUTION: Uncommon entire archipelago (Author's personal experience indicates more common Roca Redonda, Wolf and Darwin, October and November). Worldwide tropical waters.

HABITAT & BEHAVIOR: Considered open-water oceanic. Occasionally cruise along walls and steep boulder strewn slopes. Feed on plankton, baitfish, tuna, squid and pelagic crustaceans that are sieved from the water.

REACTION TO DIVERS: Ignore divers. Do not overtly react to being ridden; however, apparently are irritated. Usually dive and disappear shortly after such activities, but often remain in area, making numerous passes if unmolested.

DISTINCTIVE FEATURES: Uniform coloration with no distinctive markings.

DESCRIPTION: Silver gray to gray-brown; white to yellowish white underside. Somewhat rounded snout (compare Blacktip [next]); long, wide base pectoral fins with slender, pointed tips. Eye iris silver-gray.

ABUNDANCE & DISTRIBUTION: Occasional entire archipelago. North to Baja, including offshore islands; circumtropical, most commonly associated with oceanic islands.

HABITAT & BEHAVIOR: Cruise over rocky reefs, boulder strewn slopes and along walls. May be solitary or in small groups, occasionally in schools. Feed primarily on fishes, including other sharks and rays.

REACTION TO DIVERS: May ignore divers or make curious close pass. Usually swim away upon rapid approach or threatening movements. May be dangerous if fish blood is present (from spearfishing or fish cleaning).

HORNSHARK
Gato
Heterodontus quoyi
FAMILY:
Bullhead Shark – Heterodontidae

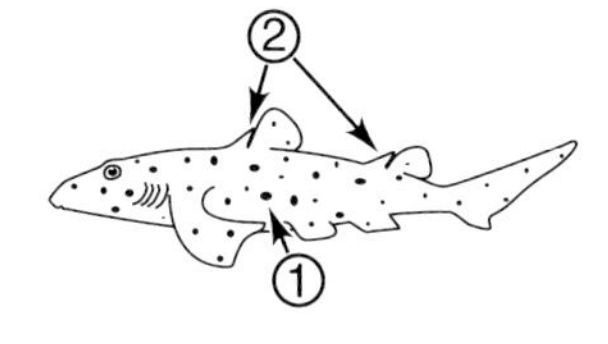

SIZE: 1½-3 ft., max. 3½ ft.
DEPTH: 10-130 ft.

WHALE SHARK
Tiburón Ballena
Rhincodon typus
FAMILY:
Whale Shark – Rhincondontidae

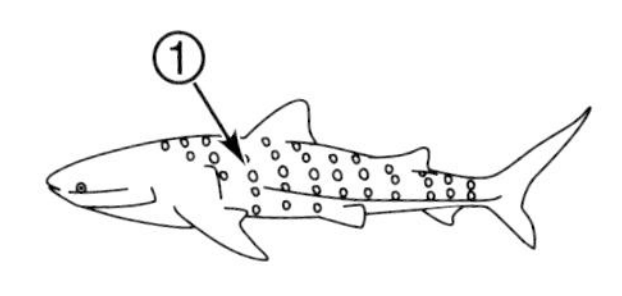

SIZE: 20-45 ft., max. 55 ft.
DEPTH: 6-60 ft.

GALAPAGOS SHARK
Tiburón de Galápagos
Carcharhinus galapagensis
FAMILY:
Requiem Shark – Carcharhinidae

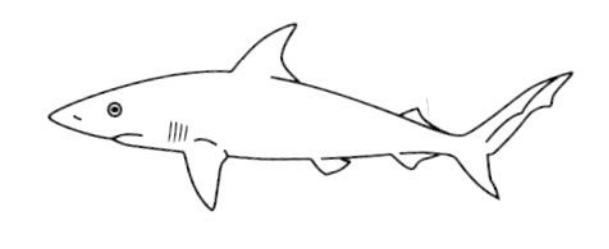

SIZE: 4-6 ft., max. 7 ft.
DEPTH: 10-100 ft.

DISTINCTIVE FEATURES: 1. Black tip and edging on all fins (except upper lobe of tail). **2. Long pointed snout** (compare Galapagos Shark [previous]).

DESCRIPTION: Black tips and edging fade with age and may be indistinct, especially on first dorsal. Silvery brown to gray on back, fading to white underside.

ABUNDANCE & DISTRIBUTION: Uncommon entire archipelago. Circumtropical.

HABITAT & BEHAVIOR: Prefer inshore waters and lagoons. Cruise over rocky reefs, boulder strewn slopes and along walls. May be solitary or in small groups. Rapid swimmer; feed primarily on fast swimming pelagic fishes.

REACTION TO DIVERS: May ignore divers or make curious close pass. Usually swim away upon rapid approach or threatening movements. May be dangerous if fish blood is present (from spearfishing or fish cleaning).

SIMILAR SPECIES: Often confused with Gray Reef Shark, *Caraharhinus amblyrhynchos*, distinguished by a more rounded snout, black edging on upper lobe of tail and lack of black edging on ventral and anal fins. No validated reports from Galapagos.

DISTINCTIVE FEATURES: 1. White trailing edges and tips on dorsal, pectoral and tail fins.

DESCRIPTION: Dark silver-gray on back fading to white underside. Snout somewhat rounded.

ABUNDANCE & DISTRIBUTION: Uncommon entire archipelago. Tropical Indo-Pacific and eastern Pacific.

HABITAT & BEHAVIOR: Prefer deep banks, channels and along dropoffs, but occasionally over shallow reefs and lagoons. Most common below 90 feet. May be solitary or in small groups. Feed primarily on bottom dwelling fishes and open water pelagics, including Eagle Rays and small sharks.

REACTION TO DIVERS: May ignore divers or make curious close pass. Usually swim away upon rapid approach or threatening movements. May be dangerous if fish blood is present (from spearfishing or fish cleaning).

DISTINCTIVE FEATURES: 1. White tips on foredorsal fin and upper lobe of tail.

DESCRIPTION: Shades of gray to brown; white underside. Rounded snout; second dorsal fin little more than half height of first.

ABUNDANCE & DISTRIBUTION: Common entire archipelago. North to Costa Rico, including offshore islands; also tropical and subtropical Indo-Pacific.

HABITAT & BEHAVIOR: Inhabit rocky reefs and boulder strewn slopes. Nocturnal; generally lie motionless during day, on sandy bottoms near rocky outcroppings, and especially under ledge overhangs and in caves. Feed primarily on reef fishes, octopuses and crustaceans; particularly adept at wrenching prey from cracks, holes and other recesses in the reef.

REACTION TO DIVERS: Tend to ignore divers. Swim rapidly away when closely approached. Creeping up with very slow movements may allow close observation. Not considered dangerous unless provoked.

BLACKTIP SHARK
Tiburón de Punta Negra
Carcharhinus limbatus

FAMILY:
Requiem Shark –
Carcharhinidae

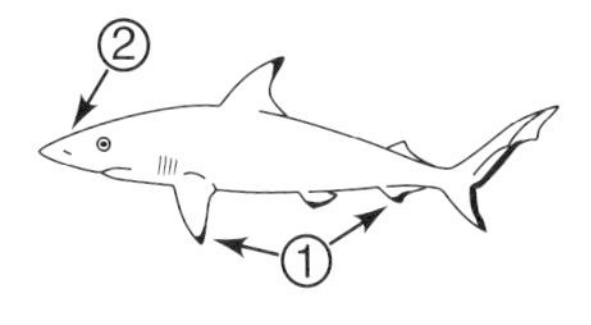

SIZE: 5 - 6 ft., max. 8 ft.
DEPTH: 10 - 100 ft.

SILVERTIP SHARK
Tiburón de Punta Plateado
Carcharhinus albimarginatus

FAMILY:
Requiem Shark –
Carcharhinidae

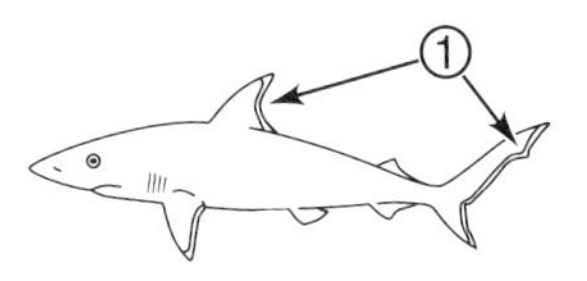

SIZE: 5 - 7 ft., max. 9 ft.
DEPTH: 10 - 1,200 ft.

WHITE-TIPPED REEF SHARK
Tintorera Punta Aleta Blanca
Triaenodon obesus

FAMILY:
Requiem Shark –
Carcharhinidae

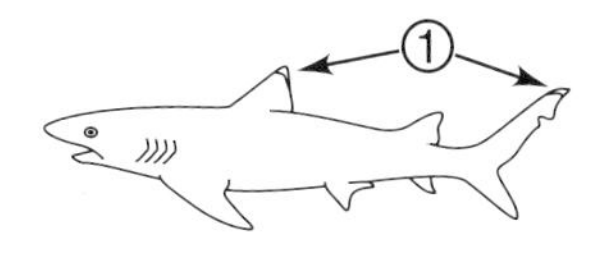

SIZE: 4 - 6 ft., max. 7 ft.
DEPTH: 10 - 100 ft.

DISTINCTIVE FEATURES: 1. Head flattened and extended to either side, with eyes set on the outer edges. 2. Front edge slightly rounded and scalloped.

DESCRIPTION: Silver-gray to gray-brown, fading to white underside. Underside tips of pectoral fins dusky. Rear edge of ventral fin straight.

ABUNDANCE & DISTRIBUTION: Abundant Darwin and Wolf; occasional balance of archipelago. Worldwide tropical and semitropical waters.

HABITAT & BEHAVIOR: Cruise over rocky reefs, boulder strewn slopes and along walls. May be solitary or in small groups, occasionally in large schools. Feed primarily on fishes, including other sharks and rays.

REACTION TO DIVERS: May ignore divers or make curious close pass. Usually swim away upon rapid approach or threatening movements. May be dangerous if fish blood is present (from spearfishing or fish cleaning).

SIMILAR SPECIES: Smooth Hammerhead, *S. zygaena*, distinguished by head with smooth leading edge; rarely observed in Galapagos.

DISTINCTIVE FEATURES: Black and gray marbling.

DESCRIPTION: Nearly circular body with only slightly extended snout. Tail thick and cylindrical to barb, then becomes a long vertically flattened, upper lobe.

ABUNDANCE & DISTRIBUTION: Occasional entire archipelago. North to Baja; also Indo-Pacific including Red Sea.

HABITAT & BEHAVIOR: Inhabit sandy bottoms and rocky, boulder and gravel strewn slopes. When moving, glide over bottom using a wave-like body motion.

REACTION TO DIVERS: Tend to ignore divers, moving away only when closely approached.

DISTINCTIVE FEATURES: 1. Pointed snout. 2. Pointed "wing" tips form diamond shape.

DESCRIPTION: Olive-brown to brown or gray. No markings. Tail thick and cylindrical to barb, then becomes vertically flattened with a rounded tip.

ABUNDANCE & DISTRIBUTION: Occasional entire archipelago. North to Canada.

HABITAT & BEHAVIOR: Inhabit, often resting, on sandy bottoms and gravel/rubble areas. When moving, glide over bottom using a wave-like body motion. May bury or cover back with only eyes protruding. Dig in sand to feed.

REACTION TO DIVERS: Tend to ignore divers, moving away only when closely approached.

SCALLOPED HAMMERHEAD
Tiburón Martillo
Sphyrna lewini
FAMILY:
Hammerhead Shark – Sphyrnidae

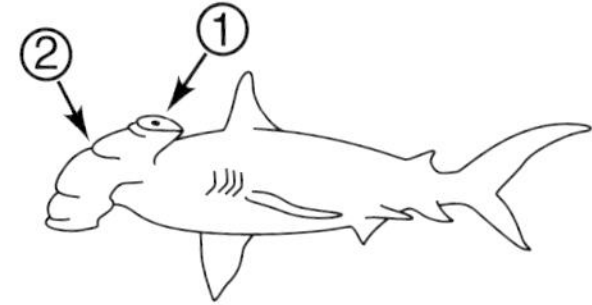

SIZE: 5 - 9 ft., max. 14 ft.
DEPTH: 10 - 600 ft.

MARBLED RAY
Sartén Marmoleado
Taeniura meyeri
FAMILY:
Stingrays – Dasyatididae

SIZE: 3½ - 6½ ft.
(not including tail)
DEPTH: 10 - 180 ft.

DIAMOND STINGRAY
Raya de Espina
Dasyatis brevis
FAMILY:
Stingrays – Dasyatididae

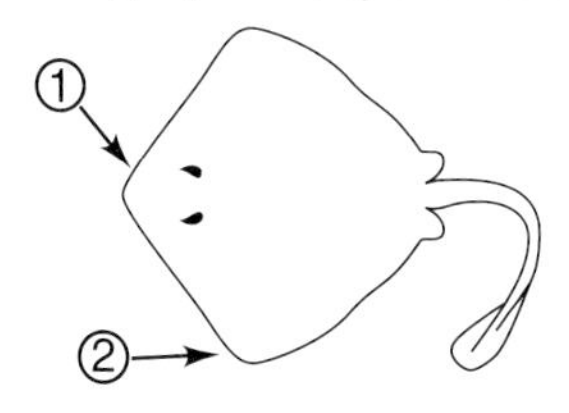

SIZE: 3½ - 6 ft.
(not including tail)
DEPTH: 10-180 ft.

DISTINCTIVE FEATURES: 1. Squarish head with two frontal lobes.

DESCRIPTION: Back shades of golden brown to brown and grayish brown; belly white. Whip-like tail.

ABUNDANCE & DISTRIBUTION: Occasional entire archipelago. Peru north to Baja.

HABITAT & BEHAVIOR: Inhabit protected lagoons and areas with mangroves, where they glide near the surface. Occasionally, over open water reefs and along walls. Often school in open water; may mix with Spotted Eagle Rays [next].

REACTION TO DIVERS: Wary; swim away upon approach. Occasionally a school may be intercepted by swimming into path of travel with slow, non-threatening movements.

DISTINCTIVE FEATURES: 1. Pointed head with flattened, tapering snout. 2. Numerous white spots and circular markings over dark back.

DESCRIPTION: White underside, occasionally with some dark spotting patterns along "wing" borders and tips. Mouth on underside. Long, thin tail with one to five venomous spines at base.

ABUNDANCE & DISTRIBUTION: Common to occasional entire archipelago. Peru north to Baja, including offshore islands; circumtropical.

HABITAT & BEHAVIOR: Cruise along walls, over reefs and sandy areas. May be solitary, often in small groups and occasionally in large schools. Stop to dig in sand and feed on mollusks and crustaceans; have also been observed feeding on barnacles in Galapagos.

REACTION TO DIVERS: Wary; swim away upon approach. Occasionally a school may be intercepted by swimming into path of travel with slow, non-threatening movements.

DISTINCTIVE FEATURES: 1. Large mouth on leading edge of head with conspicuous, movable, scoop-like fins (pectoral) on either side.

DESCRIPTION: Black to dark gray back, often with whitish patches on shoulder and occasionally other areas. White underside, often with grayish or black areas and blotches.

ABUNDANCE & DISTRIBUTION: Occasional entire archipelago. Peru north to California, including offshore islands; circumtropical.

HABITAT & BEHAVIOR: Considered oceanic. Occasionally cruise along walls and over reefs. Usually solitary, but occasionally in small groups.

REACTION TO DIVERS: Tend to ignore divers unless closely approached, which may cause them to move away.

GOLDEN COWRAY
Raya Dorada
Rhinoptera steindachneri
FAMILY:
Cownose Ray – Rhinopteridae

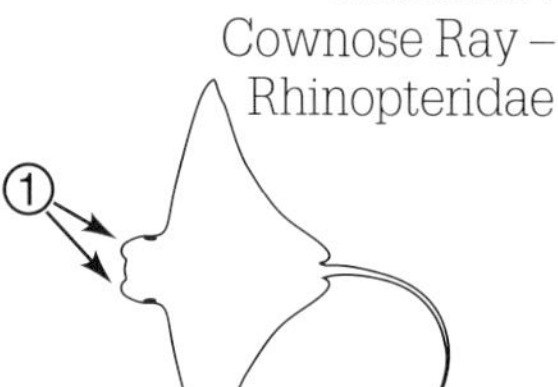

SIZE: Wing span 1½-2½ ft., max. 3 ft.
DEPTH: 0-100 ft.

EAGLE RAY
Raya Aguila
Aetobatus narinari
FAMILY:
Eagle Ray – Myliobatidae

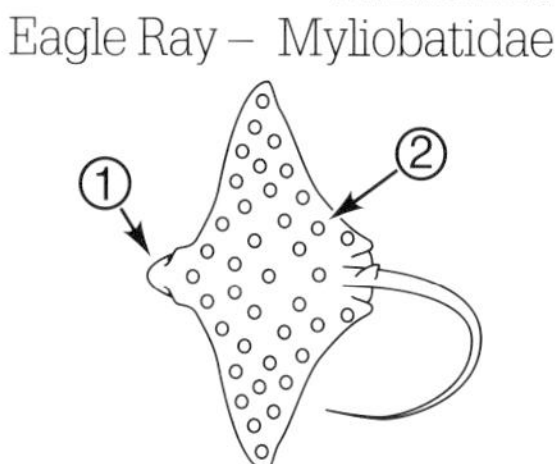

SIZE: Wing span 3-5 ft., max. 8 ft.
DEPTH: 10-130 ft.

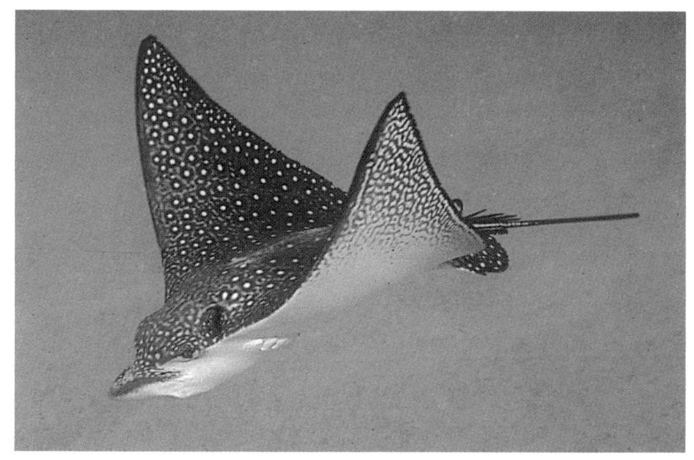

MANTA RAY
Manta
Manta hamiltoni
FAMILY:
Manta Ray – Mobulidae

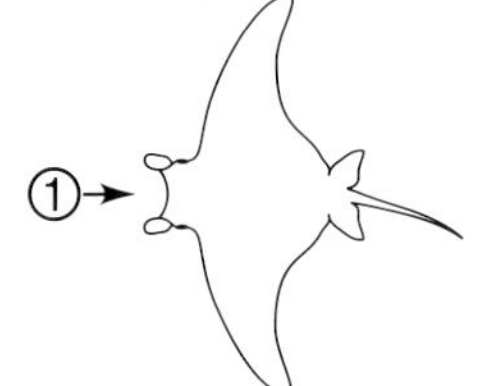

SIZE: Wing span 6-12 ft., max. 22 ft.
DEPTH: 0-80 ft.

APPENDIX

Marine Mammals, Birds & Reptiles

Sperm Whales

Several species of marine mammals and reptiles are commonly observed in the archipelago's waters. Among these are the totally aquatic mammals, called cetaceans, which include whales and dolphins. Nearly a dozen species of whales visit Galapagos, although only a few are encountered on a regular basis. Possibly the most common is the relatively small Short-finned Pilot Whale *Globicephala macrorhyncha*, which are generally observed in pods of 10-20 individuals. Because of their close relation in size they are often confused with dolphin, but can be

Bottle-nosed Dolphin

distinguished by noting their larger bulbous heads. The Humpback, *Megaptera novaeanfliae* and Sperm Whales, *Physeter catodon*, periodically sighted north and west of Isabela and Fernandina islands are the only species that dramatically raise their tail flukes when sounding, and both occasionally breach with spectacular leaps.

The most commonly spotted cetacean is the Bottle-nosed Dolphin, *Tursiops truncatus*. They regularly play in the ship's bow wake and are occasionally spotted making breathtaking leaps into the air. It is possible to snorkel with these magnificent creatures; however, they seem to be wary of scuba divers. Apparently the bubbles and sound of the equipment keeps them at bay. Several other dolphin species are also in Galapagos, but they rarely come close to either boat or snorkelers.

For snorkelers or divers, the most entertaining marine mammal in the archipelago is the Galapagos Sea Lion, *Zalophus californianus wollebacki* (a subspecies of the California Sea Lion). They apparently delight in performing a variety of "aquabatic" stunts much to the amusement of divers, streaking past like a high-performance jet fighter, with sudden turns and one or two loop-the-loops mixed with a few barrel rolls. When finished they stop a short distance away as if waiting for applause. Occasionally, the playful creatures will gently tug on divers' flippers or "mouth" a projecting snorkel. Caution should be taken with male sea lions protecting their territory and harem. They can be distinguished by their large bulbous foreheads. If a male starts barking or acting aggressive, it is advisable to quickly swim away from shore and out of its territory. Galapagos Sea Lions tend to inhabit sandy beaches and gently sloping, rock shorelines; consequently, they are generally found near visitor's landing sites.

Galapagos Sea Lions

Fur Sea Lion

Fur Sea Lions, *Arctocephalus galapagoensis*, also known as Fur Seals, are observed less frequently because of their preferred habitat of rough, steep, rocky shaded shores. Divers encounter them around Gordon Rocks. Land visitors will spot them at James Bay on San Salvador. Fur Sea Lions can be distinguished from Galapagos Sea Lions by their smaller size, more rounded faces with shorter snouts, larger eyes, and much heavier fur coats (the origin of their common name). Like their cousins, they are friendly, curious and ready to show off their aquatic skills.

Seabirds are abundant in Galapagos due to the region's plentiful marine life. A few species are encountered by divers and snorkelers. Most frequently sighted is the endemic Galapagos Penguin, *Sphenisus mendiculus*, third smallest of the family and the only penguin to live as far north as the equator. During the day, using wings as flippers, they swim offshore to feed on small fish. Underwater sightings are most frequent at Bartolome where they zip about at incredible speeds making sharp turns and occasionally performing flips.

Galapagos Penguin

Blue-footed Booby

The Flightless Cormorant, *Nannopterum harrisi*, is so well adapted to feeding underwater that the species has lost the ability to fly. The best chance of encountering this endemic species underwater is near the shore of Punta Espinosa, Fernandia—one of their primary nesting areas. If a loud "pop" is heard while underwater quickly look to open water for a diving booby plunging after a fish. More common is the sight of a Blue-footed Booby, *Sula nebouxi,* watching your activity from the surface.

Reptiles also have a prominent place in Galapagos' underwater world. The best known is the endemic Marine Iguana, *Amblyrhynchus cristatus*, studied by Darwin. It is the only lizard with the unique ability to feed at sea. With luck, these exotic creatures can be seen grazing in algae beds near the shores of Punta Espinosa, Fernandina, during the warm midday hours.

Marine Iguana

Green Sea Turtles are the only species of sea turtle that mates in the archipelago; however, Hawksbills and Leatherbacks are occasional visitors.

Endangered Green Sea Turtles are more abundant in Galapagos than anywhere on earth. Underwater sightings are frequent during their mating months from November through December, but can be expected at any time during the year. They are often found sleeping on the bottom or under ledges. With luck, a swimming Green will be curious enough to circle a diver before heading for open water.

Hawksbill Turtles, *Eretmochelys imbriocota,* are also occasionally spotted. They can usually be distinguished by their brown shell with yellow-brown, fan-like markings, but this distinction can result in an incorrect identification. Green Sea Turtles' shells are usually black to dark green, but occasionally they are brown with similar yellow-brown markings. Identification of a Hawksbill can be confirmed by the upper mouth that overhangs like a "hawk's bill". Another occasional visitor is the Leatherback, *Dermochelys olivacea,* largest of all turtles and easily distinguished by its dark brown, leathery upper shell spotted with yellow.

Green Sea Turtle on Bottom

PERSONAL RECORD OF FISH SIGHTINGS

1. DISKS & OVALS/COLORFUL

Butterfly—Angelfish—Surgeonfish

No.	Name	Page	Date	Location	Notes
	King Angelfish *Holacanthus passer*	23			
	Barberfish *Johnrandallia nigrirostris*	23			
	Threebanded Butterflyfish *Chaetodon humeralis*	25			
	Scythe Butterflyfish *Chaetodon falcifer*	25			
	Meyer's Butterfly *Chaetodon meyeri*	25			
	Threadfin Butterfly *Chaetodon auriga*	27			
	Racoon Butterfly *Chaetodon lunula*	27			
	Duskybarred Butterfly *Chaetodon kleinii*	27			
	Longnose Butterflyfish *Forcipiger flavissimus*	29			
	Yellowtailed Surgeonfish *Prionurus laticlavius*	29			
	Goldrimmed Surgeonfish *Acanthurus nigricans*	29			
	Purple Surgeonfish *Acanthurus xanthopterus*	31			
	Convict Tang *Acanthurus triostegus*	31			
	Moorish Idol *Zanclus cornutus*	31			

ID GROUP 2 SILVERY

Jack—Porgy—Others

No.	Name	Page	Date	Location	Notes
	Bigeye Jack *Caranx sexfasciatus*	35			
	Pacific Crevalle Jack *Caranx canius*	34			
	Black Jack *Caranx lugubris*	35			
	Blue Spotted Jack *Caranx melampygus*	35			
	Almaco Jack *Seriola rivoliana*	37			
	Green Jack *Caranx caballus*	37			
	Rainbow Runner *Elagatis bipinnulata*	37			
	Cottonmouth Jack *Uraspis secunda*	39			
	Steel Pompano *Trachinotus stilbe*	39			
	African Pompano *Alectis ciliaris*	39			
	Bigeye Scad *Selar crumenophthalmus*	41			
	Yellowtail Scad *Decapterus sanctae-helenae*	41			

No.	Name	Page	Date	Location	Notes
	Pilot Fish *Naucrates ductor*	41			
	Yellowfin Tuna *Thunnus albacares*	43			
	Albacore *Thunnus alalunga*	42			
	Black Skipjack *Euthynnus lineatus*	43			
	Indo-pacific Bonito *Sarda orientalis*	43			
	Sierra Mackerel *Scomberomorus sierra*	45			
	Wahoo *Acanthocybium solandri*	45			
	Barracuda *Sphyraena idiastes*	45			
	Cortez Chub *Kyphosus elegans*	47			
	Striped Chub *Kyphosus analogus*	47			
	Rainbow Chub *Sectator ocyurus*	47			
	Dusky Chub *Girella freminvillei*	49			
	Galapagos Porgy *Calamus taurinus*	49			
	Blackspot Porgy *Archosargus pourtalesii*	49			
	Silver Mojarra *Eucinostomus argenteus*	51			
	Pacific Flagfin Mojarra *Eucinostomus californiensis*	50			
	Spotfin Mojarra *Eucinostomus gracilis*	50			
	Peruvian Mojarra *Diapterus peruvianus*	50			
	Yellowfin Mojarra *Gerres cinereus*	50			
	Stripe Tail Aholehole *Kuhlia taeniura*	51			
	Machete *Elops affinis*	51			
	Yellowtail Mullet *Mugil rammelsbergi*	53			
	Galapagos Mullet *Mugil galapagensis*	52			
	Pacific Spadefish *Chaetodipterus zonatus*	53			
	Halfbeak *Hyporhamphus unifasciatus*	53			
	Ribbon Halfbeak *Euleptorhamphus longirostris*	52			

ID GROUP 3 SLOPING HEAD/TAPERED BODY

Grunt—Snapper

No.	Name	Page	Date	Location	Notes
	Golden-eyed Grunt *Haemulon scudderi*	57			
	Graybar Grunt *Haemulon sexfasciatum*	57			

No.	Name	Page	Date	Location	Notes
	Galapagos Grunt *Orthopristis forbesi*	57			
	Yellowtail Grunt *Anisotremus interruptus*	59			
	Peruvian Grunt *Anisotremus scapularis*	59			
	Black Striped Salema *Xenocys jessiae*	59			
	White Salema *Xenichthys agassizi*	61			
	Blue Striped Snapper *Lutjanus viridis*	61			
	Jordan's Snapper *Lutjanus jordani*	63			
	Dog Snapper *Lutjanus novemfasciatus*	63			
	Yellow Snapper *Lutjanus argentiventris*	63			
	Mullet Snapper *Lutjanus aratus*	65			
	Barred Pargo *Hoplopagrus guentheri*	65			
	Grape Eye *Hemilutjanus macrophthalmos*	65			

ID GROUP 4 SMALL OVALS

Damselfish—Chromis/Damselfish

No.	Name	Page	Date	Location	Notes
	Giant Damselfish *Microspathodon dorsalis*	69			
	Bumphead Damselfish *Microspathodon bairdii*	69			
	White-tail Damselfish *Stegastes leucorus beebei*	71			
	Yellow-tail Damselfish *Stegastes arcifrons*	73			
	Rusty Damselfish *Nexilosus latifrons*	72			
	Panamic Sergeant Major *Abudefduf troschelii*	73			
	Night Sergeant *Nexilarius concolor*	72			
	Silverstripe Chromis *Chromis alta*	75			
	Brown Chromis *Chromis atrilobata*	75			

ID GROUP 5 HEAVY BODY/LARGE LIPS

Grouper/Sea Bass—Sea Bass

No.	Name	Page	Date	Location	Notes
	Camotillo *Paralabrax albomaculatus*	79			
	Bacalao *Mycteroperca olfax*	79			
	Panamic Graysby *Epinephelus panamensis*	81			
	Flag Cabrilla *Epinephelus labriformis*	81			
	Gray Threadfin Bass *Cratinus agassizii*	81			

No.	Name	Page	Date	Location	Notes
	Leather Bass *Dermatolepis dermatolepis*	83			
	Wrasse Ass Bass *Liopropoma fasciatum*	83			
	Mutton Hamlet *Alphestes afer*	85			
	Barred Serrano *Serranus fasciatus*	85			
	Creole Fish *Paranthias colonus*	87			

ID GROUP 6 SWIM WITH PECTORAL FINS/OBVIOUS SCALES

Parrotfish—Wrasse

No.	Name	Page	Date	Location	Notes
	Bumphead Parrotfish *Scarus perrico*	91			
	Blue-chin Parrotfish *Scarus ghobban*	91			
	Bicolor Parrotfish *Scarus rubroviolaceus*	93			
	Azure Parrotfish *Scarus compressus*	93			
	Loosetooth Parrotfish *Nicholsina denticulata*	95			
	Rainbow Wrasse *Thalassoma lucasanum*	95			
	Chameleon Wrasse *Halichoeres dispilus*	97			
	Sunset Wrasse *Thalassoma grammaticum*	97			
	Spinster Wrasse *Halichoeres nicholsi*	99			
	Streamer Hogfish *Bodianus diplotaenia*	101			
	Harlequin Wrasse *Bodianus eclancheri*	103			
	Goldspot Sheepshead *Semicossyphus darwini*	103			
	Dragon Warsse *Novaculichthys taeniourus*	105			
	Pacific Razorfish *Xyrichthys pavo*	105			

ID GROUP 7 REDDISH/BIG EYES

Squirrelfish—Bigeye—Cardinalfish

No.	Name	Page	Date	Location	Notes
	Bigscale Soldierfish *Myripristis berndti*	109			
	Panamic Soldierfish *Myripristis leiognathos*	109			
	Tinsel Squirrelfish *Adioryx suborbitalis*	109			
	Popeye Catalufa *Pseudopriacanthus serrula*	111			
	Glasseye *Heteropriacanthus cruentatus*	111			
	Blacktip Cardinalfish *Apogon atradorsatus*	113			
	Tail Spot Cardinalfish *Apogon dovii*	112			
	Pink Cardinalfish *Apogon pacifici*	113			

ID GROUP 8 SMALL ELONGATED BOTTOM-DWELLERS

Blenny—Goby

No.	Name	Page	Date	Location	Notes
	Galapagos Barnacle Blenny *Acanthemblemaria castroi*	117			
	Red-spotted Barnacle Blenny *Hypsoblennius brevipinnis*	117			
	Blackstriped Blenny *undescribed*	119			
	Large Banded Blenny *Ophioblennius steindachneri*	119			
	Sabertooth Blenny *Plagiotremus azaleus*	121			
	Chameleon Clinid *Malacoctenus tetranemus*	121			
	Belted Blenny *Malacoctenus zonogaster*	121			
	Bravo Clinid *Labrisomus dendriticus*	123			
	Yellow-mouth Pikeblenny *Chaenopsis schmitti*	123			
	Galapagos Triple-fin blenny *Lepidonectes corallicola*	125			
	Redlight Goby *Coryphopterus urospilus*	125			
	Galapagos Blue-banded Goby *Lythrypnus gilberti*	127			
	Banded Cleaner Goby *Elacatinus nesiotes*	127			

ID GROUP 9 ODD-SHAPED BOTTOM DWELLERS

Frogfish—Flatfish—Scorpionfish—Others

No.	Name	Page	Date	Location	Notes
	Sanguine Frogfish *Antennatus sanguineus*	131			
	Bandtail Frogfish *Antennatus strigatus*	131			
	Red-lipped Batfish *Ogcocephalus darwini*	133			
	White-margined Searobin *Prionotus albirostris*	133			
	Rainbow Tonguefish *Symphurus atramentatus*	133			
	Leopard Flounder *Bothus leopardinus*	135			
	Galapagos Clingfish *Arcos poecilophthalmus*	135			
	Night Lizardfish *Synodus lacertinus*	137			
	California Lizardfish *Synodus lucioceps*	137			
	Rainbow Scorpionfish *Scorpaenodes xyris*	137			
	Stone Scorpionfish *Scorpaena plumieri mystes*	139			
	Red Scorpionfish *Pontinus* sp.	139			
	Coral Hawkfish *Cirrhitichthys oxycephalus*	141			
	Longnosed Hawkfish *Oxycirrhites typus*	141			
	Hieroglyphic Hawkfish *Cirrhitus rivulatus*	141			

ID GROUP 10 ODD-SHAPED SWIMMERS

Puffers—Triggerfish & Filefish—Others

No.	Name	Page	Date	Location	Notes
	Bullseye Puffer *Sphoeroides annulatus*	145			
	Spotted Green Puffer *Arothron hispidus*	145			
	Galapagos Puffer *Sphoeroides angusticeps*	145			
	Guineafowl Puffer *Arothron meleagris*	147			
	Spotted Sharpnose Puffer *Canthigaster punctatissima*	147			
	Spotted Porcupinefish *Diodon hystrix*	149			
	Balloonfish *Diodon holocanthus*	149			
	Pacific Burrfish *Chilomycterus affinis*	149			
	Spot-base Burrfish *Cyclichthys spilostylus*	151			
	Pacific Boxfish *Ostracion meleagris*	151			
	Red-tailed Triggerfish *Xanthichthys mento*	153			
	Yellow-bellied Triggerfish *Sufflamen verres*	153			
	Black Triggerfish *Melichthys niger*	155			
	Blunthead Triggerfish *Pseudobalistes naufragium*	155			
	Finescale Triggerfish *Balistes polylepis*	155			
	Scrawled Filefish *Alutera scripta*	157			
	Vagabond Filefish *Cantherhines dumerilii*	157			
	Pacific Beakfish *Oplegnathus insignis*	157			
	Twice-spotted Soapfish *Rypticus nigripinnis*	159			
	Mottled Soapfish *Rypticus bicolor*	159			
	Bronze Croaker *Odontoscion eurymesops*	159			
	Galapagos Drum *Pareques perissa*	161			
	Ocean Whitefish *Caulolatilus princeps*	161			
	Yellow-tailed Goatfish *Mulloidichthys dentatus*	163			
	Trumpetfish *Aulostomus chinensis*	163			
	Reef Cornetfish *Fistularia commersonii*	165			
	Pacific Seahorse *Hippocampus ingens*	165			
	Fantail Pipefish *Doryrhamphus excisus excisus*	165			
	Sailor Pipefish *Bryx veleronis*	164			
	Spotjaw Pipefish *Bryx coccineus*	164			